D0850308

Richelieu and the Affair of Cinq-Mars

Richelieu
and the Affair of
Cinq-Mars

PHILIPPE ERLANGER

Translated by Gilles and Heather Cremonesi

Elek Books London

This translation © 1971 Elek Books Limited
All rights reserved

Published in Great Britain by
ELEK BOOKS LIMITED
2 All Saints Street London N1

SBN 236 17751 6

First published in French under the title
CINQ-MARS
© 1962 Librairie Académique Perrin

Printed in Great Britain by Clarke, Doble & Brendon Ltd.
Plymouth

WHEATON COLLEGE LIBRARY
NORTON, MASS. 02766

Contents

List of Illustrations

ACKNOWLEDGEMENTS

The photographs are acknowledged to the following sources: 1, 5, 6, 7, 9, 10: Print Room of the Bibliothèque Nationale, Paris (photos by Lalance); 2: Louvre (photo by Giraudon); 3: Louvre (photo by Bulloz); 4: Musée de Richelieu (photo by M. Tremblier); 8: private collection (photo by Bulloz).

Principal Characters

Louis XIII—the Just (1601–1643)

Born at Fontainebleau, the son of Henry IV and Marie de Médicis. Succeeded to the throne in 1610 on the assassination of Henry. Marie de Médicis became Regent, delegating power to the unpopular Concini, Marshal d'Ancre. In 1617, Louis instigated the murder of Concini, and thereafter ruled through a number of favourites, culminating in the appointment of Richelieu as first minister.

Marie de Médicis (1573–1642)

Born in Florence, and married Henry IV in 1600. She became Regent on Henry's death, married her son Louis to Anne of Austria, and wielded great power until the death of her favourite Concini. Her influence secured Richelieu's appointment as first minister, but she soon quarrelled with him, and endeavoured to secure his disgrace. As a result she was banished, and died in exile in Cologne.

Anne of Austria (1601–1666)

Born in Valladolid, the daughter of Philip III of Spain, married Louis XIII in 1615, and became Regent for her son Louis XIV on the death of Louis XIII in 1643. During her Regency she worked with Mazarin.

Richelieu, Armand Jean du Plessis, Cardinal (1585–1642)

Born in Paris, Bishop of Luçon, and spokesman for the clergy in the States General of 1614. He became Cardinal in 1622, and entered the Royal Council in 1624, sponsored by Marie de

1

Médicis. He rapidly became head of affairs, and continued dominant until his death.

Cinq-Mars, Henri Coiffier de Ruzé, Marquis de (1620–1642)

Protégé of Cardinal Richelieu, educated under his supervision, Cinq-Mars was placed at Court by Richelieu. Cinq-Mars became the last and perhaps the greatest favourite of Louis XIII, and the Cardinal hoped to use him as a spy and also make use of his influence with the King. However, Cinq-Mars refused to be controlled by the Cardinal and was finally beheaded for his opposition.

de Thou, François (1607–1642)

Magistrate and close friend of Cinq-Mars, he was deeply attached to the Queen, and helped to convert his friend to active opposition to the Cardinal. He was executed with Cinq-Mars.

Orléans, Gaston d' (1608–1660)

The brother of Louis XIII, he spent his life in an endeavour to seize power for himself. He plotted against Richelieu, and later, Mazarin. He formed an uneasy alliance with Anne of Austria, and became Lieutenant General of the Kingdom on his brother's death.

Hautefort, Marie de (1616–1691)

Lady-in-waiting to Anne of Austria, Louis XIII was attracted to her and attempted to make her his mistress. She treated him coldly, but wielded great influence over him until Cinq-Mars gained ascendancy over the King.

Bouillon, Frédéric Maurice, duc de (1605–1652)

Enemy of Richelieu, he allied himself with Spain, and defeated the Royal troops at the Battle of Marfée. He was involved in the Cinq-Mars affair, but was pardoned.

Gonzaga, Marie (1611–1667)

Duchess of Nevers. Descendant of the Dukes of Mantua, she was a most ambitious lady. Cinq-Mars fell in love with her, and she encouraged him to oppose the Cardinal.

This is the story of four crucial years in the history of France. The great Cardinal Richelieu, nearing the end of his life and worn out by his efforts to make France and its King secure and powerful, attempted to consolidate his influence over the King by arranging for a young protégé to become the royal favourite. He succeeded, but young Cinq-Mars, who desired nothing but a youthful and carefree life, became influenced against him, and attempted to destroy the Cardinal and discredit him with Louis XIII. He nearly succeeded, and was one of the greatest dangers to Richelieu's sway, and one that caused the Cardinal's health to fail under the strain of counteracting it. Cinq-Mars fell, but the effort of destroying him led both the King and the Cardinal to the grave within a year of his execution.

I

The Emerging Pattern

At a time when it was fashionable to behave as outrageously as the 'Vert Gallant' (Henry IV), Madame d'Effiat was a model of marital virtue. She was a devoted wife and personally supervized the upbringing of her children—behaviour which her contemporaries regarded as almost unseemly. Her virtues had their limitations, however, for she was also a singularly proud, mean, ambitious and domineering woman.

Marie de Fourcy had married Antoine Coffier-Ruzé, Marquis d'Effiat and a captain of the light cavalry, in 1610, the year in which Henry IV's death plunged France into one of the grimmest episodes of her history. Nevertheless it was an excellent marriage. Marie's dowry consisted of 90,000 *livres tournois*, and Effiat, who already owned considerable estates in the Auvergne and Touraine, was also given the domains of Chilly and Longjumeau by his mother's brother, Beaulieu-Ruzé, then Secretary of State. This uncle who had managed to flourish at court for sixty years was an inspiring example for Effiat to follow; the Marquis himself was handsome, strong and agile and possessed every possible quality for a brilliant career.

His success was rapid. He managed to increase his personal fortune; and his wife's parsimony did not deter him from living on a grand scale. He commissioned the celebrated Métézeau, who later built the La Rochelle dyke, to tear down the old château at Chilly and replace it with a magnificent house in the best architectural style of the day. Vouet, Perrier and Sarrazin decorated it and it soon excited the admiration, if not the envy, of everyone. Festivities of unrivalled splendour took place in the great hall graced by Vouet's 'Loves of the Gods'.

Effiat's uncle Beaulieu-Ruzé had always held that it was best to be constant in one's loyalty to one's king regardless of the political climate. He had been loyal throughout the Civil Wars, which the *grands seigneurs* had so relished, and which had been

7

suppressed by Henry IV only to flare up again after his death. Effiat also lived by this principle. His devotion to his king during the troubled years of Louis XIII's minority was rewarded with the ambassadorship to Flanders in 1619, when Louis came of age.

It was five years later that Cardinal Richelieu was appointed Head of the Council.[1] France was then like a ship adrift. Royal authority 'was so unlike what it should have been that it was nearly unrecognizable. Every man measured his merit by the yardstick of his audacity.'[2] Internally the country was subject to a thinly disguised anarchy, while abroad the House of Austria took its revenge on Henry IV and prepared to crush France within a vice that spanned from Madrid to Vienna.

Louis had always loathed Richelieu. The Cardinal had been Marie de Médicis's favourite and it was only the fear of rousing her titanic wrath that forced the young King to submit to his arrogant tutelage. However, Louis soon began to admire Richelieu's mastery of intrigue. Once he realized that the ambitious priest could bring 'glory and grandeur' to his crown, he suppressed his personal feelings and gave the Cardinal whatever support and authority he required.

In fact it was only by virtue of the king's support that Richelieu maintained his position. The Cardinal found no favour with the Catholic and Protestant factions, none with the nobility and Parliament, nor with the bourgeoisie and still less with the rank and file of the population. Had his political position been based on popular support he could not have held it for six months. He had formulated his policies and drafted a truly Cartesian plan of action. But he depended on the young king to remove all possible opposition. It was Louis who said, 'I want him and that is reason enough.'

There were many at court, of course, who did not feel that the king's will was reason enough, but Antoine d'Effiat wisely chose not to be among them. He promptly offered the Cardinal his services. In 1624 he was entrusted with the delicate mission of negotiating the marriage between the king's sister Henrietta and the Prince of Wales, who later became Charles I. His success was rewarded with election to the Knights of the Grand Cross. Thereafter his talents were more fully exploited. He was a very success-

---

[1] Richelieu did not become Prime Minister until 1629.
[2] Richelieu, *Mémoires.*

Veue et Perspective du Chateau de Chilly, appartenant a Madame la Marefchalle d'Effiat, a quatre lieues de Paris fur le chemin d'Orleans.

1   The Château de Chilly where Cinq-Mars was born

2   Louis XIII by Philippe de Champaigne

ful diplomat and soldier—he was made *grand maître* of the artillery—and later was appointed Superintendent of Finance. Richelieu once asked him to 'balance the Royal accounts' during a period of financial stress. Although he was only an artillery officer, he managed this assignment so skilfully that he virtually provided the resources for the Cardinal's enterprises.

As soon as this assignment was completed he was recalled to arms. He fought so well at Veillance, where the Duke of Savoy's forces were totally defeated, that he was awarded a Marshall's baton and the governorship of the Auvergne. When he died of 'scarlet fever' at Lüzelstein in 1632, the French army in Germany had just been placed under his command. Monsieur de Pradines conveyed his heart and last will and testament to the inconsolable Madame d'Effiat.

She was left with three sons and three daughters. The youngest daughter died in infancy, while the eldest, Charlotte, was forced to take orders and mourn her passing youth in a convent, a fate she shared with so many of her rank. The life of the second daughter Marie was equally sad. At the tender age of nine she was married to the widower Gaspard d'Alègre. The little girl grew to adore him. The marriage, however, could not be consummated. The Cardinal, who had the unfortunate habit of expressing concern for his friends' welfare by intervening in their family affairs, soon realized that little Marie would be an excellent match for his cousin the Duc de la Meilleraye. Her parents were cooperative enough and ambitious enough to consent. The heartbroken little girl was removed from her beloved Alègre and remarried to the duke. As she was already rather unstable, this shock completely unbalanced her. When she was eighteen she left her harsh world during a miscarriage. Her surviving son, who later became the Duc de Mazarin, inherited her mental instability.

Martin, the eldest son and heir to the Effiat title and domains, was already a soldier when his father died. His mental faculties were also rather weak. He liked to cut up the tapestries at Chilly to resole his worn shoes; he died in 1645 completely out of his wits. Jean, the youngest son, went into the Church, for which he had no calling, and his exuberant nature inevitably involved him in scandals which marred his career as a court *abbé*.

The perpetuation of the house of Effiat thus fell to the second son Henri. He was born on March 27, 1620. He was spared the religious career that usually awaited the younger members of noble families, for his father handed over to him a large estate in Touraine which Beaulieu-Ruzé had originally acquired from Jacques de Broc. The Castle of Cinq-Mars, which dominated the estate, was an old fortress with magnificent terraces. The outer walls were 135 feet long and 45 feet wide; the keep had three surrounding walls and could easily withstand a siege. Twenty-five towns and villages belonged to whoever bore the feudal title of Marquis de Cinq-Mars. When he was ten, Henri was appointed chief bailiff and lieutenant-general of Touraine.

The Cardinal could be a ruthless enemy, but he was loyal and generous to those who served him. His sense of duty to his family was particularly strong. The sacrifice of poor little Marie to the Duc de la Meilleraye made the Effiats his relatives. On the death of Effiat the duke persuaded his mother-in-law to submit to the Prime Minister's despotic will and make him the protector of her fatherless children.

Richelieu often visited Chilly, which the Marshall d'Effiat himself had had so little time to enjoy. He soon came to regard the house as his own. It was here that he carried on many of the government's secret activities. Political prisoners were spirited away to the mysterious château to be questioned and perhaps even silently eliminated down some *oubliette*. It is said that there was a terrible tipping chair which could dispose of unsuspecting victims during the interrogations. Richelieu, encircled as he was by conspirators eager to assassinate him, felt no compunction in resorting to the methods of Louis XI.

The little Marquis de Cinq-Mars saw the more convivial side of the Cardinal's nature. Richelieu was quick to see the luckless Martin's lack of capabilities and gave his attention to the lively, intelligent and handsome Henri. Although he was usually flint-hearted, he may have felt some fleeting affection for the son of his dead friend. But Henri must certainly have been terrified by the awesome Cardinal clad in his striking scarlet robes. He was equally in awe of his fierce mother, who was now absolute head of the family. He grew up under the domination of this twofold tyranny, at a time when convention prevented his being shown the kind of affection he obviously needed.

*   *   *

Henri did everything with 'consummate grace and ease'. He inherited Marshall d'Effiat's handsome features but not his manly self-confidence. He had a charmingly languid air, slightly touched with sadness; his dreaming, seductive and troubled eyes betrayed the weakness and the instability of someone easily hurt. He concealed this weakness in frequent and totally arbitrary outbursts of violence. Had he been brought up in the twentieth century he would have been studied, cared for and possibly given stability and confidence, but this was quite inconceivable in the seventeenth century. The educational theorists of the time rigorously avoided 'softening' youth, which had to be broken from infancy to strict discipline and complete submissiveness. Children ate at the far end of the table, bareheaded, in contrast to their elders, and in silence. They sat only when given permission, and, before the last courses were served, they rose, took their plates, bowed low to their parents, and quietly withdrew to their quarters. 'Well brought up children with wise mothers never speak save in whispers and are always to be found in their mothers' rooms,' Angélique Arnauld used to say; and Henry IV, who was regarded as an excellent father, used to tell his son, the Dauphin, 'I am the master and you, sir, are my servant.'

Madame d'Effiat's disposition inclined her to tighten rather than relax this rigorous control; her ambitions, in fact, intensified her authoritarian nature. It was to be Henri's duty to maintain and increase the Effiat's recently acquired fortunes which could easily have been jeopardised by the Marshall's untimely death. Madame d'Effiat felt, therefore, that she should retain absolute control over her son and bring him up with a rod of iron, an end to which she devoted all her formidable energies. But she went too far. She permanently crippled his self-confidence. Henri bitterly resented his own weakness and spent much of his life in impatient and awkward revolt (with one disastrous exception) against those who tried to control him.

When Henri was fifteen, Richelieu decided that he should attend Monsieur de Benjamin's Academy in the Rue Vieille du Temple. The Cardinal himself had drafted the military academy's founding statutes: Monsieur de Benjamin was to concern himself with 'modelling the young men's manners. No man was better suited to instruct the young in the rules of virtue than he.' Besides virtue, Cinq-Mars learnt 'all that concerns the profession of arms' : geography, mathematics, surveying, the art of fortification, fencing, riding, dancing, and many other skills. The Cardinal, in a paternal role, 'insisted on receiving detailed accounts of the young men's progress'.

Cinq-Mars's letters show that he also received the usual thorough grounding in the classics and that as an adolescent he showed a particular fondness for the fashionable novels of his day. He and the rest of his generation grew up under the spell of *Astrée* and its Code of Love. Thus at sixteen, when the ailing Monsieur de Benjamin decided to close down his academy, our young man was longing to get out into the world and do great and noble deeds, longing to live out his 'Carte du Tendre'.

Richelieu appraised his protégé with his notoriously perceptive 'eagle eye' and saw a vigorous impetuous young man, handsome as a Greek hero, bursting with laughter, eager to rush at life and swallow its pleasures whole. He decided to terminate his studies and send the young Lieutenant-General of Touraine, now also Lieutenant in the government of Bourbonnais, to court. The previous year, 1635, France had begun a war against Spain and the Emperor, a war which eventually lasted a quarter of a century; new companies were added therefore to the King's Guard and Cinq-Mars was given the command of one of them. He was also, of course, presented to His Majesty, who ignored him totally.

* * *

Cardinal Richelieu was directing a colossal operation, which had reached a decisive point. His plans had gone smoothly, but the scale of the whole undertaking now threatened to overwhelm him. At the same time his popularity was at a low ebb. He was the object of even greater disgust and hatred than in 1624. He was still admired but his only support continued to be the king's will and the general belief in royal authority.

The King had written to his minister saying, 'Rest assured that I shall love you to the very last.' But the King never lifted the protective sphinx-like mask which he donned before the Cardinal. In reality Louis was not the 'illustrious slave' that Madame de Motteville was to describe, although he was quite willing to appear so at court. He may have disdained to share his minister's glory, but every single decision that went towards establishing that glory was first referred to the King, who studied, weighed, and finally approved it. His family, his confessor and the whole of his immediate circle insisted that the Cardinal was ruining his kingdom; there were many who eagerly awaited the King's slightest signal to rid him of this scourge. Richelieu knew this. The examples of the assassinated Concini, the liquidated Buckingham, the murdered Wallenstein always loomed large and clear before him. He knew that a mere word or a mere silence could as easily dispense with him.[3] This explains why 'this great genius who performed nothing but miracles', as Corneille put it, was condemned to wait upon his master's every change of mood, to watch for the very slightest intimation of a frown that could herald his downfall. Richelieu's sudden bouts of feverishness were but reactions to his master's frequently equivocal, if not mysterious silences. This situation explains why he had to be a courtier. He became a consummately subtle, vigilant and artful courtier, as well as a highly versatile actor, a master of the tearful scene, and of sudden improvizations. The King once said to him in anger, 'Lead the way, for they say you are the true king.' To which the Cardinal riposted, seizing a blazing torch, 'I lead but to illuminate your way.'

In the end Louis and Richelieu were united by the political confusion of the times and by the dangers that faced them both : each knew he was indispensable to the other. The minister's existence hung upon the king's fate and the kingdom's fate depended upon Richelieu's existence. The King wished to be kept informed of every detail of the affairs of state; Richelieu gave far more time and energy to the relatively small area that comprised the King's offices than to the remaining areas of the world. He threw a tight network of spies over the entire court, drawing priests, doctors, court favourites and servants into his mesh. After twelve years of practically ruling alone, however, his apprehensions had not diminished. They had in fact become obsessive. As we have seen there was some justification for them and 1636 was a particularly eventful year, in which a terrifying, successful invasion had finally been turned back at Corbie only to be followed by an almost fatal attempt on his life.

The cold and steely outer casing of the 'Scarlet Courtier' con-

[3] Louis XIII had chosen, for instance, to keep such a silence when the Duc de Luynes's second, Déagent, had said at Vitry, when speaking of Concini in the King's presence, 'The King wishes him dead.'

cealed an anxious, intensely emotional man, worn down by illness and by the almost superhuman tasks he shouldered. It was only natural that he should come to regard the affairs of state as being inextricable from his personal survival. He could not afford to allow any moral scruple to take precedence over this concern. Nor could he afford ever to forget it. Even Cinq-Mars's astonishing good looks entered this concern. It suddenly occurred to him that this boy might win the King's affection as Baradas and Saint-Simon had already done.

Saint-Simon, now a duke and peer, had started life as a humble stable page. Until he was nineteen he was nothing but a rough and ready rustic of no great subtlety or wit although he was lively and nice enough. His Eminence himself had introduced Louis XIII to the lad, who had then become the royal favourite. On the Day of Dupes in 1630, when Richelieu thought that his ex-patron Marie de Médicis had contrived his downfall, it was this same 'smelly little chap' who had led the Cardinal to his master and consequently saved the day for France.

Richelieu felt that he had the right to expect even greater loyalty from the son of his old friend Effiat, whom he had protected and helped bring up. At that moment Louis's affections were divided between two women, the proud Marie de Hautefort and the gentle Louise de La Fayette. Both women loathed the Cardinal and both worked for his downfall. If Henri managed to supplant these two, Richelieu would be relieved of this added burden and would be able to devote himself wholly to the greater glory of France.

The King had not yet even noticed Cinq-Mars; the young man himself regarded the King as a distant divinity whom he wished to serve but whose personal characteristics repelled him. The Cardinal was ready to spin the web which would fatally ensnare them both.

II

The Vain Struggle

Cinq-Mars joined the court. The young man was eager for excitement and glory and thus found the court a baffling experience. The monarch himself would personally have preferred a monastic existence but the demands of government, his own sense of duty and tradition, and the pomp that inevitably surrounded his position forced him to participate in the dazzling spectacles given at the Louvre and Saint-Germain. He did all he could to dim the brilliance of these official displays. He tried to abolish duelling and to banish extravagant fashions by passing sumptuary laws, but nothing could induce the French to cease converting their fortunes into lavish attire or forego the pleasure of slitting each others' throats.

Henry IV's son was a sickly and neurasthenic King. He was his own whipping boy and he was masochistic. He did not, however, share the Spanish princes' morose habit of moping over ancestors' tombs; he was an active, athletic man. He devoted as much energy to war, travel and hunting as he did to politics. Hunting was a passion and an escape. Once when it was raining he expressed the frustration of a huntsman denied his favourite pastime by banging on the streaming windowpane and muttering to one of his servants, 'What a bore!' Hunting released him from his obsessions and made him feel more at ease, especially at his beloved Versailles. 'This little playing-card castle, which even the humblest of gentlemen would not boast of owning', was set in a subdued and melancholy countryside with a few scattered farms and vineyards surrounded by marshes and vast dense forests well supplied with game. It was here that His Most Christian Majesty realized that there was much misery beneath so much splendour and that he was destined to live between these two extremes.

His Majesty had other pastimes which revealed a childish

15

streak in his habitually grim nature. He liked making trellises, preserves and armour as well as gardening and casting coins.

Then one day the royal craftsman decided to reveal his aptitudes for composing, decorating and dancing. The magnificence of the last Valois was revived at the Louvre and the Hôtel de Ville. The royal family and the nobility intermingled with hundreds of artists. Hosts of people, whose social status was defined by their brilliant attire, gasped in admiration at weird and wonderful spectacles whose splendour our grey age cannot conceive. Processions of giants and dwarfs, mythological deities, knights, enchantresses, tight-rope walkers and exotic animals peopled the pageants and farces. Their costumes were sewn with gold and precious stones. The 'hypochondriac king' himself was known to dress as a clown or a devil or a farcical Mahomet and dance before his court.

None of this, however, could persuade the court to excuse his tense reserved nature, his halting speech and awkward gait, or the diffidence with which he expressed his feelings. His ascetic ideals were out of tune with the gallant, adventurous, theatrical gestures favoured by the fashionable *précieuse* heroines of the day. His virtues were stoical.[1] They were not understood or appreciated by a court which had been weened on *Astrée* and seduced by the *Cid* and which nevertheless remained Rabelaisian to the core. The king did not have the grace of a Céladon or the heroic dimensions of a Rodrigue or the robustness of a Gargantua. His restive nobility regarded him as a martinet who frowned upon anything connected with pleasure, who disapproved of festivities, duels, intrigues, lechery, independence. Everything he did provoked their mockery. Madame de Chevreuse called him 'the fool', when her seductive ploys were spurned. Her words were not forgotten. Wits composed pithy epitaphs to while away the time until they were rid of this nuisance :

> Here lies the king whose pastor
> Let him strut upon a puppet stage.
> His virtues might have earned a valet's wage,
> But they were not the virtues of a master.

[1] The *Manual of Epictetus* was one of the most popular books of the day and gave rise to a philosophy whose enduring success was assured by the works of Guillaume Du Vair.

It was only when the King was dead that these same cruel haughty gentlemen appreciated his true worth. When they were made to bow under Mazarin's hard yoke they paid him belated homage.

Queen Anne of Austria could have lent lustre to a cheerful and brilliant court, as she did indeed during her regency, but her dampening husband prevented her from doing so. He even went as far as forbidding her her own circle of friends. At thirty-five she was slightly heavy but she still retained much of the beauty and attraction that had fascinated Buckingham and had even stirred the Cardinal. His Eminence had been known to grant her request and dance a saraband for her dressed in a green habit trimmed with little silver bells. The request had been a joke and his compliance had made him the laughing stock of court. She never finished paying for it.

The greatest queen in the world led a miserable harassed life. She was the Prime Minister's enemy. She was distrusted by her husband and was constantly watched and spied upon. Her sterility exposed her to still worse indignities. She was everything that Louis XIII was not : sensual, greedy, lazy, muddle-headed, flirtatious. The king loathed her elaborate toilette, her chatter, her Spanish powders and scents. He accused her of being more like an Infanta than a French Queen. He was convinced that she had played a part in the Challois plot to kill him because she wanted to marry Monsieur, his brother, and he resented this to his dying day. He performed his conjugal duty only to perpetuate his line, and since he had dedicated France to the Virgin in the hope of begetting a son, his visits to his 'intimate enemy' had become few and far between.[2]

His court was thus a very different one from that of Francis I or Henry IV, despite its superficial brilliance—for the Queen was attended by splendidly witty and lively ladies-in-waiting : the Princess of Condé and her daughter, the future Duchess of Longueville, Princesses Marie and Anne Gonzaga, Madame de Montblazon, Madame de Hautefort, Mademoisilles de La Fayette, de Chémerault, de Ponchâteau, de Vigean, d'Escars, de Saint-Louis and twenty others who made up her peerless retinue.

Cinq-Mars enjoyed the company of the spirited, bellicose,

[2] Louis XIII's impotence is fictitious, as his doctor's journal proves. Anne of Austria suffered three miscarriages before Louis XIV was born.

wild and gloriously vain young men of the day. They all wanted to dazzle the world with their extravagance. Cinq-Mars was determined to make a name for himself. Life was sweet, springs and summers were spent on the battlefield and winters were for pleasure and Paris. His prowess on the battlefield and in the bed-chamber excited the admiration of his peers. His handsome features had an anxious, ingenuous and even mysterious look that inspired friendship as well as love. But he had little chance of winning this sort of distinction at the court of Louis 'The Chaste'. It was at the Hôtel de Rambouillet and in the other *salon* societies outside the court that such recognition was won. He was soon adopted by the glittering *Précieuses* beneath the painted ceilings of their noble houses and in the chambers of those ravishing Marais hostesses. He knew all the notorious 'libertines'. Des Barreaux, who was the most infamous of all, was nicknamed the 'Illustrious Debauché' or 'Théophile's widow',[3] even though he was then madly in love with a provincial girl called Marie Delon de Lorme. These libertines were an enclave of free-thinkers in an essentially religious age. Anything sacred was subject to blasphemy. Conservative conformism was ridiculed. They brazenly published scandalous verse and 'revelled in orgy'. They believed in an aggressive materialism. Madame d'Effiat obviously disapproved of these reprobates, but Henri admired their defiance of God and the Devil, of Church and Parliament. He met them at their favourite cabarets, at the Pomme de Pin in Rue de la Juiverie near Notre-Dame, at Coffier's in Rue du Pas-de-la-Mule, at Cormier's in Rue des Fossés-Saint-Germain-L'Auxerrois, where they drank heavily and recited wickedly salacious poems.

The young Marquis also enjoyed the more refined intellectual pursuits of the Marais salons, where literary jousts benefited from his sharp wit. He still had, however, to prove himself a mettle-some swordsman. He fought and defeated Louis Foucault, Comte du Daugnon, in a duel and became the talk of Paris. The duel was the more dangerous as duelling had recently been made a capital crime. The Cardinal, however, was secretly delighted to see that his protégé had proved himself and so turned a blind eye.

Cinq-Mars was handsome, witty, courageous. He could not fail to captivate both the court and the capital. He acquired the right mistresses and won devoted friends, the closest of whom

[3] After the poet Théophile de Viau, who died in 1626.

was Henri de Massue, Marquis de Ruvigny, whom he loved like a brother, and who was respected and very popular despite his Protestant faith. Henri came by these trophies so easily and they followed his emotionally deprived childhood so quickly that they were bound to give him an exaggerated opinion of himself. He began to feel that nothing was beyond his reach. He was a dashing young peacock who preened himself with disarming presumption. He was sure of a dazzling future and until his dreams came true he and his companions would live life to the hilt, a life of battles, duels, romances, adventures and mad-cap escapades, of chases, swordfights, silken ladders and drunken street brawls, a life that glittered with the intoxicating illusion of total freedom.

The Marquis de la Force was negotiating the sale of his office of Master of the Robe to Monsieur d'Aumont; the King was ready to give his consent but Richelieu asked him to delay. Cinq-Mars did not consider the transaction could affect him and so ignored it, but Richelieu soon drew his attention to it. He wondered whether a dandy so concerned with his own appearance might not be pleased to concern himself with the king's as well. The young man rejected the suggestion. The very idea of being forced to share the King's most intimate life, of having to listen to his confidences and bear the brunt of all his moods in no way appealed to him. The post of Master of the Robe may have been an important and highly coveted one but he knew it to be a euphemism for slavery. He had just begun to feel free for the first time in his life and had no intention of becoming the slave of a gloomy, cantankerous, maniacal prince. He mastered his awe of the Cardinal and refused. Richelieu did not press the point. He gave the young man a condescending, knowing smile and dismissed him.

*   *   *

Then in March 1637, when Father Gordon relinquished his post as confessor to the King, the Marquis de Cinq-Mars had the honour of escorting his Jesuit successor, Father Caussin, to the Louvre. He could not foresee how this implacable enemy of Richelieu's would affect his own future. Father Caussin immediately became involved in the politics that surrounded Louis's love life. The King was then tragically in love with Louise de La

19

Fayette. He had started courting the sweet young girl in order to make Marie de Hautefort jealous, with the unexpected result that they both fell in love with one another. It was a chaste, sad and timid love. Louis and Louise were to be seen huddling together in alcoves, at the hunt and at court ceremonies, whispering sweet nothings. This would have been the full extent of their relationship if politics had not intervened. Richelieu, delighted with Hautefort's fall from favour, promptly offered his services to La Fayette, only to find that his enemies had already won her sympathies. The pious Louise was shocked by the Cardinal's approaches. She was convinced that it was her personal mission to reconcile the King with his Queen and to liberate the French people from the Cardinal's tyranny. She gave herself zealously to these tasks. Richelieu outmanœuvred her by playing on her piety and giving Louis a rival for her affections who was none other than God. He ordered Father Carée, the young lady's confessor, to lure her into a convent while Richelieu played on Louis's religious inclinations making it impossible for him to stop her pursuing her calling.

Father Caussin did his best to thwart Richelieu's stratagem. He persuaded La Fayette to stay at court for the sake of France by fanning her horror of Richelieu. The King's intimate life thus became the political instrument of the Cardinal on one hand and of the rival Spanish-led faction on the other. Richelieu's ends were finally served by the inherent frailties of the relationship itself. The exasperated ascetic mastered his timidity and asked Louise, 'Would you like me to keep you at Versailles as my very own, subject to my wishes?' The virgin recoiled in terror and the shamefaced suitor regained his self-control. 'Their mutual fear of each other induced them to part.'[4]

This incident made him realize that he could not afford to become attached to any one person, for it might lead him to neglect his Christian duty to God who was the true Sovereign of the State. He could only be harsh towards others if he were harsh towards himself. He sent the Cardinal a tear-stained note and Mademoiselle de La Fayette entered the Convent of St Mary of the Visitation on May 19. Louis lapsed into despair. He might even have abdicated had there been anyone less despicable than his brother to succeed him.

Father Caussin was not so easily deterred. He assailed the

[4] Madame de Motteville.

King with the threat of damnation if he persisted in waging a sinful war and refusing to live with the Queen. Louis would hear these arguments again during his interminable visits to the Convent of the Visitation where he went to see Louise, now in her novitiate habit.

Richelieu was thus constrained to fight off internal enemies while conducting a gigantic war. At this point he again took up the matter of the Marquis de la Force's position with Cinq-Mars and this time he exorted and scolded. Henri fought back tooth and nail. His affair with Mademoiselle de Chémerault, who was Madame de Hautefort's best friend, reinforced his determination not to yield to the Cardinal. This beautiful creature excited in him all the exalted, sublime sentiments of *Astrée*. 'Let the soul love the soul, which is its equal, rather than the body, which is inferior.' These shepherds of Lignon, however, did not sacrifice all physical pleasures to metaphysical joy. Wits of the day observed that when they set out to attain the summits of chaste love they were wont to rest from their journey at half-way house.

Given Cinq-Mars's refusal, the Cardinal was forced to look elsewhere. He did not look very far. Mademoiselle de Chémerault was ambitious and had a natural gift for intrigue and far fewer scruples than her suitor. She did not refuse the Cardinal's offer. When Richelieu spoke to the King about her, however, he was silenced. 'I have resolved', Louis said, 'not to become involved with anyone ever again.' The King was deluding himself, for his interest in his *Aurora*, the proud and brilliant Marie de Hautefort, soon reawakened.

Summer came. In July Richelieu obtained conclusive evidence that the Queen, despite the war, had been corresponding with her brother, the King of Spain, as well as with the Duke of Lorraine and with England. Anne did not hesitate to give false testimony but she knew she had been discovered. She was in danger of being publicly denounced and dismissed to a convent. Louis would probably have been glad of the chance to be rid of her. Her undoing would have brought him closer, in a mystical way, to Louise.

The Cardinal, however, considered the alternatives and decided that the conspirators' desires for a united Royal Family also suited his own ends. The Queen, who never tired of plotting his downfall, ironically was the only person who could fulfil his greatest hope by giving birth to a Dauphin, a hope which his adversaries naïvely shared. He therefore decided to treat himself to the pleasure of being merciful to a dangerous enemy. The daughter of the Habsburgs had to eat her pride and even humbled herself to say, 'Your Eminence is so full of goodness.' She even tried to press his hand in gratitude. Louis forced himself to bestow a kiss of peace, which he gave with his lips and not with his heart.

Meanwhile Louise de La Fayette and Father Caussin were still under the illusion that a reconciliation between the King and his wife would be the Cardinal's undoing; and they continued their efforts to achieve this useless end. On December 5 a series of romantic coincidences served their cause by leading the reluctant Louis XIII into the conjugal bed at the Louvre.[5] On December 8 Father Caussin, certain of victory, further inveighed against Richelieu. He described the destruction caused by the war, the resulting distress of the population, and the sacrilegious alliance with the Protestants. He insisted that the King be responsible for the welfare of his kin. The tirade ended with the dramatic presentation of a letter from Marie de Médicis, who had been in exile for six years.

Louis was deeply moved by this portrayal of his distressed kingdom. It exacerbated his insomnia, anxiety, doubts and guilt. The following morning he instructed Father Caussin to restate his case before the Cardinal at Rueil. He would follow him and 'uphold all he had said'. But the tables were turned on the Jesuit. An order bearing the king's seal exiled him to Rennes as from the following day. Richelieu had scored another victory. It was one of those situations which constantly arose to threaten his very existence and which he survived as always, unscathed but not unshaken.

He turned on Cinq-Mars and subjected him to another round of intensive persuasion. Henri continued to oppose him with the negative obstinacy which is peculiar to the weak. He put up a desperate fight against the minister's violent temper and refused to accept the dubious honour which was being thrust upon him. Richelieu was disappointed and angry. Having dealt with the chaste virgin and the King's confessor he still had to find a new favourite. That old ditty cropped up again :

[5] Cf. Philippe Erlanger, *Louis XIV*.

The King's heart alights
At the pretty sight
Of his Hautefort, his delight,
Whose sweet lips of ruby
Smile for her Louis.

But Louis's heart, in fact, was as unaffected as it had been when he had resorted to using a pair of tweezers to remove a suspicious message from Madame de Hautefort's bodice.

'Banish the word desire', he told Boisrobert, after reading a poem dedicated to his beautiful mistress, 'for the King desires nothing.' And then he quoted one of his favourite expressions: 'God would not that adultery ever enter my house.'

He nonetheless allowed himself to be dominated by Marie, whose *Précieuse* name was Hermione. She was not capable of the epic furies of Racine's princess, nor did she have Hermione's eagerness to be married—she waited until she was thirty before choosing a husband—but she did have her pride, haughtiness, courage and cruelty, none of which she spared her sighing suitor. When her beauty eventually faded, it was described as being 'stronger and nobler rather than mellowed and graceful'. She had an essentially pitiless, overbearing nature and could not abide anyone who preferred hunting to the subtler pursuits of the *'Carte du Tendre'*. Whenever conversation strayed from the King's outdoor pleasures, it invariably deteriorated into a bickering match. It was a strange relationship cemented by mutual irritation, vexation and 'martyrdom'. Marie never pretended to prefer the King to the Queen. She took delight in avenging the Queen, and Anne of Austria heaped all her bitterness and boredom on the 'lover' and not on the 'mistress' as might have been expected. Madame de Motteville once wrote of Louis, 'His was an habitually bitter soul whose only joy was the relishing of its present sorrows.' These sorrows were what bound him to his dearly beloved tyrant.

In January 1638 the incredible news broke out: after twenty-two years of marriage, Anne of Austria was finally pregnant. The king renewed his vow to the Virgin in the hope of obtaining a Dauphin who would decide the fate of France. But his hostility and coldness towards his wife continued. Marie de Hautefort, ever devoted to her Queen, was determined not to let the Cardinal rob the Queen of her glory in her motherhood. The haughty creature decided to win the King over by treating him kindly. Louis XIII was quite delighted but Richelieu quaked. He could not afford to let this little schemer play with the King and poison his mind at will. It was essential to be informed of everything that passed between them. Their trifling exchanges terrified the scourge of Europe.

The Cardinal went to Madame d'Effiat to point out that her son's indiscretions threatened to ruin his fortune and future. A career which could make him the King's favourite had been offered him and he had foolishly refused it. If he persisted, he and his family could expect nothing further from him. He need not have gone so far to excite the ambitious woman to action. She swooped down on her son, who had never had the courage to disobey her. But he made a last stand.

Richelieu was setting about the problem in another way : the King began to hear people talk of Cinq-Mars. He had scarcely noticed him although he had been in his Guard for eighteen months. But now the courtiers in the Minister's service voiced their delight with Cinq-Mars and manœuvred conversations round to praise 'this young man in the very flower of his youth, who distinguished himself by his striking appearance, his elegant manners and lively wit'. One night as His Majesty was retiring his retinue talked of nothing else.

The King finally took note of the object of all this praise and was struck by his beauty. When he spoke to him he was pleased by his manner. Richelieu then reminded him of Marshal d'Effiat and showed his approval of his son, suggesting that the office of Master of the Robe might suit him perfectly. This enthusiasm roused the King's suspicion. Nonetheless he chose to forget his half-promise to Monsieur d'Aumont and raised no obstacles.

This end accomplished, the boy's intransigence still had to be broken. Madame d'Effiat used all her authority to threaten and frighten Henri. She did not want to lose the Cardinal's support. And Richelieu became peace-maker.

Henri would have needed a will of iron to withstand such pressure. He capitulated, fully aware of the consequences of his defeat. On his eighteenth birthday, March 27, 1638, he was made Master of the Robe.

3   Richelieu by Philippe de Champaigne

4   Portrait of Cinq-Mars

III

Adonis and the Stoic

Mathieu Le Nain has left for posterity a portrait of the handsome and gallant Master of the Robe. The finely modeled face is surrounded by an exquisitely curled wig. The gentle eyes have a slightly malicious glint which emphasizes the sensual mouth. The Marquis is dressed in a white satin doublet trimmed with aiglets and a pair of gold embroidered breeches finished with a cascade of lace that overlaps his top-boots. His cuffs and collar are of fine Venetian lace. A magnificent gold baldric lies across his chest.

Madame d'Effiat's avarice had never permitted Henri to offset his good looks with fine clothing. But now that he was Master of the Robe and had all the clothiers of the land at his feet, he began to amass at no great expense a fantastic collection of clothes. The inventory of his estate confirms that when he died he possessed fifty-two outfits valued at fifty to a hundred *livres* each, not to mention all the cloaks, hats and accessories. One such outfit comprised : 'A surcoat, doublet and breeches in nut-brown cambric, the surcoat lined in the same cambric, the breeches lined in white satin and the doublet in linen-grey satin; each garment edged in silver and gold lace, the buttons being embroidered with gold and silver; the breeches trimmed in Scottish satin aiglets and gold and silver lace.' Then there were the plumes and jewels and those strong and costly scents with which dandies were supposed to anoint themselves.

As Cinq-Mars was responsible for choosing the King's apparel, the clothing industry assumed that this paragon of elegance would persuade the monarch to dress less austerely. Cinq-Mars did, in fact, try to influence the King in this way but to no avail. His Majesty would not dress more lavishly and reproached the young man for his indiscretion. Their relationship thus started on the wrong foot. The King often scolded the rascal. Louis enjoyed being sanctimonious. His tormented soul found gratification in reprimanding his charming novice and instructing him in the ways of virtue. Cinq-Mars controlled himself and kept a cheerful face because he was sure that he would not have to endure such rebukes for long. His instincts told him that they were harbingers of royal favour.

*   *   *

Was Henry IV's son simply an unhappy man or was he a great king? He was probably both and he was certainly also a very unhealthy man and a conscience-stricken Christian. His ill-health is extensively documented : he had contracted tuberculosis when he was twenty-one. However, he had 'an iron constitution', as his excellent physician Héroard observed. It was this constitution which enabled him to live to be forty-two despite all the barbarous remedies prescribed for him by the Faculty of Medicine after Héroard's death. If his royal status had not commanded the indefatigable attentions of all the Diafoiruses of the time his malady might have been held in check still longer. In fact, his physicians were often astonished by his miraculous recoveries when they had given him up for all but dead and stopped treatment. They never noticed the relation between recovery and the cessation of treatment. The laws of medicine were as inflexible as those which governed tragedy. Even a crown prince dared not disobey them. In one year alone, the fearsome Bouvard, whom Louis was publicly to blame for his death, prescribed forty-six bleedings, two hundred and twelve medications and two hundred and fifteen enemas.

The court never ceased to marvel at the King's physical endurance. He was not to be deterred by the foulest weather, wind, rain or snow. He would lay his hands on the heads of eleven hundred ailing subjects at a time, stay in the saddle for seventeen hours at a stretch, walk eight leagues without stopping to rest, and share his soldiers' lot till the battle was over. He always rose before six o'clock and never retired before midnight. Nature rebelled and Louis paid the toll for maintaining this pace. At thirty-seven, this 'slight Jupiter with a pointed beard' had an anxious, pale, feverish face. His personality also suffered. His dwindling strength made him more restless, more eccentric, more obsessed by lugubrious thoughts, and aggravated his spiritual torments.

He had not inherited his father's scepticism. He feared God and enjoyed hearing his choir sing His praises. He was devout to the point of superstition. His beliefs were absolute; his religious observances, like all his formal behaviour, were impeccable. He built chapels and was truly devoted to the Virgin. He never was guilty of the religious hypocrisy of contemporary monarchs, for his belief in kingship constituted a second faith to which he was no less passionately devoted. It was unfortunate that his duty to the Church so rarely coincided with his duty to his kingdom. His Most Christian Majesty could dedicate France to Notre Dame with one hand and stave off the Pope with the other. He made alliances with Protestant kings and waged a fierce war against His Catholic Majesty. He persecuted his wife and brother and he forced his mother to suffer and die in exile, sacrifices that always weighed heavily on him. These perpetual conflicts wore him down.

A lad of eighteen could scarcely be expected to grasp the complexities and grandeur of such a sovereign. Living at such close quarters with him, he was bound to notice all his pettiness, his foolishness, his blunders, his ill-humours, his contradictions. The King was not an easy man to understand. In fact he was unpredictable. He was timid but given to terrible fits of violence. He was an over-sensitive, suspicious, jealous despot who was capable of assigning so much power to his Minister and yet could be ridiculously intimidated by his mistress's slightest frown. He was indecisive but stubborn, a rigid moralist with a taste for puerile pleasures, a wounded soul given to passing stringent judgement on others. He was a compound of anguish and conviction, of pride and self-effacement, dynamism and submissiveness. It probably never struck Henri that this singularly awkward person, whose sheer meanness did not stop at denying the court ladies an ordinary bowl of soup, might personify the very ideal qualities celebrated by Corneille in the *Cid*, a play which had enjoyed a great success the previous winter. In fact, the second Bourbon king's reign displayed 'the triumph of the will applied to uncommon duties',[1] in the best Cornelian manner.

Had Louis not been born a King, he would never have attained much distinction. As it was, however, he created an ideal of what the King of France should be, which was a too

[1] Jules Lemaître.

oppressive model for such a mediocre man to follow. This ideal was superhumanly endowed with miraculous powers, which enabled him to heal his ailing subjects. His word was sacrosanct and any resistance to his commands was an unpardonable crime. Sovereign, state and country were a single supernatural entity to which all other considerations were subordinate. It was natural that lesser men kiss the feet of the man who embodied these ideals, as it was that his subjects should say, 'Rule well and all that we have is yours, Sire.'

Corneille would exalt this suppression of the individual and magnify the importance of the autocrat whose personal fortune was one with the fate of the whole world. Long before Louis saw *Cinna*, he emulated the Prince who was master of himself and of the universe. This concept of kingship was the very antithesis of Louis XIV's imperious ego-idolatry. Louis XIII's king was the semi-divinity who demanded total submission from his subjects, while sacrificing his personal existence to his ideal of kingship. He was the absolute monarch and the servant of his people; his omnipotence was divinely granted for their protection. From the very beginning of his reign he had had to face the discrepancy between the weak man he was and the king he wished to be. And being aware of the discrepancy he made constant and enormous efforts to live up to his model. These efforts were all the more poignant because he would not allow anyone to help or even to witness them.

'I should not be King had I the sentiments of ordinary men.' With these words he refused Montmorency's blessing. They define his ambitions exactly. They would have been less pathetic and less Cornelian had they been truer, for Henry IV's son *was* subject to 'ordinary' sentiments. He participated most in the human condition when he needed most to eschew it. His conscience dictated that he overcome these sentiments; he tried to obey and eventually his regal functions absorbed his personality.

Louis applied equally rigid principles to his love affairs, despite his disastrous marriage. Anne of Austria's complicity did not throw him into Marie de Hautefort's arms; she was never his mistress. When Saint-Simon offered to be their go-between, Louis scolded him, 'It is true that I am in love. I could not help this because I am a man and men are subjects of their senses. But I am also King and can thus be certain of obtaining whatever I

desire. The more I am King, the more I am obeyed, however, and
the more I must remember that God forbids me this. He made
me King that I might obey His command and make all those
obey me whom He has made subject to my command.'

Louis's scrupulous continence occasionally relaxed when he
took a fancy to a young girl or a youthful courtier. He treated
both sexes identically, was susceptible to both and all his infatua-
tions followed the same pattern. He poured out his soul, wrote
childish, long-winded letters, flew into rages and made amends.
He was a masochist whose idea of amorous bliss was to feel completely dominated by his beloved, to whom he could unbosom
himself endlessly and confide all 'the movements of his heart'.
Marie de Hautefort's imperious tyranny over him satisfied his
secret desire for this type of relationship. Henri must have laughed
at this strange pair or even felt sorry for them.

Throughout the Queen's pregnancy Louis and 'the Creature'
quarrelled incessantly. He tried to appease her by promoting her
to tirewoman with little effect. When he wrote to Richelieu
about affairs of state he often broke off to bemoan his miseries :
'The Creature is always angry with me . . .' 'The first day of our
reconciliation she treated me most coldly although I was most
submissive . . .'; 'This evening I thought I should award Madame
de Hautefort a pension of 1,200 *écus* . . . to show her how I shall
always return her ill-humour with kindness . . .'; 'Each day I discern that ill will which she bears me and, loving her as I do, I
can but despair . . .'; 'One never knows how to conduct oneself
with a person who finds fault with all that one does to please . . .'

The King's patience eventually came to an end. On August
25 he decided to leave her. The next morning they were reconciled. 'Their affection won through,' Chavigny wrote to Richelieu,
'and the reconciliation was easily effected and the King, who
had approached the encounter drawn and very nervous, emerged
from it in good spirit and his stomach went down without recourse
to the usual remedies.'

Ten days later Anne of Austria was in labour. Her condition
aroused some concern. Madame de Hautefort was upset and on
the verge of tears; Louis reprimanded her coldly, 'Keep your
thoughts on the child. There will be ample opportunity for
mourning the mother later.' When the future Louis XIV was
born and Château Saint-Germain resounded with jubilation,

29

Marie had to 'urge him to go to the Queen's side and kiss her'.

France was overjoyed at the news. So was Richelieu. The fruition of the Spanish faction's plot gave him solid ground on which to operate and guaranteed his ultimate success. His mortal enemy, Gaston d'Orléans, the King's brother, was now no longer heir. The Cardinal's future no longer depended upon the waning strength of a sickly monarch, and the birth of a son satisfied in Louis that universal need for posterity. He gave prayers of thanksgiving. But he was incapable of unadulterated joy and soon began to feel strangely jealous of the little child who was already worshipped as a rising sun.

The God of War had begun to favour France. Richelieu was concerned to find the King under the spell of a dangerous woman at such a time. She strove to undermine policies she did not understand and could only upset her hapless 'lover's' moral judgement. Cinq-Mars was not making the progress Richelieu had expected, even though the King's ears rang with the young man's praises. But the King was growing used to him and the Cardinal had reason to hope for the future. For the time being Richelieu had to turn his attention to more pressing problems. He asked Mademoiselle de Chémerault to inform him of everything she saw and heard between her close friend Marie de Hautefort and the King. She did not refuse the distasteful task. Cinq-Mars's behaviour would also fall 'within her province'. And as if this were not enough, she was instructed to provoke quarrels between the King and his beloved, and, most cunning of all, she was to attract the King's attention to the young man who was in love with her.

Henri did not realize that he was walking into a snake pit. His cheerful spirit often performed the miracle of soothing His Majesty's temper when Marie's biting tongue provoked his ill-humour. In the autumn of 1638 the courtiers in waiting noticed signs of an important change : the 'hypochondriac' had begun to smile openly at his Master of the Robe's lively jokes.

*   *   *

Monsieur Delon de Lorme was a loyal and upright man. He had tried unsuccessfully to preserve his daughter from dangerous liaisons. The adventurous girl finally settled down in Paris with

Des Barreaux in a delightful house in the suburbs of Saint-Victor. The libertine poet had named his retreat 'Cyprus Isle'. It was from here that he indiscreetly advertised his joys and pleasures :

> Love, thou glorious god of gods, I die and
> rise again,
> Your gifts award me so much glory and such
> joy.

His decision to introduce his conquest to Parisian society was his greatest indiscretion. He took her with him everywhere and presented her to the celebrated Ninon de Lenclos, who then plied this new discovery with all manner of advice. She was instrumental in transforming the provincial girl into an irresistibly beautiful coquette who radiated joy. Marie Delon became Marion de Lorme; she was twenty-five when she embarked upon the career which was to make her immortal. Despite the influence of the Church, people were not puritanical in the nineteenth-century sense. No door was ever closed to her because she was the mistress of an infamous man. Her incredible beauty graced the noblest houses and the most opulently bourgeois homes.

Cinq-Mars met her and was dazzled. He courted her ardently and she did not discourage his attentions. She was attracted by his dandy good looks and his prestigious position as Master of the Robe flattered her growing aspirations. She loved Des Barreaux, however, and would not betray him. Henri was forced to play the role of 'pining lover' as dictated in the Hôtel de Rambouillet's code of love.

Cardinal Richelieu kept careful track of what happened throughout the kingdom, but he made a special point of knowing everything that went on at court. He knew Des Barreaux well : he had saved the famous debauché when he committed 'some outrage against a young Jesuit'. And he also kept a very close watch on Cinq-Mars. He was especially interested in anyone who could 'enslave' both a libertine and a prince charming. Abbé Boisrobert, who was his closest confidant, kept him abreast of every intricacy in this double intrigue. He was so lyrical in describing the young lady's charms that he excited something more than the Cardinal's curiosity.

There was a popular jingle that was sung in Paris at the time :

Those who praise His Eminence
For his saintly continence,
Flatter him, at the very least.
For as the maxim goes in Rome,
A saint is but a cunning priest
Who only makes love at home.

The cunning Cardinal's amorous life was, in fact, common knowledge. The saraband incident had made the court roar with laughter and joke endlessly about his weakness for the Queen. His affair with his niece, Madame de Combalet, who had become the Duchess of Aiguillon, also added spice to the chronicles. Indeed, it was Marie de Médicis's jealousy of her which alienated her from her ex-protégé. Madame de Chaulnes and Madame de Fruges were among the few women of real social standing who bestowed their favours on the Scarlet Courtier; he recruited the majority of his conquests from lower social rungs. Monsieur le Cardinal now wished to become acquainted with the most celebrated beauty of the day. Boisrobert brought Marion and her friend Ninon de Lenclos to lunch in the Château du Rueil's magnificent park while fountains plashed and violins played serenades. Richelieu watched from the secrecy of his window. He studied Des Barreaux's mistress carefully. The next morning Boisrobert began making arrangements for a tryst between the two. Contemporary reports disagree on the conditions stipulated by the two parties, but it is known that Marion did not resist the lure of the Cardinal's purple. She arrived at the Cardinal's palace disguised as a page. Richelieu also wore an unusual outfit—a linen-grey satin habit trimmed with silver and gold lace, lace-trimmed boots, and a plumed hat.

How their encounter proceeded remains a mystery. Marion later boasted of carrying away a 'trophy'—a ring worth sixty gold pistoles belonging to Madame d'Aiguillon. The politician never lurked very far behind the Cardinal's diverse façades, even when fortune smiled on him : it seems that no sooner was he satisfied than he tried to recruit her as an agent. He proposed that she spy on Cinq-Mars. But when Des Bournais, His Eminence's valet, went to deliver a hundred gold pistoles to her and to ask her to return to the Cardinal's palace, the young woman scornfully refused and threw the money into the messenger's face.

The story ran round town, much to the Cardinal's discomfort. Marion became famous. Des Barreaux forgot his short-lived humiliation and gloated over his victory. He immediately sat down to write a poem on 'His Mistress's Preference For The Author Over His Sometime Rival, the Cardinal', which ended in a triumphant couplet :

> I had it from her lips and from her mouth
> so faithful,
> That she would rather die than again be
> playful.

But Des Barreaux was tempting fate. The adventure had only made the lady the more desirable to Cinq-Mars. And no young woman who yearned to conquer Paris and revel in its pleasures could hold out against an Adonis who occupied one of the most important posts at court. She yielded and Cinq-Mars returned her passion. They were blissful lovers and soon became the talk of the Marais. The defeated Des Barreaux sank into despair, vainly casting curses upon the traitress :

> My angel you no longer are,
> Nor shall I praise you from afar.
> This sighing heart of mine
> I disclosed to you in every line.

And Marion merely laughed. She was unmoved by the great cynic's downfall. The prince of libertines was so deranged that he was actually converted : 'He made an utter fool of himself and went about kissing all the relics he could lay hands on,' the heartless Tallemant remarks.

For a time, Cinq-Mars and Marion were the happiest and most fêted lovers in Paris. Richelieu was annoyed and Madame d'Effiat was horrified. Henri was no longer so afraid of his mother and her reprimands only threw him back into his lover's delightful arms. He did not, however, relinquish Madame de Chérmerault. They continued to be lovers and the treacherous lady continued to report to the Cardinal.[2]

Henri was not aware of the slightest threat to his future. He was no longer troubled by the King, whose benevolence had not yet begun to curtail his pleasures. These triumphs naturally went

[2] Some of these reports are mentioned in Richelieu's *Mémoires*.

to the eighteen-year-old boy's head. His family background and his own inclinations did not temper his success with the necessary circumspection. Our young Marquis was convinced that his success was entirely due to his own merit. Adonis became Narcissus. And as youth and grace add lustre to all things, his reckless vanity added to his charm.

IV

The Workings of Fate

The ensuing winter proved both bitter and glorious for Louis. The capture of Brisach had been crucial. The Emperor was cut off from the Netherlands; a wedge had been driven between the talons of the Habsburg eagle. Victory now seemed possible, though still far off. The hero of the Pas de Suze, whom Bassompierre had credited with an 'assurance and valiance in battle which even the late King, his father, never displayed', had originally thrown himself into the war with much less anxiety than Richelieu. Three years of war had made them change places. The minister advocated war with ferocious tenacity while the King yearned for peace. His Most Christian Majesty's health was declining. He was increasingly tormented by the ailments which Callot described in such detail. He trembled at the prospect of having to meet his 'Sovereign Judge' before he had ended this sinful war.

His people's sufferings also worried him. He had always been well loved by his people, but now he was becoming painfully aware of the diminishing number and volume of 'Long live the king!' salutes that accompanied his travels through the country. Then, no sooner had the troubles in Périgord died down than the Norman 'Bare-feet' began slitting tax collectors' throats and committing other atrocities. Another cycle of violence, counterviolence, sentences and executions ensued. Overwhelmed by his public responsibilities Louis continued to endure his private martyrdom.

He was surrounded by intrigue, espionage and duplicity. La Chesnaye, one of his valets, was a secret agent of the Cardinal's. Mademoiselle de Chémerault spied on both Cinq-Mars and Madame de Hautefort. Madame de Hautefort, in turn, reported her hapless lover's every word to the Queen. Louis often wished to sever this bond. 'The King wanted to break loose,' wrote Chavigny to Cardinal de La Valette, 'but he could not find the pretext.' Later he wrote, 'The Hautefort matter has not yet been

35

decided, but I think it is over and done with.' But it always seemed to mend. Louis was fascinated by Hermione, and would have accepted his bondage if the Cardinal's legion of agents had not undertaken to liberate him. They told him of how she ridiculed him and provoked unpleasant incidents and misunderstandings.

Once an incredible rumour was broadcast that the Marquis de Gesvres had dared talk of marriage with the King's favourite and that she had not been outraged by it. The King, however, was appalled. His anger swept through the court. The Duc de Gesvres, the rogue's father, was made to endure a Homeric diatribe, whereupon he rushed back to his son to make him sign an oath that he would never again pretend to the hand of the Queen's tirewoman. The Marquis was disgraced. Louis regained his equanimity slowly. Such minor dramas became melodramas in the hypochondriac's mind. His daily letters to his minister betrayed a curiously distorted sense of proportion. Madame de Hautefort's cruelties were given as much weight as the affairs of state.

In this sinister world where even the simplest pleasures were suspect, Cinq-Mars was a breath of fresh air : he radiated youth, and liveliness. He was a happy and fulfilled lover. Louis was drawn to the young man's obvious charm. Henri even had the fortunate knack of loving both Marion and Mademoiselle de Chémerault without rousing their jealousies, although each obviously knew of the other, since his affairs were on everyone's tongue.

Marion's beauty made her immortal, but her rival's beauty was just as dazzling. 'She was remarkable,' La Rochefoucauld wrote of her, 'and her delightful intellect was no less pleasurable than her beauty.' She was not financially independent—she was called the 'Pretty Pauper'—and she was therefore forced to be a resourceful schemer. But Cinq-Mars ignored such considerations. He sometimes spoke of marrying the schemer and sometimes the hussy.

When Marion was made to go home with her parents to their château at Baye, he galloped after her in hot pursuit. Travel was hazardous in those days. The Master of the Robe's haste attracted suspicion. 'A band of men concerned with catching thieves overtook him and bound him to a tree. Had no one come

forward to verify who he was, they would have carried him off
to prison.'

Madame d'Effiat took a dim view of her son's 'libertinage'.
Marion de Lorme had not yet become an experienced courtisan
but she did her best to play the part in style and was consequently
incredibly extravagant. One can easily imagine how she must
have worried the parsimonious Madame d'Effiat. Ruvigny, whose
gallantry and military prowess Cinq-Mars greatly admired,
advised him to break away from his mother's intolerable control.
Cinq-Mars mustered up his courage and left his mother's home
after a particularly violent scene to take up residence at
Ruvigny's 'by the Couture Sainte-Catherine'. He spent his nights
with Marion and punctuated his days with no less than four
visits to her, each in a different suit of clothes. Madame d'Effiat
choked with rage, but the few months which the young man
spent with his lively companion, a time entirely taken up with
the pursuit of love, were probably the happiest in his life.

Cinq-Mars suspected that Ruvigny was the lover of a very
noble and worthy lady because he pursued his love with such
secrecy. Henri would see him leave impeccably dressed every
morning for the Hôtel de Rohan. At first he thought the object
of his pursuit was the Duchess herself. On further reflection,
however, he realized that Ruvigny was too proud to share his
mistress with another man, for it was well known that Madame
de Rohan[1] had a number of lovers, one of whom was Monsieur
de Ferzay. Henri decided to trick Ruvigny into telling him who
his mistress was. He told him 'I nearly boxed a fellow's ears on
your behalf. He said some foolish things about you and Mademoiselle de Rohan.'

'Then you very nearly did me a grave disservice,' Ruvigny
replied.

Cinq-Mars swore to keep the secret. He would have been
very happy if all his friends had been like Ruvigny and if his
secrets had always been amorous ones.

Louis d'Astarac, Marquis de Fontrailles, harboured other
secrets. This 'gentleman of Languedoc, hunchbacked aft and of
wondrous ugly face before' was a born conspirator, dedicated to

[1] The Duchess of Rohan was Sully's daughter. Her daughter, Ruvigny's
mistress, eventually married Chabot and founded the family of Rohan-
Chabot.

a life of intrigue. He was remarkably intelligent but obsessed with the need to avenge the humiliations of his physique. He would have liked to impart some of his strength and courage to the Duc d'Orléans, who despite his enthusiasm for intrigue was always prepared to betray his collaborators. Richelieu knew of Fontrailles's shady dealings, but was unable to interefere with them. He disliked the man intensely. One day, when Richelieu was on his way to an ambassador's offices, he found the hunchback in the antechamber. 'Out of my way,' he said, 'you should not present yourself to the ambassador for he has no love of monsters.'

Fontrailles gnashed his teeth and swore under his breath, 'You devil, you may stab me today, but I shall do the same to you one day if it is the last thing I do.' Later the Cardinal beckoned him in and tried to laugh the incident off; but the hunchback never forgave him.[2]

Fontrailles had perceived Richelieu's intentions and guessed that the King would fall prey to Cinq-Mars's charms. He thus set out to win the young man's confidence. Henri, who could never resist intelligent, strong-willed people, did not reject Fontrailles's friendship. Fontrailles 'became his intimate friend, entering his rooms at any hour he pleased, receiving the young man's confidences', and whispering all manner of dangerous counsels in his ears. The role of evil genius suited him to perfection.

François-Auguste de Thou was a very different sort of friend: he was the guardian angel. He was the son of an illustrious parliamentary family who had known Henri since early childhood. His father owned the property of Villebon, near Chilly. His extensive travels took him to England, Flanders, Italy, the Levant, and gave him a precocious experience of the world. At nineteen he was made Parliamentary Counsellor. He was then made Magistrate and an officer of the quartermaster's staff, through which he received a wound and was enabled to reveal his military gifts. His career promised to be brilliant. But it was abruptly curtailed by a chivalrous if rather ill-conceived gesture. At the Queen's behest, the young counsellor advanced the necessary funds to save Madame de Chevreuse's jewels. These had been pawned just before the treacherous lady had been forced to flee

[2] Tallemant des Réaux.

after the exposure of the same conspiracy that very nearly brought about Anne of Austria's downfall. De Thou's chivalry was reported to Richelieu who gave the impetuous gallant a thorough dressing down and summarily placed him in the category of the untrustworthy. Thus disgraced and reduced to the ignominious post of 'Director of the King's Library' he became a subscriber to the widespread opinion that the Cardinal was a detestable satrap and a plague on the kingdom. He was convinced of this, or rather he believed he was, for he was essentially loyal and scrupulous and yearned to attain Christian perfection. He had studied theology from his earliest years and had spent much time in meditation and in the search of absolute truths, which had the effect, however, of tormenting him and making him the more indecisive. His normal state of anxiety was taxed to breaking point when he fell in love with the glowing and very devout Princess Guéméné. His love for her was bound to be guilty and even sinful, for despite her piety she offered him temptations which he struggled to resist. His old wound was painful and also taxed his nerves. He felt a need to work for noble causes and for the good of others.

He began to regard the terrible Minister as the embodiment of all evil. It was his duty to destroy him. 'He took it into his head to contrive his downfall convinced that in worldly terms it was the greatest possible achievement and that it would be the best way of serving his God.'[3] This obsession soothed his fevers and exorcised his demon. Despite his austere demeanour he was very fond of young Cinq-Mars, whom he intended to rescue from his youthful flush of riotous living and lead back to God. Henri recognized and admired his friend's 'exceptional merit', his 'lofty soul', his courage and his 'noble penchants'. He may have made light of his stuffiness, ridiculed his scruples and called him 'His disquietude', but respected him.

One day de Thou had the same intuition that Fontrailles had had : he also perceived what role the Cardinal wished the Master of the Robe to play. He was thrilled. His earthly mission was now revealed. Heaven had predestined him to prepare the scatter-brained youth to be 'the King's guardian angel' and the saviour of the state.

Cinq-Mars was so involved in his various love affairs that he

[3] Le Vassor.

failed to notice the webs that were being spun about him. Richelieu, Fontrailles and de Thou filled his ears with advice as to how to conquer Louis XIII, each for completely different reasons. Cinq-Mars listened. His successes multiplied and fortified his self-confidence and ambition and his former timidity disappeared. It might be fun to play the pretty wench and seduce a devout neurotic king. A young man's hot head could easily be turned by the fabulous tales of Epernon or Luynes or Buckingham, whispered to him by experts in temptation.

*   *   *

Louis XIII had evaded the trap he knew the Cardinal had laid for him for some time. Nonetheless he finally yielded. The Cardinal's direct pressure had roused some interest in the Master of the Robe. But it was Cinq-Mars's youthful spontaneity which eventually broke down his defences. When Marie upset him he sought comfort in Cinq-Mars's pretty face and his almost childish laughter. Then one day, he suddenly discovered the personality behind this face. He saw Cinq-Mars in a completely different light.

On March 27, 1639, the King wrote of Madame de Hautefort to the Cardinal, 'The attachment continues.' At the beginning of May, Madame de Hautefort could still upset him, as La Chesnaye, the Cardinal's spy-Yeoman of the Bedchamber, reports : 'His malady is a form of self-torment. Having sufficiently tormented himself and all those about him, he [the King] was restored to reason. He even took it into his head to get down on his knees and beg our forgiveness . . .' Louis solemnly proclaimed, 'I love her more than all the rest of the world together.' By May 25, however, when his Majesty left Saint-Germain to take command of his army, Richelieu had reason to believe that his plan was taking effect. Louis XIII arrived at Abbeville on May 30, he was to leave on June 4. It was during these four days, according to Montglat, that 'he began addressing Cinq-Mars more than was his wont'. The Court noticed this new familiarity immediately. Substantial evidence indicates that it was at this time that he yielded to the new emotions which had been tempting him for some time.

It seems probable that this was a new experience for him. The young king was not even eleven years old when Luynes,

5 Marion de Lorme

6 François Auguste de Thou

7 Princess Marie Gonzaga

8   The Queen, Anne of Austria, by Van Dyck

who was then thirty-three, comforted him in his unhappiness and helped the boy to overcome his infatuation for him. Baradas was a coarse blockhead and that ex-stableboy Saint-Simon, 'The Manurist' as he was called, was hardly less boorish. Louis loved Luynes as a hero, Baradas as a faithful animal and Saint-Simon as a confidant.

A good deal of malicious speculation surrounds the nature of these relationships. When Luynes took power (the king was then fifteen), the Tuscan ambassador wrote, *'La buggera ho passato i monti'* ('Buggery has crossed the Alps'). It seems difficult to believe that 'the only reason for these spiteful insinuations was the universal envy that attended Luynes.'[4] The King's 'Italian' inclinations were as obvious as those of his illegitimate brother César de Vendôme. However, Louis was devoutly religious and always regarded the sexual act as shameworthy. This would indicate that he did not follow his inclinations. Furthermore he had remarkable powers of self-control. His childhood miseries may have thrown him into Luynes's arms—he used to have his mattress placed alongside his friend's bed to ward off his nightmares, or so he claimed. But it was very unlikely that he should have participated in 'a thousand piggeries' with Baradas; and his famous reprimand to Saint-Simon would become meaningless had any such relations existed between the two. In any case, none of his past loves resembled his lightning attachment to Cinq-Mars. In fact, it became something more than an attachment. 'It was a total infatuation, an obsession, a sort of madness. Now no one ever sees Louis diffident and indecisive. No, there will be no glancing, thinking or turning back.'

Thus it was at Abbeville that Cinq-Mars learned that he had become a favourite. He may not have been surprised at being the object of such passion, but he was probably astounded at its violence. He had heard of nothing else for two whole years and then all at once the dance was on. He may not have calculated the outcome of these two years' efforts. It would have been impossible to predict Louis XIII's passions.

Cinq-Mars did not have the virtues of a saint but he had his own inclinations to contend with. He was not given to any such 'deviations', to which he had obviously been exposed in the company of the libertines. Louis's attachment presented him with a

4 Louis Vaunois.

dilemma. How could he possibly refuse a man whom he had effectively seduced, especially when this man was a king, the Lord's anointed one, the absolute lord and master of all souls and properties? Even a young thorough-going womanizer like Cinq-Mars might find some excitement in the conquest of the sacred person to whom God had entrusted France.

The affair has provoked much bitter controversy. Many modern historians have shrunk in horror before this scandalous hypothesis and rejected it out of hand, while others have elected to give Louis XIII the benefit of the doubt. But his contemporaries had no doubt whatever. Perrault wrote to the Prince de Condé, 'His Highness will be able to recall what he knew of King Henry III's affection for Monsieur d'Epernon and remember how he behaved and how he could give him presents.' Vittorio Siri tacitly shared this opinion. So did the dignified Henri Arnauld, the future bishop of Angers, a brother of the famous Jansenists, who frequented the Hôtel de Rambouillet, 'and who always had first-hand knowledge of what went on at court and in the city'. He kept President Barillon, then in exile, informed as to every development in the Cinq-Mars affair. Tallemant des Réaux draws his facts from eyewitness informants whom he never fails to name. His *Historiettes* were long regarded as a collection of scandalmongering petty gossip and were dismissed as unreliable. Today his non-conformism is felt to warrant considerably more attention. His realistic accounts of the seventeenth century should often be preferred to other more ornate descriptions.[5]

We cannot therefore ignore the probability of a most unusual relationship between the two men, in which the vanity and curiosity of the one gave free reign to the other's passion.

[5] cf. Antoine Adam, *Introduction à la nouvelle édition des Historiettes de Tallemant.*

V

Monsieur le Grand

The King, having taken Hesdin and several other towns, proceeded on to Stenay to inspect Marshal Châtillon's troops, then entered Mézières, where he stayed for four days. It was there, on July 26, that some of France's foremost officers gathered and dined together. The Duc de Nemours was among them: 'He was as witty and handsome a prince as any [he was Prince of the House of Savoy] but he was a young hothead.' That evening he showed his annoyance at Cinq-Mars's meteoric rise to royal favour and at all the rumours that surrounded the upstart. He set about needling the Master of the Robe.

Social rank then demanded that a mere gentleman respect his superiors. He was not expected to retaliate to any insult a prince might choose to hurl at him. Henri ignored such considerations. He allowed himself to be impetuous and did answer for himself. The Duke was taken aback and proceeded to redouble his attack; Cinq-Mars redoubled his counter-attack. Nemours was furious and flung a cherry stone at the insolent upstart's face, only to have another cherry stone shot back at him, which caught him in the eye. He sprang at Cinq-Mars and they started struggling with each other. The other guests finally succeeded in dragging them apart.

This childish incident shocked the court and split it in two factions. Henri could count on those who recognized his potential and not on those who wished his downfall. The King soon heard of it. It was expected that Louis, who always demanded strict conformity to formal etiquette, would decide in the prince's favour. In this case, however, he reproved Monsieur de Nemours for his conduct. He defended the Master of the Robe's position and bestowed favours on the young Marquis's apologists. The King's surprising reaction caused a scandal. The incident served to convince everyone that Cinq-Mars had indeed become his Majesty's favourite. Louis provided further proof of his favour by starting to call Henri 'dear one' before a speechless court. Even the older courtiers had never heard of such a flagrant indiscretion : Henry III had been scandalous enough but he would never have dared flaunt his affections so publicly.

The beginning of the seventeenth century saw the rise and exercise of absolute power as well as the advent of royal favourites. The two were inextricably linked : witness Spain, England, and France, where Marie de Médicis had choosen Richelieu. Only twenty years before the celebrated Francis Bacon had described a favourite's superb and yet precarious position for Buckingham : 'You are the king's shadow. If he commit some error, it is you who have committed it, or have permitted it, and you will have to pay the consequence. You may even be sacrificed to please the multitude. You must be his constant watchdog.' But Henri was not acquainted with these shrewd words. He was content to bask in the reflected glory of an absolute monarch. He was only nineteen and yet he had the world at his feet.

Henri's strange victory was followed by three unique, unproblematical, joyful months. Louis rode across his kingdom directing sieges, inspecting his fortresses, breathing the smell of gunpowder, leading a life which kept his persecuting demons, his ailments and manias at bay. The habitually tormented King even managed to feel happy. That active summer and early autumn, he and his favourite enjoyed the best months of their tragic friendship.

Louis made no effort to conceal their relationship. When Cinq-Mars joined the court again at Langres after he had spent a few days in Paris, Louis actually sent the royal coach to meet him at Châtillon. Nonetheless His Majesty had just sent Madame de Hautefort a 'casket' which had raised many a speculating eyebrow.

The king travelled throughout the Ardennes and Champagne until the end of August. He then went down towards Savoy to rescue his sister Christine, Madame Royale. She was the Duke of Savoy's widow and the Regent of his Duchy until her young son came of age. She had been forced to flee from Turin when her brother-in-law, an ally of Spain, had marched on her.

The king and the Cardinal met at Dijon and proceeded to Grenoble together, where Madame Royale threw herself at her brother's feet. Louis comforted her and sent a rescuing army to

Piedmont. He continued to Lyons, went to Roanne on the water-way, participated in the festivities of All Saints Day at Montagris, and finally returned to Fontainebleau on November 3.

The Cardinal's presence on these journeys afforded him the opportunity of observing Louis and Cinq-Mars at close quarters over an extended period. He had reason to hope that this relationship might rid him of Marie de Hautefort, which he would regard as a personal triumph. 'The Cardinal's instructions to Cinq-Mars to insinuate himself into the king's affections reveal this minister's acute genius,' wrote Vittorio Siri. Henri was so delighted with his new-found glory that he was quite prepared to listen to his protector's advice. He was also prepared to believe that Hautefort constituted a threat to his good fortune and agreed that she would have to go. With this in mind Henri began to sulk more and more noticeably when they were on their way back to Paris. Louis noticed and worried. He finally asked Henri why he was so sullen.

'Alas, sire,' Henri answered, 'when His Majesty sees Madame de Hautefort again he will no longer love me and the court will wonder what I could have done to lose my master's favour.'

He would not be reassured or cheered. Madame de Hautefort inadvertently helped his scheme by treating the King to her cruel mocking tongue when they met. The Cardinal's spies immediately reported these dissonances back to him. The King turned to his favourite and did his best to make his handsome face smile. He gave him a gift of 1,500 écus and hinted that he would make him First Equerry, a post which Baradas and Saint-Simon had held before him. Henri swore he would never enjoy anything again unless Louis promised 'not to look at Madame de Hautefort ever again'. Louis finally gave in and he probably did not regret his decision, for 'although it may not be impossible to have both a friend and a mistress, *he* found it difficult to reconcile the two.'[1]

*   *   *

Louis went to great lengths to appease this young man whose sensibilities he believed to be as delicate as his own. He even swore a veritable oath of allegiance to him : 'I have given you my heart and I swear I shall never share it with another.' When

[1] Montglat, *Mémoires*.

this declaration was broadcast to the royal retinue, it assumed the importance of a new statute. Chavigny, the Cardinal's right-hand man, wrote to Mazarin, a fellow collaborator, 'We have a new favourite at court, Monsieur de Cinq-Mars, who depends wholly on Monseigneur le Cardinal. The King has never shown such violent passion for anyone.' But did Henri 'depend wholly on Monseigneur le Cardinal'? The impetuous adolescent was conscious of his new power and had begun to wonder how best to liberate himself from his old protector and from his imperious, meddlesome mother. He intended being master of his own destiny.

François de Thou may have helped him reach this ambitious decision or Henri may have made his own mind up. What is certain, however, is that Henri set about trying his strength against those who thought him their puppet. He first decided he would have none of being made First Equerry, a post the King and the Cardinal had chosen for him. He set his cap at becoming Master of the Horse, which was one of the most important and highly prized offices in the kingdom.

It was a dangerous move and Henri played it daringly and with unexpected Machiavellian skill. He spread conflicting rumours that he would secretly marry Marion de Lorme and alternatively that he had already done so. This had the effect of propelling a horrified Madame d'Effiat to Parliament to obtain an 'injunction' against the marriage. She even filed a suit against Marion accusing her of 'rape and seduction'. Louis was distraught and Richelieu furious. Henri sulked and took exception to it all and never revealed his true motives. The King tried to humour him by nominating him First Equerry. Cinq-Mars was indignant.

'As I am already Master of the Robe, this post could not possibly elevate me. It was awarded other favourites with whom I do not wish to be compared. Is the son of a Marshal of France to be put on the same footing with mere "pages" who were delighted to have the opportunity of shedding their livery?'

Louis was crestfallen and asked 'what would make him happy'.

Henri continued playing his game and refused to answer. Louis pressed and he finally announced that 'either he would remain what he was or he would accept the post of Master of the Horse'. Richelieu was astonished by Henri's gall. His own nephew, Marshal de Brézé, had sought the post for years, but it was tenaciously held by the old Duc de Bellegarde.

The King would not listen to the Cardinal. The situation was threatening his health, for 'the least of his passions disrupted the economy of his entire person'. Henri had to be placated and pleased at all costs. Louis dispatched Monsieur de Saint-Aoust to prostrate himself before Bellegarde to ask him in His Majesty's name to relinquish his post in exchange for a considerable sum of money—five hundred thousand *livres*. The old man hesitated, sighed and recalled his own youth, for he, too, had been a favourite. He had been Henry III's last *mignon* and Gabrielle d'Estrées's first lover. He was a legendary seducer whose charms had conquered many a princess and many a fashionable young person. Now the poor old man was left with his memories to console him in his disgrace. But detested as he was by the Cardinal, childless and with one foot in the grave, he was scarcely in a position to gainsay his master's request. The sometime *mignon* may even have been amused by the idea of serving the same sort of fortunes he had enjoyed half a century before. But none of these considerations weakened his bargaining powers. He demanded that the office of the Master of the Robe be awarded his eldest nephew, the Marquis de Montespan (the future father-in-law of Louis XIV's mistress).

The terms for Bellegarde's resignation were still being negotiated when the Queen joined Louis at Fontainebleau—the Queen and her retinue, including Marie de Hautefort. Louis was uncertain as to the outcome of both the Marion de Lorme situation and the Bellegarde case. He was at Cinq-Mars's mercy and the rascal played on his anxieties like an accomplished coquette. One thing was certain, however: Madame de Hautefort had lost her hold over Louis. She would not believe it, as she was convinced that her mere presence would soon enslave him again. In fact, all she did merely hastened her own downfall. Louis's affections were otherwise engaged and she meant less than nothing to him. As Richelieu once put it, one did not fall from Louis's favour by degrees but headlong.

The court was astonished that Louis should introduce Cinq-Mars to the Queen and 'in words that fully revealed his passion'. When Marie de Hautefort appeared he gave her an icy look and said nothing to her. It was at Fontainebleau that Louis took every opportunity of displaying his exceptional attachment to Henri. He even went off to the hunt on horseback in order to

47

leave his carriage behind for his favourite, who was not an early riser.

* * *

Louis finally approached Madame de Hautefort in the company of Cinq-Mars on the evening of November 7.

'Madame,' he said, 'my affections are now entirely for Monsieur de Cinq-Mars. I understand that you are pleased to malign him. This grieves me. Should you continue, you will have cause to repent. I wish you to know that I shall punish those who have the effrontery to conspire against me.'

He turned his back on the speechless and furious woman. The court hurried to pay their respects to His Eminence and to the Master of the Robe. Henri was still not satisfied.

The following day, November 8, the nomadic, erratic King decided to leave Fontainebleau. At a very early hour an officer called upon Madame de Hautefort to deliver a note which bore the King's private seal and which banished her from the court. The proud young woman blushed with shame. She tore the letter up and chased the officer out, shouting that the letter was not from the King and that she would believe its contents when he communicated them to her directly.

An hour later, as Louis was stepping into his carriage, a veiled woman appeared before him. She brusquely disclosed the face of an angered goddess, bowed and begged His Majesty to explain his order, which belied all his promises. The King did not appear in the least concerned. On the contrary, he donned that near-inhuman expression that he wore when refusing Montmorency's and others' blessings. He nonetheless politely held his hat in his hand throughout their long and painful farewell.

'Get married,' he said. 'I shall provide for you.'

Marie refused to listen and demanded further explanation. When finally she had lost all hope, she asked, 'What then will become of me?'

'What you would have become had you left the court every time you threatened to do so.'

These were the last words they exchanged according to Henri Arnauld, who witnessed the scene. 'She has been provided', he adds, 'with assets worth a hundred thousand *écus*:[2] she will

---

[2] The king had given her the port of Neuilly for thirty years.

marry very well; her virtue and courage are held in high esteem.'

Madame de Hautefort left the court, and did not return until the death of her one-time adorer. But she was not the only one to leave. Louis may have felt frantic, but he did not yield to Cinq-Mars without exacting his own pound of flesh. Bellegarde's capitulation would prevent Cinq-Mars's dreaded marriage to Marion, but she was not his only rival. Mademoiselle de Chémerault would have to be sacrificed to the ambitious young man's career. Louis may also have learnt of her excellent services to the Cardinal. 'The Pretty Pauper' was to share the tirewoman's exile and bowed out of the chronicles of the time.[3]

On November 8 the king slept at Villeroy. The next day he called on Madame d'Effiat at Chilly castle. He did not go to negotiate a reconciliation between mother and son, but to impose one at the grasping lady's expense. Madame d'Effiat was forced to surrender 'whatever personal effects Henri might require'.

On November 10 the King arrived at his beloved Versailles accompanied only by servants and personal staff. Amid the forests, marshes and the autumn mists, the melancholy huntsman was in his element. He could spend his days with Cinq-Mars in this temptation-free haven and savour a kind of happiness that rarely came his way.

Meanwhile, the lawyers of the kingdom were working overtime. For sixty years the church and Parliament had argued over clandestine marriages. Many young people married precipitously and secretly to avoid parental, and even royal, disapproval. During the wars of religion this practice had increased. Many a rich heiress was forcibly carried off in the midst of the general commotion and then made to marry her abductor. Parliament sometimes annulled such unions and sometimes upheld them. It varied from province to province. The Church violently objected to these decrees that dealt with marriages, as it regarded them as a civil infringement on their domain. Under Henry IV, lawyers

[3] There are several contradictory accounts that deal with Madame de Hautefort's disgrace and with the so-called clandestine marriage. Having examined all the texts, we have adopted the ones which we consider to be the most acceptable. Dreux de Radier and Tallemant differ greatly in their versions of the marriage. No historian who has since treated the subject has thought fit to follow the incidents of Louis's and Cinq-Mars's life in chronological order. This method makes the truth accessible.

had started to draft legislation which would reconcile all factors, but they did not manage to make much headway in the bog of legal minutiae. Then, suddenly, when the King and the Prime Minister learnt of young Cinq-Mars's marital impulses, they ordered their lawyers to work something out immediately. The lawyers and clerks worked day and night drawing up a statute, just as Bellegarde's last defences were falling.

On November 13, Saint-Aoust returned with the old favourite's resignation. Two days later the new Master of the Horse was sworn in. Henri thus became *Monsieur le Grand*. On November 19 His Majesty signed a law on civil marriages which conceded a nominal victory to the Church, even if it did leave some scope for flexibility. The law, in fact, stipulated that, on pain of annullment of the marriage and confiscation of all estates, which would be donated to the hospitals, 'the marriage banns shall be proclaimed by the curate of each of the contracting parties with the consent of fathers, mothers, tutors or trustees, if they be children of families or in the keeping of others, and that the marriage shall be celebrated before four bona fide witnesses other than the priest who shall receive the consent of the parties and join them in matrimony in accordance with the formal practices prescribed by the Church'.

Louis breathed freely again : his 'dear one' would no longer be prey to fallen women and petty intriguers. 'He could not suffer that those whom he honoured with his friendship should marry and yet he was a chaste man and wished his subjects to be chaste.' Lavisse and Mariéjol, who wrote these lines, may have allowed discretion to blunt their perception.

Cinq-Mars rejoiced. The loss of the dangerous Chémerault was a small price to pay for this triple victory : a double victory over the king, who had made him Monsieur le Grand in his twentieth year and yet could not prevent him from being Marion's lover; and a further victory over the Cardinal before whom he had finally proved his independence and power. The dizzy hothead did not realize that in sounding this advantage so loudly he might be heralding his own destruction.

* * *

Richelieu flew into one of those rages that could make Europe tremble. He was furious that Henri should defy him and win his independence, that the boy he had always regarded as his own creation had proved that he was capable of achieving his own personal ends. He jabbed at his bedroom tapestry with his cane and beat his servants as he always did when he was in one of these tempers. Then he became reflective and uneasy. He realized it had been a serious, if not fatal, mistake to create such an ambitious headstrong favourite. Henri might well prove to be his downfall. Marie de Hautefort had been a less redoubtable antagonist, for all her bought allegiance to the Spanish party, which the king had known about in any case. Although Richelieu distrusted women, it even crossed his mind to bring her back from exile and break Henri before it was too late.

But it was already too late. Louis XIII would never countenance the removal of his favourite after he had gone to such extremes to secure his good graces. Richelieu thought it wiser to conceal his fury and make the best of the situation rather than launch into a doubtful battle. A dispute between the king and his adolescent friend soon rewarded his prudence. He was asked to play the role of arbiter.

Cinq-Mars was convinced his battle was won and over for ever. His admirable caution and restraint left him overnight. He had controlled himself all during their travels through France. He had conducted himself irreproachably throughout his daring game of setting up a loose woman as rival to His Most Christian Majesty. And he had emerged victorious. But youth rebelled. No sooner had he been made Monsieur le Grand than he rushed off to make love to Marion with all the pent-up ardour that had accumulated during those frustrating months. The lovely young woman hastened to broadcast the news of their reunion, delighted at the chance of snubbing those who had thought this unlikely after their clandestine marriage had failed to materialize. The Queen of the Marais was now named Madame le Grand.

The King was deeply hurt. Louis was very possessive, very pious and misogynistic and he thought Cinq-Mars was monstrously ungrateful. He took a masochistic delight in needling his lovers into hurting him—as Marie de Hautefort knew only too well. He was, however, afraid to discuss the real cause of his despair with Henri. He picked quarrels on the pretext of taking exception to the young madcap's extravagance : Henri had just bought a golden coach. They thus had a quarrel just a week after

Cinq-Mars's triumph. And it acquired epic proportions. Louis upbraided the young man harshly, denounced his careless extravagance, his debauched tastes, his dissipation, his laziness. He threatened dire punishment if he did not renounce his dissolute ways. Henri did not give an inch. He no longer looked upon Louis as his king, but as an infatuated, jealous, feeble, bickering man who was also something of a hypocrite. He answered bitingly. He would neither waste his youth nor be incarcerated. He then returned to Marion to sulk, as he knew this would produce the best results.

Louis made himself sick with sorrow. He turned to his minister, told him of his favourite's depravity and wickedness. Richelieu was pleased to have the opportunity of reaping his revenge : he summoned Monsieur le Grand and scolded him thoroughly. His Eminence's reprimands had a different ring from those of the King. The mere sight of the scarlet robes could revive Henri's old terror of the Cardinal. He promised to apologize and make amends.

The incident was the sole topic of conversation at court for some time. The great Cardinal wrapped in the pride and pomp of his Roman purple had become a paternal arbiter between the King and his 'dear one' !

Louis was so overjoyed that he wished to give gossips written proof of the restored harmony. This is how the following extraordinary document was written :

> We, the undersigned, certify to whomsoever it may concern that we are most satisfied and contented the one with the other and that we have never been in such perfect mutual understanding as we are at present. In witness whereof we have signed this document :
>
> > Louis
> >
> > By my command : Effiat de Cinq-Mars
> Written at Saint-Germain the twenty-sixth of November 1639.

The king wrote to the Cardinal on the same day, 'I appreciate your concern for my welfare. I felt a little unwell last night and was constrained to take a small remedy this morning. I may take medicine this evening. The certificate I enclose will indicate how well your reconciliation of yesterday has succeeded : when you intercede to lend your assistance nothing can go wrong.'

And the rainbow shone radiantly. Louis had the portrait of his favourite painted.[4]

[4] Monsieur de Nyert, His Majesty's head valet, was to recount to Tallemant des Réaux, who is our source, certain intimate scenes which provide ample food for thought. 'Fontrailles once entered Monsieur le Grand's bedchamber at Saint-Germain rather abruptly and discovered him being rubbed from head to foot with oil of jasmine. He got into bed and said rather unconvincingly, "Ah, that's much better." A second later there was a knock at the door. It was the King. It would seem he was oiling himself for combat.'

'On one of his trips the King retired at seven o'clock. He was in a state of disarray. Two great dogs leapt onto the bed, upsetting the bedclothes and kissing him. He sent word that Monsieur le Grand should undress and come to him. When he came he was dressed as a young bride. "Come to bed. Come along!" said the King impatiently. He had the dogs taken away but did not have his bed freshly remade. The *mignon* had scarce climbed into bed when the King started kissing his hands. When he noticed that Monsieur le Grand, whose affections were otherwise engaged, was not responding to his ardour, he said, "Dear one, what is the matter? You seem so sad."'

VI

Rows and Wrangles

In the winter of 1639-1640 the events that were to change the course of European history began to take shape. The King wanted peace more than ever. He called a convention of diplomats to Cologne to seek a peace settlement, but their search was to last eight years. Father Joseph, the 'Grey Eminence' of foreign affairs, died and Richelieu recalled from Italy the only man capable of succeeding him, Giulio Mazarin. Mazarin had once been Papal Nuncio in Paris. He now resigned from the service of the Holy See and openly entered that of His Most Christian Majesty. He had been involved in French politics for some time. He returned to the Louvre on January 5, 1640[1] as a naturalized Frenchman after four years' absence.

While Richelieu and Louis XIII pursued peace, they continued to plan the spring campaigns. They would have to fight on four fronts: Artois, Piedmont, the Basque country and Roussillon. News from Roussillon was promising despite the Spanish victory at Salse. Catalonia was preparing to shake off her Spanish yoke and separatist delegates came to Paris to ask Louis XIII to be their king. These vast and costly campaigns would require new taxes and further sacrifices. Richelieu was confident that victory would soon reward his efforts, but other worries claimed his attention. He confessed to his close friends, 'I am only a cypher signifying nothing unless a greater figure stands before me.'

The figure was the old, fragile sovereign, whom Richelieu had to protect from illness, worry, doubt, nervous attacks and bouts of mysticism, or the unfinished edifice of France's grandeur would come tumbling down and bury its architect beneath the debris. Louis XIII's peace of mind was as important to Richelieu as the strength of his armies. This is why he thought Cinq-Mars important and why, despite the recent humiliation, he continued

---

[1] This date alone refutes those who insist that Mazarin was Louis XIV's father.

to hope he could make use of him. He swallowed his pride in the expectation that the young fool would soon stop sowing his wild oats and help him manage His Majesty's moods. In any case, the king was so completely devoted to him that the Cardinal's best way of managing both of them was to appoint himself their protector and arbiter. He would have to devote as much attention to keeping them on good terms as to the conduct of war, intrigues and the business of government.

Richelieu's efforts to be conciliatory, however, and all his good intentions met with poor results. When Cardinal de La Valette died he left a number of ecclesiastical benefices vacant which the Minister then redistributed, reserving a somewhat meagre abbey for Jean d'Effiat, Cinq-Mars's reluctantly ecclesiastic brother. It then appeared that Louis had become fond of this foolish youngster whom he jokingly called 'the little Cardinal' and he was infuriated by Richelieu's slighting appointment. He tore the order to pieces and insisted that Effiat be awarded the best abbey available. Richelieu had to obey. It was the Cardinal's turn to be furious. His retinue quaked yet again. For days Rueil and the Cardinal's palace buzzed with possible ways of getting rid of the favourite. The rage abated and Richelieu took hold of himself. He would stick to his plans, but he began to hate his former charge.

*　　*　　*

Henri tried to reconcile his 'duty' with the pursuit of pleasure He loathed life at Saint-Germain. 'The court was always there and entertainment consisted in wooing foxes from their holes and blackbird hawking in the snow in the boring and totally unremarkable company of a dozen hunters.'[2] Cinq-Mars felt so self-confident that he was certain he could lure even the primmest of Capetians into a life of debauchery. Indeed this was the only time that the son of the Vert Galant was known to stay up drinking, dancing and feasting. The Master of the Horse did foster splendour, as his position demanded; or at least he did manifest it in his own person. He invited the lords of the land to magnificent feasts and balls. He dressed sumptuously. The court began to regain some of its past Valois brilliance, though not for long. The King was haunted by the image of his people's misery and felt

[2] Montglat.

guilty. He had not only inherited his Protestant grandmother Jeanne d'Albret's tuberculosis but also her toughness, sense of duty and puritanism. He soon resumed his morose habits and issued a new sumptuary edict. Saint-Germain became boring again.

Cinq-Mars could not bear the gloom. 'He was a very young man and thus had not the wit to dissimulate his sentiments. He openly expressed his dissatisfaction at being denied the pleasures of Paris before the King . . . He was not content to revel in the exalted favours he enjoyed but spent his days complaining bitterly to his friends, claiming that they enjoyed far greater liberty than he, yoked as he was to a singularly boring person.'[3]

The excitement of charging across France and plotting and conducting skilful intrigues dimmed and passed. Louis returned to his old self : he preached, moralized, talked of God, burdened Cinq-Mars with all his worries and endless accounts of his dogs and birds of prey. He also insisted that Henri never leave his side. Marie de Hautefort had not been subjected to such tyranny. Henri could not endure it. 'Ambition, which is the passion of maturity, was of little interest to a young man seduced by passions of a more youthful nature', and certainly could not relieve his intolerable burdens.

The King was in the habit of retiring early, which enabled Cinq-Mars to gallop off to Paris and make love to his Marion. The young lovers would then join the gleeful band of Marais libertines at the Hôtel de Rohan where they actively participated in the nightly festivities. When the sky began to pale, Cinq-Mars would leap back in the saddle and race back to Saint-Germain in time to assist the King's rising.

This routine of sleepless nights, love-making and nocturnal jaunts which were daily followed by the exasperations of his duties to the King soon took its toll on his appearance and conduct. Louis reacted by becoming worried and irritable. He started to fear that he had become an object of revulsion and made himself sick with apprehension. His jealousy caused him to have his favourite watched, and so he got to know of his escapades. They began quarrelling again. As soon as the King awoke he would scrutinize his beloved's face and if he discerned the slightest look of fatigue he would pounce on Cinq-Mars and reproach him

[3] Montglat.

9   Louis XIII and Madame de Hautefort

10 The execution of Cinq-Mars

bitterly. Henri would either deny his imputations or answer back impertinently.

The Cardinal's agents carried back all these developments to him immediately. The ambitious La Chesnaye was one of his agents; he had helped bring about Madame de Hautefort's fall from favour. He had hopes of 'changing his role from that of confidant to that of favourite'. He hated Cinq-Mars, but he disguised his hatred so well that he became his confidant. This enabled Richelieu to be a well informed peacemaker. After each quarrel Cinq-Mars was paternally scolded and the King suitably soothed. 'I am concerned to hear of His Majesty's present discontent,' wrote the Cardinal to Louis. 'I am writing this morning to inquire after His Majesty's disposition, knowing that he left here (Rueil) yesterday feeling dejected. I beg His Majesty's leave to proffer the following counsel: *should he not voice his discontent immediately it is roused, should he not inform His Master of the Horse of his will and pleasure, these dissonances will continue to plague him.* It is impossible to be young and also truly wise. His Majesty can make good his subjects' frailties by guiding them in his wisdom. I would beg His Highness to decide to act upon these counsels for the sake of his wellbeing, as I am convinced that they will produce the best results. I entreat him to give the matter thought and beg leave to remain to the very last his most humble and obedient servant.'

The Cardinal was responsible for another truce. The treaty stipulated that the favourite should no longer frequent the 'gentlemen of the Marais'. Louis felt something akin to revulsion for these men for their impiety and for the open homosexuality practised by their patron Théophile. He feared that Cinq-Mars might be wooed away from him. As it was, the young man seemed to prefer women. Mademoiselle de Chémerault, 'who had entered religion in Paris',[4] had taken up with him again. Not that this prevented him from visiting Marion's crimson-damasked bedchamber. These irresponsible escapades upset the King's equanimity and interrupted the Prime Minister's work.

'One evening he [Cinq-Mars] met Ruvigny at Saint-Germain and said, "Follow me, I am going to see La Chémerault. Two horses are waiting for me in a ditch near by." When they got to the ditch, they found that the groom had fallen asleep on the

[4] That is, she lived in a convent.

ground and that both horses had bolted. The Master of the Horse felt exasperated. They went into the town in search of other horses and then noticed that a man was following them at a distance. It was a Guardsman of the Light Cavalry, one of the spies the king had put on to his Master of the Horse. Cinq-Mars recognized him, called him over and spoke with him. The man pretended he had thought the two friends were about to fight one another. Cinq-Mars told him that that was not the case and the Guardsman rode off. Ruvigny advised the Master of the Horse to return and spare the King irritation. He should go to bed and then two hours later call his Gentlemen in attendance to help him dispel his sleeplessness. In this way he could shake the King's faith in his spies' information. For the King was bound to hear of his escapades the next day. The Master of the Horse did as his friend counselled with the result that when the King the next morning said to him, "You went to Paris, I hear," Cinq-Mars brought forward his witnesses, the spy was confounded and he was able to go into Paris on the three nights following.[5]

* * *

The Queen liked the Master of the Horse. She never demonstrated any of the jealousy she had towards her friend Madame de Chevreuse (when the latter had tried to seduce the King) and towards Mademoiselle de La Fayette, to whom she was so indebted. Since the near-miraculous birth of the Dauphin a year before, her situation had changed and she was forced to operate with greater discretion and deviousness. Before the Dauphin's birth, when she had been the sterile, ignored wife, the suspected and treacherous accomplice of the enemy, she had lived in constant fear of being subjected to a humiliating divorce or even a criminal's trial. Her best prospects had then been a dishonourable widowhood or seclusion in some convent. But as the mother of the next King of France her future held greater charms. She had to prepare for her future and for her possible widowhood. She had to be careful, prudent and cunning. She could not count on faithful supporters, who were, in any case, rather scarce. Her political ally, her dangerous and seductive brother-in-law Gaston d'Orléans, would immediately become her rival and contest her position as regent if the King died.

[5] Tallemant.

The King and the Cardinal had the means to prevent her from becoming regent before they left the scene. Fortunately for her, however, they both suspected and feared Gaston more than they did the King of Spain's sister. When Louis died it was certain that the Cardinal would assume the tutelage of the future Louis XIV himself, but then the Cardinal was unlikely to survive the King. It was nonetheless essential that she play for time and avoid making mistakes. Above all she must not incur the King's anger.

This is why the Queen was so charming to the King's favourite. And Cinq-Mars was easily won over by his sweet and lovely Queen. He also had an ulterior motive: he hoped that a reconciliation between the royal couple might give him more freedom. He set about bringing them together as Marie de Hautefort and Louise de La Fayette had done before him. On Christmas Eve at Saint-Germain, the King took everyone by surprise by ordering that his 'pillow be placed' in his wife's bed. Thus was Philippe, the founder of the House of Orléans, ancestor of all the Catholic princes alive today, conceived. One wonders whether the strange atmosphere which surrounded this event might have influenced the temperament of the future Monsieur, Louis XIV's brother. Many and mysterious are the ways of nature.

Henri's servitude was not, in fact, relaxed by these marital intimacies. The King's tyrannical passion for him continued and the young man defended himself with the same mockery and ill-temper as before. They resumed their rows on the very first day of the year, and they continued over a period of several weeks, interrupted by the occasional, short-lived reconciliation. 'The Cardinal and the Master of the Horse were aloof and cold towards each other,' observed Henri Arnauld. 'His Eminence was displeased by the Master of the Horse's frequent quarrels with the King.' The man who was becoming the 'greatest King in the world' was reduced to despair by the slightest sign of ill temper, by the merest note of harshness he detected in his beloved.

On January 23, 1640, Louis wrote to his Minister, 'I shall go hunting. My sorrow is so great that nothing can please me. The Queen is well and we have reason to believe she may be with child. I was reconciled with my Master of the Horse last evening. I hope he will be more prudent in future.' But Henri refused to be prudent. On January 29 Henri Arnauld related the following to President Barillon : 'His Eminence spent two days in Paris. He was not at ease and returned on Friday to make peace between the King and the Master of the Horse, who had just quarrelled again after the two great disputes they have had in the past fortnight. Nothing good will come of this.'

At first Henri took a secret feminine delight in these rows. He always emerged from them victorious, despite his apparent submissiveness. But the game began to pall when his jealous master's recriminations became really bitter and the Cardinal's scoldings grew more threatening. Tallemant indicates that Henri was beginning to find the King's 'caresses' odious. Cinq-Mars was regretting and cursing his fortune, which a few months before had seemed so blessed and joyous. Where were the gay boisterous days of his eighteenth year? He never stopped bemoaning their loss to the King who was invariably hurt by his complaints. Henri did not control his tongue in deference to the King. He would lash out at Louis remorselessly and the King was saddened despite the childish nature of the assaults.

'Monsieur le Grand', wrote Henri Arnauld, 'has taken it into his head to refuse to go hunting with the King. No one dares broach the subject with him.' This was a way of spoiling the unhappy King's greatest pleasure and depriving him of whatever mental solace he usually gained from hunting. But Henri gained nothing by this as he alone had to bear the brunt of the King's resulting nervous tension. Henri began to feel the strain and it started to show through his coquettish antics. He had nervous attacks and hysterical crying fits. His friends did not know how to soothe him. If he had been a twentieth-century screen idol and not a seventeenth-century favourite, these hysterics would be known as a nervous breakdown.

At the beginning of February Louis had gout. Richelieu was disturbed to see him so downcast. He set his skilful mind to devise some sort of diplomatic solution and he succeeded. February 11 witnessed a complete reconciliation. 'Monsieur le Grand is now more in favour than ever,' Arnauld remarked the following day. The Cardinal's pleasure at his success was soon soured. The insufferable wretch had snubbed him once again. A deliriously happy Louis had promised his 'dear one' the county of Dammartin, whose revenues were worth 23,000 *livres*. Then Louis expressed his desire to enjoy the pleasures of the reconciliation in peace and away from Paris. But dutiful as ever, he did not leave before checking with Richelieu that the interests of the state would not suffer from his absence. Richelieu kept him waiting anxiously for a fortnight and then wrote to Chavigny in an acidly ironical vein, 'The King may go to Chantilly without fear of prejudicing his affairs. I think he could do no better than to amuse himself . . . I am pleased to hear of Monsieur le Grand's reinstatement. As you may well imagine, I should prefer to see him before the King's departure, but I would not ask him to come here [to Rueil]. I shall judge his intentions by his actions.'

Cinq-Mars was not wise enough to be wary of the Minister's growing irritation. Dammartin was given him on condition that His Majesty retain the usufruct[6] and that the title revert to the crown in the event that he died without leaving an heir. This had prompted the young man to announce jocularly, 'I am the King's heir and he is mine.'

*   *   *

Louis XIII was not always the jealous lover, nor were hunting and religion his sole concerns and topics of conversation. His serener moments were spent in confiding the more serious aspects of his life to his friends and trying to explain some of the Cornelian dilemma posed by his kingship. Nor did Cinq-Mars lend an unsympathetic or heartless ear on such occasions, he would stop playing the spoiled child and feel an admixture of pity and admiration for his stoical friend who was capable of making such supreme sacrifices for his country. But like nine-tenths of his fellow Frenchmen, he was quite incapable of appreciating Richelieu's work. He would accuse the Cardinal of barbarous cruelty when the King spoke sadly of his exiled mother, whom he would never see again, or of his brother, whom he was forced to persecute, or those friends whose heads had rolled, or of the war against Catholic peoples whom he was forced to fight with the aid of Protestants, all of which weighed heavily on his conscience.

Louis said that Richelieu was 'France's greatest servant', but this inquisitorial despot's personality and methods did cause Louis much suffering. 'I should not be King had I the sentiments of ordinary men,' Louis insisted, although he did have such sentiments, of which he was not always master. When he confided in

---

[6] Richelieu insisted on this clause, but it was revoked in June.

Cinq-Mars, it was an indulgence, a way of finding some ephemeral solace by sharing his burdens and anxieties which he usually hid beneath his inscrutable expression. He always regretted his revelations and would hasten to swear the young man to secrecy. This exposed Cinq-Mars to very grave dangers, for Richelieu wanted to know precisely these sentiments and revelations. Richelieu had pressed him repeatedly that winter with disastrous results. Henri would not answer the Cardinal's questions to his satisfaction. His Eminence did not wish to lose what little hold he had over the young man, who struggled so hard to free himself. He decided it would be unwise to put too much pressure on Henri for the time being; he could still rely on La Chesnaye for such information.

It was at Chantilly that Monsieur le Grand learned of the valet's duplicity. His suspicions were roused when he surprised Richelieu whispering heatedly with his supposed friend in the garden—a conversation 'which ended with His Eminence dismissing him like a schoolboy'. Henri set about obtaining sufficient proof to expose and destroy the spy. The King had to be humoured and prepared before he launched his attack. Then, on March 21 Louis XIII wrote to Richelieu, 'I slept very well last night. It is my hope that Monsieur le Grand and I shall have no more misunderstandings. When next I see you I shall tell you of La Chesnaye's wicked ways.' The favourite had worked hard and well and his efforts were rewarded when 'the King entered the Gentleman's Chambers in the company of Cinq-Mars and brusquely ordered La Chesnaye to quit the court at once for being a seditious sower of discord'.[7] Louis fumed at the thought of all the painful wrangles the traitor had engineered. 'Having maltreated La Chesnaye thus, Louis turned to his retinue and said, "At least he was not a gentleman." He called him knave and threatened him with his cane.'[8]

The valet sought refuge with the Cardinal, but His Eminence refused to receive him and ordered him to disappear. Richelieu never supported his agents once they committed the folly of being caught. He was, nonetheless, furious.

Henri felt rather uneasy at this complete victory and so he also ran to the Cardinal to 'explain the reasons which had made the

[7] Vittorio Siri.
[8] Tallemant.

King rid himself of La Chesnaye'. He was greeted with fire and brimstone : the Cardinal 'reprimanded him severely for his short-comings which he foresaw would finally have dire results unless he mended his ways once and for all'.[9] Cinq-Mars thought he could stem the Cardinal's ire by 'saying that the rogue had caused trouble with the King which had hindered him from fulfilling his duty to His Eminence', but he could not have said anything worse. Richelieu decided to take the rash creature at his word. As Monsieur le Grand seemed so well disposed, the Cardinal would be pleased to pardon him on the condition that he stepped into La Chesnaye's shoes and reported back every single word the King ever said. Cinq-Mars saw the trap and refused point-blank. Richelieu lost control and gave vent to all he had with-held. He told him how and why a dandy who had no greater claims to fame than the possession of a pretty face had been made to rise to such exalted heights, why he had been chosen and why Richelieu had foisted him on to the King. Henri d'Effiat was a total nonentity, an insignificant nothing and Monsieur le Grand was even less than nothing. The only existence he had was that of a servile instrument created in the interests of the Cardinal for his own designs. It was a shock, a rude awakening. Cinq-Mars was barely twenty, and despite his precocious experience of the world, he knew little of the wiley deviousness of politics, of the base dealings of politicians acting in the interests of the state. He did not like Richelieu but he feared him and would never have dreamed that a friend of his father's would sanction serving him up to Louis XIII to make a spy of him. Henri expressed his humiliation, his disgust, his rage and then fled, weeping con-vulsively.

The following day his brother-in-law, La Meilleraye, now Marshal of France, visited him. La Meilleraye was startled by the chaotic situation. He reasoned paternally with Henri, impres-sing upon him the dangers that might ensue as a result of his behaviour, and persuaded him to return to Rueil. The trembling youth stood once again before the scarlet robes. La Meilleraye took up Henri's defence and with a great flurry of words, 'declaimed his apology'. His Eminence condescended to show some indulgence. The victorious Marshal begged his brother-in-law to return the Cardinal's great kindness by immediately 'offer-

[9] Father Griffet.

ing a written, signed pledge to the effect that he would tell the Cardinal all that the King might say'. Henri was tempted to consent, but he had his pride, courage, and a good deal of obstinacy. He declared that to do so 'would be signing his own damnation', whereupon he took his leave and walked out. La Meilleraye gave him up dramatically and went to pay his compliments to La Chesnaye.

This was a declaration of war. Richelieu did not forgive offences and humiliations he was made to suffer. This child had once been the object of his hopes, of his generosity, and had then proceeded to wound his pride by winning Marion's love; then he betrayed his confidence, then foiled his manœuvres, and finally presented him with an adversary in place of the submissive creature on which he had counted.

As for Cinq-Mars, he had received a blow which his friends did their best to aggravate. Fontrailles fanned his rage; de Thou his indignation. Both, however, convinced him that he should fear the tyrant's vengeance. Henri saw the wisdom of their arguments. The admirable Minister truly had a vile soul. He was too young to understand that such a man would regard the refusal to commit an evil or ignominious deed for the good of the state as tantamount to treason.

VII

The Arras Affair

It was the early spring of 1640. That year France was to recover her ground and Louis the Just would live through his finest hours.

It was to be a year of victories and it was the year when *Horace* and *Cinna* were first performed. A few lucid minds began to see the emergence of a new France eager for pre-eminence, a powerful, impetuous, magnificent France of brilliant men, of Condé and Turenne, of Descartes and Pascal, of Corneille and Poussin.

The King and his Minister felt the resurgence of this new life, but Parliament, the nobles and the people ignored it. Revolts, dissent and plots continued to proliferate. Three Spanish spies disguised as hermits were discovered and confessed that they had been hired by French princes, by the Duc de Vendôme in particular, to assassinate the Cardinal. This dampening discovery did not, however, interfere with the preparations for the campaign which Louis hoped would finally bring his desired 'blessed peace'. He applied himself to the task with something akin to passion. And the God of War, as Richelieu put it, did work miracles for them in Piedmont. The Comte d'Harcourt defeated the Marquis of Leganez and recovered Casal. They had to push northwards and complete the campaign by taking Arras and thus Artois.

The conquest of Arras was a risky undertaking. The town was an important Spanish stronghold. The Catholic King's subjects and Richelieu's enemies sang the jingle:

> When Arras by France is beaten,
> Cats by mice will be eaten.

The army was enlarged to two hundred thousand men and the campaign was entrusted to three marshals: Châtillon, Chaulnes and La Meilleraye, to whom Richelieu announced, 'You will answer with your heads if you fail to take the town.' Louis XIII had planned the siege during a relatively peaceful sojourn at Chantilly.

The King and his favourite continued to squabble. Louis had given up trying to conceal his jealousy of Marion. He dared not exile the impudent young woman, but he ordered her to leave Paris whenever he was to be there. Richelieu also disapproved of Monsieur le Grand's liaison with the woman who had snubbed him. Marion defied them both. She encouraged her lover to be as debauched, insolent and extravagant as possible. Louis did not have the courage to deal with her himself, nor the strength of will to ignore their relationship. He was being made to look as ridiculous as Molière's Arnolphe and Bartolo; the situation was becoming dangerous.

Richelieu had felt it essential to terrorize his Marshals to ensure military victory and now he turned to the equally essential task of pacifying his master. He would have preferred to remain arbiter-general of their extravagant quarrels himself, but his recent encounters with Cinq-Mars had been particularly explosive and required a sort of mediation he could no longer provide. He turned to the Secretary of State, Sublet de Noyers, and asked him to shoulder this responsibility with the same solemnity and gravity with which he had once conferred the protection of the kingdom into his hands. The King and Cinq-Mars admired this great steward who had been responsible for the singlehanded resurrection of the army. It seemed ironical, if not ridiculous that a war minister should have to referee an intimate lovers' quarrel on the eve of a major offensive. The situation would have been truly farcical had the individuals involved not had the power to influence the outcome of the war itself. Noyers proved himself to be as excellent a peacemaker between these incompatible combatants as he was a military organizer. The Cardinal knew he had won when the King left Chantilly for the north on May 7.

On May 9 at Soissons a new 'reconciliation' was concluded in the form of a treaty. Louis XIII dictated a solemn document to Noyers:

> 'This day of the ninth of May, the King being at Soissons, His Majesty has consented to give assurance to Monsieur le Grand that throughout the duration of this campaign he will have no quarrel with him, and, should it occur that the said Sieur le

Grand offer him any cause for complaint, it shall be brought, without malice, by His Majesty to the attention of Monsieur le Cardinal, in order that His Eminence advise the said Sieur le Grand to correct the cause of His Majesty's displeasure, this being done for the sake of all His subjects that they may continue to find their strength and sustenance in His Majesty's person. These terms have been agreed by the King and my said Sieur le Grand in the presence of His Eminence.

> *Signed:* Louis
> Effiat de Cinq-Mars.'

His Eminence appears to have forgotten his grudges for he gave his blessing to this truce, which favoured Henri. Henri elected to act rationally and sensibly and did not flaunt his advantage. Paris was a long way away and Marion was at her family château at Baye. Then on May 20, a joyous King wrote to the Cardinal, 'I can assure you that Monsieur le Grand and I have attained a perfect understanding.' Henri, however, decided that his discretion and co-operation should be rewarded.

*   *   *

The only authentic glory the seventeenth-century gentleman could win was to be found on the battlefield. The social functions, the purpose and the authority of the nobility, its preeminence, its privileges and its abuses were tried and justified on the battlefield. When Henry IV restored a long-forgotten state of peace to France, the gentry lost their military profession and were forced into unemployment which reduced them to subsisting on royal generosity. When Louis XIII came to power and war broke out, young nobles were again afforded a thousand and one opportunities of excelling themselves in the service of the King, or in that of opposing factions.

The favourite had already proved that he was a 'man of mettle', but he had not yet distinguished himself in battle. A year before it would have satisfied him to achieve this recognition by the mere demonstration of valour, but now his growing ambition and pride spurred him to attain more lasting recognition. His intentions were good but his aspirations were so lofty as to appear childish. He decided that the laurels of a victorious general would forever safeguard him from being treated 'like a schoolboy', and

Monsieur le Grand complained 'of the vile inaction which prevented him from acquiring the reputation of a man of arms which he had always longed to win'. Louis was distressed to see his beloved dejected. The King was troubled but he was also a soldier and he sympathized with the young man's ardour and was even proud of it.

Arras was under attack by mid-June. A Spanish army commanded by the Infante-Cardinal, the Queen's beloved brother, marched to rescue the besieged town and to counter-attack the besiegers. The French were cut off from their supplies and their situation was critical. An immense convoy of six or seven thousand heavily escorted carts was requisitioned to save them from starvation.

The siege held the general public in suspense. 'News is eagerly awaited,' wrote Henri Arnauld. The outcome of the war was in the balance. Every young Frenchman wanted to take part in the decisive battle. Cinq-Mars decided to win the desired victory himself. He asked the King to give him the command of the troops that were to force the blockade. Louis hesitated for a moment. He was reluctant to be separated from his beloved, but he was touched by the bellicose impatience of a boy whose frivolity he had so often criticized. The seductive ploys and persuasions Henri adopted to win command of the army could have won him the crown jewels. Louis finally consented.

A general of twenty was, perhaps, about to make history. Richelieu was astounded and horrified by the news. He rushed to the King and launched into one of his long Cartesian discourses to prove the danger of entrusting the outcome of the war to the inexperience of a young dandy who was better suited to amorous debauchery than military strategy. But a mere look from the King silenced him. It was one of those times when the Cardinal could hear the whistle of gunshot as he confronted his 'illustrious slave'. He feigned submission, bowed and left.

That evening Monsieur le Grand was summoned before His Eminence. Richelieu, like most great statesmen, was a gifted actor. He played this scene brilliantly: he started by adopting the right paternal pitch in which to warn the young stalwart against being over-impetuous; then in a voice redolent of pathos he evoked the sorrows that would befall the kingdom if the Arras operation failed; he finally donned his terrifying mask and swore he would never countenance a folly which might prove disastrous for the whole country. Cinq-Mars was no match for Richelieu. He was overwhelmed and hypnotized by all these modulations and by the grave content of the Cardinal's delivery. By the time Richelieu adopted a dulcet tone in which to suggest he make the stoical gesture of spontaneously renouncing the disproportionate honour which had been bestowed on him, he had already given ground. But this great sacrifice merited compensation. The flower of the nobility were to form a corps of 1,400 volunteers and they would not fail to acquit themselves gloriously in battle and thus win fame and recognition for their prowess. Monsieur le Grand would be given the command of these 'Immortals' despite the presence of three princes. This would enable him to exhibit his abnegation as well as his valour.

Henri capitulated. He told the King of his decision in the most touching terms and Louis was filled with admiration and tenderness for his consideration and courage. Meanwhile Richelieu hastened to make amends with his old enemy du Hallier, who was one of the army's best strategists. Du Hallier (later called Marshal de l'Hôpital) was given general command of the operation and Monsieur le Grand was put in charge of the volunteers.

Then at the last minute the King showed signs of weakening. Cinq-Mars feared the King would make him remain with him at the army headquarters in Amiens. Louis let him go but made him promise to write to him twice a day. Henri was wild with joy at the prospect of leading such a brilliant detachment: he could just see himself prancing behind drum and standard down the path of glory, François de Thou riding at his side. But his vainglorious dream was to be tempered by reality. The Duc d'Enghien, the Prince de Condé's son, and the Ducs de Mercoeur and de Beaufort, His Majesty's nephews,[1] refused to take orders from a mere gentleman. Bitter quarrelling erupted between the young men. But the King kept an eagle eye on them all and the princes were made to accept Cinq-Mars.

The great day arrived—August 2, 1640. The Spaniards attacked the half-starved besiegers. Marshal Châtillon had two horses killed beneath him before the relief army arrived, and the battle was almost lost. The enemy held the fort of Rantzau:

[1] They were grandsons of Henry IV and Gabrielle d'Estrées.

'Someone came to tell the Marshal that all was lost and that the entrenchments were falling.' Châtillon reined back the young soldiers from rushing into the fray. He was reluctant to let Monsieur le Grand face the enemy. 'Wait,' he said, 'wait until they have done their worst.' He finally gave the order to charge and was promptly struck in the shoulder by a musket shot. The Volunteers 'charged so fiercely that the Spaniards were pushed back from the entrenchments to the far end of the battlefield.' Cinq-Mars acquitted himself remarkably. His horse was shot from beneath him but he leapt up and fought on while spiteful onlookers were eager to discern a certain all-too-natural pallor. The princes and their friends were heard to whisper that 'Monsieur le Grand looks better in the ballroom than on the battlefield'. But such remarks were quite unjustified, as Henri was soon to prove. When he saw the infantry assembling to lay siege to the fort of Rantzau, he hurried to join them. But Châtillon, who had remained at his post despite his wound, was reluctant to let him expose himself to such danger, for if the favourite died or was disfigured Louis XIII's wrath might well descend on his head. The Marshal decided not to allow the volunteers to lead the assault. 'I had Monsieur le Grand removed from the lines by the force of my own entreaties and orders,' he wrote to Count Charost. 'Everything turned out well.'

The favourite was safe and sound and the battle was won. Châtillon felt he would ingratiate himself by exalting Cinq-Mars. His report stated, 'Monsieur le Grand arrived with many notable volunteers. Had Monsieur de Châtillon not restrained him by entreaty and by order, which he was obliged to obey, he would have charged the fort that the enemy had just regained. His arrival was welcomed by the officers and troops who had withstood the enemy's onslaught for two continuous hours.' The *Gazette de France* sounded its trumpets on Cinq-Mars's behalf. The August 8 issue read, 'Our volunteers were commanded by the Master of the Horse, who acquitted himself with such excellence that those who witnessed his charge at the enemy's squadrons deemed him a worthy heir of the titles and virtues of his father, the great marshal who accomplished the feat of leading His Majesty's armies to victory in Germany, even though he was on his deathbed.'

Châtillon's zeal and the *Gazette*'s eulogy were ill-placed, according to the Cardinal. He had never expected to see his one-time *protégé* win such a dangerous halo. Théophraste Renaudot, the editor of the *Gazette*, was severely reprimanded. He then published an official account of the Arras engagement and retracted the first report indicating that it had not been the official one. Richelieu himself dictated the text. Cinq-Mars was not even mentioned, nor was François de Thou. The *Mercure* went even further and coolly attributed the command of the volunteers to the Duc d'Enghien.

Since his departure from Amiens, Henri had not thought of his promise to write to Louis. His continued silence turned Louis's initial fury into sheer misery, which Tallemant claims actually made him weep. As the King's resentment did not diminish, the Cardinal took the opportunity of minimizing his favourite's accomplishments by reporting that the brazen boy had behaved like a coward. Richelieu knew his 'warrior king' would think such behaviour despicable. 'He told His Majesty in mocking tones that he had been very grateful to the Generals for guarding his [Cinq-Mars's] person so zealously; that the accident that had befallen his horse had so frightened him that he had not recovered in time to join the army in the retaking of Rantzau; and that it was a pity that he had not chosen to demonstrate some of the valour which he had flaunted before the fray.'

Arras fell on August 9. On the fifteenth the King dealt with all the amnesties and the necessary procedures for the occupation of Artois, which was now restored to France for good. A fortnight later Cinq-Mars joined him at Chantilly. Louis had rehearsed a terrible reception for him but his anger dissolved at the sight of the boy tanned by the winds of battle. Henri proffered a host of good reasons to explain his negligence and he was very charming. Their reconciliation was complete. 'The understanding between Monsieur le Grand and myself is very great,' wrote His Majesty to the Prime Minister. 'Yesterday's clouds have now passed.'

Louis, who had always been reluctant to befriend any of the Cardinal's creatures, was now secretly pleased to find that the Cardinal and Monsieur le Grand had fallen out. It was his turn to seize the opportunity of rending the two asunder and ensuring that they would never be reconciled. He told Henri of what Richelieu had said about his performance at Arras. Cinq-Mars was astonished for it was considered almost a crime to question a

71

gentleman's courage and the injustice of this particular insult exacerbated the outrage. The naïve boy was convinced that Richelieu had wanted to dishonour his old friend's son because he was annoyed that Cinq-Mars had refused to become his spy. Monsieur le Grand had hated the Cardinal since that day and now he swore to reap his own vengeance.

* * *

On September 7, the King returned to Saint-Germain where the Queen, who was eight months pregnant, awaited him. He went to see the two-year-old Dauphin, whom he thought looked 'very much prettier'. Cinq-Mars wanted to fondle the infant, but the future Louis XIV would have none of it and shrieked with fury. His father's intervention merely doubled his fury. The King was angry. He gave the Queen a 'livid look' and said, 'My son cannot bear the sight of me. His upbringing seems most strange. I shall see to it that it is changed.' That evening he wrote to Richelieu about the incident concluding, 'My son is . . . very wilful.' (Henry IV had once said the same of him.) 'I am not prepared to suffer his ill-humours.' Then, two days later, 'I am ill-pleased with my son. No sooner did he set eyes on me (I was accompanied by Cinq-Mars) than he cried as though I were the devil incarnate, and then he always calls for his mother. His evil temper must be made to disappear and he must be removed from his mother's keeping as soon as possible.'

A distracted Anne of Austria sent a messenger to ask for the protection of her enemy the Cardinal. The court was excited by the incident for quite a week. The King threatened to take the Dauphin away from his mother and entrust him to the care of guardians if his conduct did not radically improve. Everyone knew that these guardians would be the King and his favourite. On September 13, however, Louis obtained some satisfaction: 'My son begged my pardon on his knees,' he wrote to His Eminence, 'and then played with me [and Cinq-Mars] for more than an hour. I gave him some toys and we are now the best of friends.'

The Master of the Horse's intimate participation in family matters indicates the extent of his favour and even his power, despite the events of the previous months.

On September 21, Anne of Austria gave birth to a second son, to the great joy of the sombre monarch. A few days later the King went to Monceaux. He informed Richelieu that amid this gentle countryside, which autumn had made the lovelier, his soul was at peace, which was an almost unique experience for such a king. He was hunting wolves and he and Cinq-Mars were 'happy together'.

F

VIII

The Femme Fatale

Marie Gonzaga, Duchess of Nevers and Rethel, Princess of Mantua, was descended from Nordic adventurers and sophisticated Italian despots. Her ancestors were Albrets, Lorraines and Paleologues. She was the daughter of the Rhine through the Clèves and the daughter of the Renaissance through the Dukes of Mantua. Her coat-of-arms thus bore both the arrogant Gonzaga eagle and the mystical Clèves swan. She was a tough hardheaded princess (Albret), courageous and ambitious (Lorraine), and a somewhat illusionistic Greek besides (Paleologue), whose father had hoped to become emperor of Byzantium.

Her family was a remarkable and extraordinary one. Her grandfather Louis Gonzaga was the third son of the Duke of Mantua. He married Henriette de Clèves and became Duc de Nevers. He was one of Catherine de Médicis's principal counsellors. He was also the young Henry III's mentor and accompanied him on his trip to Poland. He was remembered and respected for his singular wisdom and moderation even though he had helped to organize the St Bartholomew's Day Massacre. Henriette de Clèves became the mistress of the magnificent Annibal de Coconnas, the glamorous idol of the day. In the Bartholomew Massacre he was said to have slain some thirty heretics with his own dagger. Henriette mourned him publicly when he was condemned to death for attempting to kidnap the Duke d'Alençon and the future Henry IV. His head rolled off the executioner's block immediately after that of Queen Margot's beloved La Mole. It was at this time that another remarkable and extraordinary Gonzaga, Louis Gonzaga's namesake and cousin, was in the process of becoming St Louis Gonzaga.

Henriette de Clèves's and Louis Gonzaga's son Charles was an extravagant gadfly. He astonished Rome with his fabulous ambassadorship. Then he undertook to wage war against Louis

XIII. He occupied Champagne, in fact, before he had come of age. Then he went on to organize a campaign to recapture his rightful inheritance of Constantinople. He set sail, but his fleet, and with it his hopes, went up in flames.

He was compensated for some of his losses in 1629 by the fortuitous death of his cousin Vincent II which gave him the Duchy of Mantua. Mantua was a key principality in Italy. Neither the Emperor nor the King of Spain wanted to let it fall into the hands of an ally of France. They tried to give it to the Duke of Savoy, but Richelieu intervened and war broke out. Charles was finally recognized Duke of Mantua and Marquis of Montferrat in 1631. His sons had disappeared at a very early age and he was left with three daughters, Marie, Anne, and Benedicte.

Louise-Marie Gonzaga was born in September, 1611. She lost her mother when she was seven and was then brought up by her aunt Catherine Gonzaga, Duchess of Longueville, who took pains to educate her as an Italian princess. She also gave her an ardently religious education as well as elaborate instruction in all the superstitions then prevalent in the land of her paternal ancestors. Marie divided her time between churches and pilgrimages on the one hand, and astrologers, magicians and alchemists on the other. When she died she left a considerable work on 'the great profession'.

Marie Gonzaga possessed that supreme pride and that passion for grandeur and 'glory' which Corneille personified in his heroines. She followed her father's exploits with avid interest and was overjoyed when he became Duke of Mantua. Unfortunately the Duchy could never be hers, but this did not concern Mademoiselle de Nevers, as she was then called, for she had greater designs in mind. When she was at an age when most girls pine for their first love, Princess Marie was dreaming of crowns; for no throne was beyond the young lady's reach. This is what she would request of the Virgin of the Dove, also known as the Virgin of Good Love, when she went to prostrate herself before her image in the Church of Saint-Etienne de Nevers. A portrait painted of her when she was fifteen shows her young face encircled with enormous pearls. The face is one of a determined but charming girl. The child's smile recalls that of a slightly malicious Reims Angel, but her eyes are not the kind that would lower readily.

When she was seventeen, Mademoiselle de Nevers distinguished

75

herself amid the Queen's beautiful ladies-in-waiting. She was not one of the fragile, heart-wrenching, simpering creatures subject to the 'vapours' who wrung so many fashionable hearts in the eighteenth century. The gentlemen of her day were once described as 'wild bucks held at Christian bay', and their female companions held their haughty heads high above their mettlesome bodies. They loved good food and the smell and din of battle, and, despite the 'Carte du Tendre', they enjoyed their warriors' lusty embraces. These headstrong women managed to persuade their suitors that they would only bestow their love on those who truly merited it; aspirants were thus convinced that no effort was too great for such a recompense. This enabled the women to smooth down their men's rough edges when it suited them, or, when the need arose, to give fire to the men's natural mettle and to their taste for danger and rebellion. Marie was the equal of all these Amazonian *Précieuses*, but was unfortunate in her choice of suitor. No other woman in France would have dared set her cap at such a man.

In 1628 Monsieur, as Gaston d'Orléans, the King's brother was called, was heir apparent to the throne and the favourite son of the Queen Mother Marie de Médicis, who was still the ruling deity of the court. He was also the hope of Richelieu's adversaries. At the age of twenty he was already a widower. The contrast between the lugubrious Louis XIII and this jasmine-scented prince charming who sauntered about with his hands shoved into his pockets, whistling like an oriole, was indeed remarkable. He was as handsome and scatterbrained as a page, and his grace and charm reminded everyone of Henry IV. There were many who wanted to see Monsieur become the defender of the Cardinal's victims and the feudal and Catholic[1] order which this scarlet tyrant sought to destroy. When, however, the plot that was to seize power in his name was discovered Gaston showed little integrity and none of the courage of his convictions. He promptly denied friendships, betrayed colleagues, and sacrificed Chalais's life in order to save himself.

Marie de Médicis intended to marry him to one of her relatives, the sister of the Grand Duke of Tuscany, but Marie Gonzaga interfered with her plans by capturing his hitherto fickle heart. Richelieu, who was still managing the mother's raging

[1] In the domain of foreign policy.

tempers, promised to foil any plans the young couple might have of marriage. But Monsieur was genuinely in love. He started writing love poems to his beloved despite his earlier sarcastic sallies against the *Précieuses* and their simpering suitors :

> Youthful goddess who new delights
> Augment today my secret cares ...
> To your beauteous eyes I pledge my heart.

A sonnet bearing his signature would arrive almost daily at the Hôtel de Nevers, where he was to be seen sighing in the best *Astrée*-shepherd manner. Marie could realistically dream of becoming Queen of France.

The War of the Mantuan Succession interrupted the idyll abruptly. The Cardinal had Gaston appointed general in command of the French army, for which he would receive the sum of 50,000 *écus*. Gaston was to restore the Duke of Mantua to his estates but the restoration was not to win him the Duke's daughter. The Cardinal had made a deal with him that the appointment and the glory he would win would in fact cost him Marie Gonzaga. He was to renounce all plans he might have of marrying her. The rogue actually subscribed to the unchivalrous bargain, but he was not given the chance to reveal his intentions. Louis XIII, who had suffered Marie de Médicis's preference for his younger brother throughout their childhood, drew the line at conferring so great a military honour on him. He decided to command his armies himself. Gaston, thus freed and furious, proclaimed his firm intention of marrying the princess. He abandoned the army and the King near Grenoble and turned back for Paris. In the meanwhile, Mademoiselle de Nevers and her aunt had set out for the Alps. The Queen Mother posted a hundred horsemen led by Sieur de Cahuzac after them, fearing that they would encounter Monsieur. This disturbing escort descended upon the two ladies at Coulommiers, and proceeded to accompany them, not to Mantua, but to a prison in the forests of Vincennes. Monsieur was thwarted. He withdrew to Orléans to play the sulky rebel, where he received a volley of angry letters from his brother. Then he took refuge in Lorraine.

Peace was not restored to the royal fold until January 1630. Gaston made a rowdy return to Paris and spent his very first day back in the company of his 'mistress' with whom he stayed until midnight. Everyone was more convinced than ever, that Mademoiselle de Nevers would become Madame, the future queen. But reasons of state interfered again. The Mantua affair was far from being settled and Marie realized that a marriage contracted against the King's will might be the undoing of her father Duke Charles. She sacrificed her personal sentiments to her filial duty in the manner of a truly heroic princess. On January 28 after a heart-rending scene, she and Gaston bid each other an eternal adieu.

Richelieu had never really wanted to persecute the young lovers. Their troubles sprang from the terrible Medici Queen Mother's ancestral hatred of the Gonzagas and from the King's sibling jealousy. The Cardinal was trying to ward off the crisis which finally exploded at the end of the year and which opened the dangerous rift between him and his former protectress. He had served the Queen Mother's designs in an attempt to molify her rage. Gaston and Marie, however, were unaware of the Cardinal's motives. They were convinced that this cruel tyrant was exclusively responsible for all their misfortunes. They both hated him. Gaston became a conspirator again, while Marie began gathering new recruits for the anti-Cardinal faction at court.

Marie fell under suspicion which was only aggravated by her friendship with Anne of Austria. Thus the years and opportunities for making an illustrious marriage passed her by. She was nearly twenty-six when her father died. Since Salic law applied to the fiefs of Mantua and Montferrat, these went not to her but to her young nephew. Rethel and Nevers, however, legally reverted to the eldest Gonzaga. Marie was recognized Duchess and entered Nevers on May 29, 1637. She inherited all her family's French possessions which had been sorely depleted by Charles's recklessness. She was determined to gain distinction and rule nobly. She refused to relinquish the minutest fraction of her inheritance to her two sisters, who were promptly locked up in a convent. But the limited confines of her Duchy, which she ruled from the court, were incommensurate with her ambitions.

The fruitless years continued to pass her by until Marie Gonzaga reached the age of twenty-nine. Men continued to be charmed by her, though her beauty was now more majestic than seductive. The imperious Duchess was still bent on attaining supreme achievements, but it seemed increasingly unlikely that her duchess's diadem would ever become a royal crown.

*   *   *

Cinq-Mars had savoured the pleasures proffered by Marion de Lorme, Mademoiselle de Chémerault and various other lovely ladies of easy virtue. He had had such a feast that he occasionally suffered from a mild case of amorous indigestion. He had started to long for that sublime, passionate love that poets and novelists depicted. Never had literary fashions imposed such refinement of sentiment and such heroic overtones on such a rough and thoroughly Rabelaisian society as at this time. The *Cid* elaborated upon and intensified the rather insipid models set by Urfé and Scudéry. When Marion de Lorme applied her wit and skills to the art of love, she became a Greek-comedy courtesan. She was incapable of the disquieting turbulence of a true tragic heroine. Monsieur le Grand had now reached the stage where his reputation and his desires demanded a mistress capable of such grandeur.

Cinq-Mars had known Princess Marie since he had come to court, as she was one of the Queen's retinue. She was one of a hundred haughty noblewomen of exalted ancestry and 'virtue' who boasted numerous suitors, but she was by far the most majestic and subtly seductive woman at court. The King's favourite admired her greatly. We know little of how this admiration evolved. Their initial interest in each other probably sprang from their joint realization that they might well serve each other's ends. Cinq-Mars could dream of becoming a prince if he married the exalted Duchess of Nevers. His increased status would fortify his position at court and moreover the marriage would certainly stun and dazzle an astonished court, city, Cardinal, and the King himself. Marie, on the other hand, was an enemy of the Prime Minister. Her fortune was not enormous. And she was fast approaching thirty. She had also begun to realize that her exceptional fate might never materialize. If, however, she conquered the charming gadfly who controlled Louis XIII and if she could induce him to gain complete control and even to govern in his name, her ambitions would be fulfilled, for such a fate was truly fitting for a woman of her ancestry.

The princess and the favourite looked at each other through

the eyes of their respective illusions. Then nature took over. The charms and graces and even the fundamental frailties of the pretty boy moved the Amazon's heart and Henri was completely captivated. Henri's fragile, unstable, even feminine side was attracted by the lady's bold authoritarian character. His mother had been such a woman and her maternal tyranny had disposed the young man to enjoy subjecting himself to a woman who was nine years his senior and who could give him the support and help he needed at this juncture in his life. Marie's beauty and her aura of queenly majesty toppled whatever other barriers remained.

The relationship was accepted as fact by September 1640, when the King and Queen were at Saint-Germain. Henri resumed his escapades to Paris to visit Marion and the dangerous society of the Marais, but this did not prevent him from becoming the Duchesse de Nevers's 'lover'. This word should not be misconstrued. It is used here as Corneille used it : Henri 'committed his faith' to the princess. He 'sighed' for her and proved his passion for her publicly in a thousand ways. He swore to sacrifice 'his blood and his life' for her should the need arise. These gestures entitled him to her 'favours', to her smiles, ribbons and token kisses. This love game produced remarkable results. Marie remained mistress of herself, despite her genuine feelings, but Cinq-Mars yielded himself up to the new experience of passionate love and let it control his whole life.

*　　*　　*

This is how Cinq-Mars felt when he followed the king to Monceaux. Marie may have been responsible for his brief period of rational behaviour, which so delighted the king. But he was not capable of controlling himself for long. The life of a rustic Nimrod, which held such joys for the King, always bored the young man and now aggravated his distress at being away from his beloved. He took his restlessness out on the King in the most childish way by creating unpleasant situations. At such times Louis's letters show peculiar signs of weakness, which were unusual for a man who displayed such great physical and moral strength in the face of the most overwhelming odds.

'I would beg that you excuse me if this letter lacks good reason,' he wrote the Prime Minister. 'I have been out of sorts since one o'clock yesterday when it pleased Monsieur le Grand to quarrel with me and thus disturb my peace. Thankfully I have witnesses who will bear me out and prevent him from denying anything. Had he not received Monsieur de Noyer's letter, which he was obliged to bring me, I would not have seen him at all, as I have not done since three o'clock yesterday afternoon, since when he has decided to keep to himself, as I fear he will continue to do. Monsieur de Noyers will tell you how I showed him all possible tenderness and friendship the evening before last. The more one shows him love and appreciation the more certain is he to take objection and be ill-humoured. I believe he will try to justify himself to Monsieur de Noyers but I would ask that you give no credence to anything which you do not have directly from me in his presence and in that of Gordes who witnessed all that happened. I was so angry that I scarcely slept last night. I was quite out of humour. I will not continue to suffer his ill-manners. He has gone too far.'

The King of France was made to endure the insolence of a poor subject and humble himself by pleading his case to the arbiter of conflicts. He could not sleep. He made himself ill. He would tolerate it no longer. But the favourite's merest gesture or smile were enough to gladden his heart. The evening of that distressing day, the two were once again reconciled and another messenger set out for Rueil.

'I write this note for fear that you may worry over what I wrote this morning. As soon as Monsieur le Grand decided to return to my company, I received him gladly and we are both happy and together again.'

*　　*　　*

The King returned to Saint Germain and Cinq-Mars to Marie. Their relationship was a fabled romance in the Hôtel de Rambouillet style : passions soared to an incredible pitch because the Princess refused to allow Cinq-Mars to violate the literary laws of chastity. The court knew of their love and gossiped and commented and speculated but no one ever cast the slightest doubt on her proud virtue. Tallemant shared this conviction : 'He often came to see her at night. Their respective positions at court inevitably fostered a certain intimacy, but no one has ever suspected them of anything untoward.'

'Their respective positions . . .' Henri's desires and ambitions

81

craved an early marriage. Marie let him be the first to speak of this fantastic project. She heard him out and she gave him time to measure the light-years that divided an Effiat from the ruling Duchess of Nevers. Then, when her suitor had duly sounded the depths of despair, she told him how he might span this distance that separated them. She drew his attention to how Monsieur de Luynes, the humble little falconer whom Louis XIII had loved as he loved Monsieur le Grand, had managed to become a Duke, Constable and the Keeper of the Seal. There was no reason why Cinq-Mars should not also aspire to such promotions, which would then make him worthy of the hand of a Gonzaga.

This artful suggestion set the hapless youth's mind racing. He began to plan feverishly. He was naïve enough to think that Richelieu would help him achieve his aims. For Cinq-Mars, Richelieu was omnipotent. Their relations, however, had deteriorated badly, since the favourite had refused to go to Rueil after the Arras affair, despite the Cardinal's wrath and the warnings of his emissary, Saint-Aoust. Monsieur le Grand suddenly decided to heed his mentor, and allowed himself to be persuaded to call on his former protector. He listened submissively to the inevitable dressing down, begged forgiveness and promised he 'would treat His Eminence in a more fitting manner'. He believed this token submission 'fortified' his position with the Cardinal. He then decided to make peace with his mother to whom he confided his intentions. Madame d'Effiat was pleasurably surprised and gave him a good deal of encouragement. None of his friends came forward to warn him. Ruvigny had too great a respect for the supreme rights of love and the pious François de Thou and the cynical Fontrailles were delighted to see their frivolous friend finally embarking upon the right path.

Passion can dull even the sharpest of minds, let alone that of a twenty-year-old gadfly. Henri had decided to ask the king to make him a duke and a peer. He thought he was being an artful strategist when he went to beg His Eminence not to oppose his desires.

Richelieu never ceased being astounded by this creature's incredible nerve. Cinq-Mars's request shocked him and also worried him. He was aware of Marie Gonzaga's hatred of him and did not underestimate the intelligence, determination and ambition of Gaston's ex-fiancée. He saw the snare which was set to trap him and had no alternative but to destroy it and Cinq-Mars's hopes at once. He did not waste his cunning skills on him. He dealt with the sapling quite brutally. He bluntly declared that 'he could not believe that Princess Marie had so forgotten her birth and station that she would stoop to such a lowly mate'.

'You must remember that you are but a mere gentleman raised beyond your station by favour alone, and that the Marquis de Sourdis paid your brother [Martin] an inordinate honour when he gave him his daughter. I cannot think how you dare even think of such a union.' Henri tried to justify his temerity by muttering that he had his mother's approval. 'If what you say is true,' thundered the Cardinal, beside himself with rage, 'your mother is also a fool. And if Princess Marie has entertained such a notion, she is an even greater fool than your mother.'

Richelieu, like Napoleon, excelled himself in scenes of anger. He could work himself up to volcanic rages during which he would crush his victims with a torrent of sarcasm and insults. Henri crumbled. He had great trouble in containing his tears and barely made it back to his carriage gasping and choking. 'When he returned home someone noticed that the buttons down his doublet had burst.'[2]

[2] G. de Pitaval.

IX

The Advantageous Quarrel

After that scene, Cinq-Mars's fortune began to bear on the fate of France and of the world. Henri did not have the strength to master his despair. He shuttled between depression and mania. He imagined fantastic revenges. He played with the idea of withdrawing from the court and its intrigues, and even from the princess herself. He was too feminine, however, not to take his disappointment out on his totally innocent victim, the King. He wanted nothing of the King for the time being, and so he made him his whipping boy. Louis was therefore subjected to a thousand capricious injustices. He defended himself and he rebelled, but he never thought of banishing his dear executioner, despite Cinq-Mars's real efforts to achieve this. 'When he knew that something would please His Majesty and that the alternative would displease him, he always chose the alternative.' But to no avail. It seemed he could not be too detestable. Cinq-Mars did not understand Louis at all—which was just as well for him. His best schemes were not schemes but instincts. Father Griffet betrays his own lack of perception when he muses, 'A favourite who behaves so badly should not excite such fear.' And he shows his lack of subtlety when he adds, 'The King's love for him was so strong that all that should have destroyed it did but increase it.'

The sixteen-year-old Louis may have declared, 'I must prefer justice to pity'—Richelieu coined the declaration—and Richelieu may have written to Louis, advising him that 'Kings must punish and be harsh and exacting to those who disrupt the order of their realms; they should never take pleasure in their destructive antics.' But the implacable prince was a living paradox. The barbaric punishments inflicted on him as a child, his moral lassitude after his father's death, his mother's harshness and injustices, his court's open disdain had all helped to make him the pitiless but masochistic man he was. The King who refused blessings and who signed the all-too-frequent death warrants

84

may even have taken a secret sado-masochistic delight in doing so. It may have been his way of revenging himself on his cruel governess Madame de Montglat with her fearful disciplinary cane. And yet he had adored his tormentress as he adored his detestable mother.

The same monarch who ordered the erection of so many scaffolds, experienced a voluptuous joy (as Marie de Hautefort had realized) in being snubbed and thwarted, bullied and martyred. Cinq-Mars's childishly tyrannical behaviour cost the rascal nothing and gained him even greater power over the King. These unintentional tactics served him more than he knew. Louis might grumble and groan while he masochistically enjoyed his discomfort, but he also genuinely regretted his favourite's obvious suffering. Knowing the Cardinal to be the author of this misery, he conceived a grudge against him.

It may only have been a slight grudge, a slight change of attitude, but when such a change came from the demiurge himself it gained monumental proportions. The Cardinal's faithful collaborators were the first to detect the winds of change. Chavigny wrote, in code to Mazarin, who had been away for a few months on a mission, 'The King, the Cardinal, and Cinq-Mars are exactly as you last saw them at Amiens, but for the fact that H.R.H. has recently changed towards the Cardinal-Duke. I confess that I fear the outcome of it all, but Monsieur de Noyers continues to assure me that there is no cause for alarm.' Then on November 6 he insists, 'I am on better terms than ever with His Eminence. He has told me of his feelings for that certain person whom you know well, whose insufficiency is a source of constant trouble to him. I cannot write in any greater detail but I feel sure that you will understand what I mean.' Eight days later a letter written in Italian informed Mazarin that His Eminence was anxious to find a solution to a most distressing situation and that he did not know where to turn.

A subterranean war was being waged and the public were beginning to notice signs of discord. Superficially the trouble appeared to be between the King and his favourite, who were indulging in a series of incredible scenes. They left Saint-Germain—which deprived the young man of his princess and of the last of his self-control. On November 22 the King wrote to the Cardinal from Livry :

'I have kept my peace until now before writing to you to see if Monsieur le Grand's ill-humour might pass. But nothing has changed since I was last at Rueil. Although I have been twice to his chamber to beg him to forget anything I may have said or done to displease him, he insists that I do not love him because when he requests something which is unjust or contrary to justice or good usage I refuse him. He would also have me inform him of my plans four or five or six days hence, when I myself do not know what I shall do an hour before I do it. These are the causes of his discontent. This is how he humours me when he knows that I am worried by my son's malady and were it not for the long hours I spend hunting (for when I am at the lodge I have to suffer his arrogant, aloof presence), I should have a merry time indeed! I can no longer abide his airs. He considers everything unworthy of him and refuses to see or talk to anyone. I would prefer not to importune you thus but you are the only person I can wholly trust and to whom I can turn in my discontent. I bid you good day and hope you are well.

Louis.'

'He is as slothful and dilatory and negligent of his duties and commitments as ever.' Three weeks later another battle broke out at Versailles and Henri stuck to his new strategy of 'aloof arrogance', indifference, and offended dignity. On December 13 the King wrote to the Cardinal, 'We have no cause to complain of Monsieur le Grand, for since yesterday, he has but uttered commonplaces. We can say in his favour that he has shown me no anger; nor has he shown any sign of good spirits.'

The young man may have been pining away but he certainly did not deny himself any of the joys of life. The King continued to reproach him in vain for his extravagance and frivolity. Henri Arnauld wrote, 'Monsieur le Grand has ordered some of the most beautiful furniture anyone has ever seen. The court has never seen such a magnificently laid and served table.' The King had a truly magnificent favourite. The Master of the Horse would escort the King in his own coach, which was more sumptuous than the Queen's. He resumed his visits to Marion who furnished him with the pleasures of profane love while Marie Gonzaga proffered the nobler glories of sublime love.

If the princess would have him, Henri would become the envy of all France. But the princess had 'her pride', and she still insisted that her 'lover' prove his worthiness. Cinq-Mars had no idea how to achieve worthiness and his plight reduced him to tears of frustration.

The New Year's festivities were peaceful enough but a new clash broke out on January 5 (1641). The King decided to deal severely with him this time. He dispatched Cinq-Mars to Rueil with a letter instructing Richelieu to give him a thorough trouncing and the Cardinal did just that. He lectured and raved for a whole gruelling hour. However, His Eminence decided to reinstate himself as peacemaker now that his recalcitrant protégé had become an adversary. He sent Henri back to Louis with a fairly mild letter which assured His Majesty of Monsieur le Grand's new resolutions. But Louis was not in a conciliatory mood when he received the missive. He wanted to escalate the quarrel and therefore seized upon the first pretext that came to mind.

'Monsieur le Cardinal informs me that you wish to please me in all things and yet you continue to persist in displeasing me on the one account I especially asked him to have you amend: I refer to your sloth.'

Henri had borne too many insults for one day and felt he had reached the end of his tether. 'His Eminence did speak to me of this but I cannot mend these ways and I shall never be otherwise,' he exploded. The King was taken aback by Cinq-Mars's violence and he tried to be conciliatory without capitulating. 'A man of your condition who pretends to the command of armies and who has expressed such a desire to me cannot on any account afford to be slothful.'

'I have never had such a pretension.'

'To which,' wrote the King in his account of the exchange to the Cardinal, 'I replied that he had, but that I did not wish to dispute it further. You know what he is like.'

Louis was definitely looking for a quarrel: 'I then returned to the question of his sloth saying that this vice rendered a man incapable of accomplishing noble deeds and that it only befitted the pleasure-damned souls of the Marais, where he had been weaned.' The King became so excited with his own invective that he got carried away: 'And that is where you will make me send you if you continue to behave in this manner.'

'I am quite ready to go any time.'

'If I were not wiser than you,' Louis retorted, struggling to beat a dignified retreat, 'you know what I should say to that.'

Then he added piously, 'In view of your obligations to me you ought not speak to me like that.'

This had no effect at all on the insolent fellow. On the contrary. 'I want none of your favours. I should like you to take every single one back and keep them. I can do very well without them. Furthermore I would be just as happy to be Cinq-Mars as Monsieur le Grand, and as for altering my way of life, I cannot and will not live in any other way.' The outraged King left his room, crossed the hall, and descended the palace steps. Cinq-Mars pursued him and they continued quarrelling loudly as they passed before the mocking eyes and ears of the courtiers. When they reached the courtyard, Louis shouted, 'Seeing that you are in such a temper, you will do me the favour of getting out of my sight.'

'With pleasure.'

'I have not seen him since,' the King noted sadly as he gave the Cardinal a detailed account of the whole squabble. 'All that I write took place in Gordes's presence (the captain of the guards). Then he added in a postscript, 'I showed Gordes this note before sending it to you and he agrees to its accuracy.'[1] This was the absolute monarch who would have a man beheaded merely to justify a whim.

Cinq-Mars continued to play cat and mouse with him. The next day, at eight in the morning, Richelieu was informed of the following incident. 'Last evening Monsieur le Grand asked Montespan to inquire if I should be glad to receive him. Then he changed his mind and sent word through Montespan to say he was unwell and could not come.'

His Majesty was obsessed by the need to prove everything he said was true. 'I ask you to refer to my two memoranda to Messieurs de Noyers, Count de Guiche, de Sénecterre, Bautru, and Saint-Aoust, who are his friends, so that you may ascertain which of us has been in the wrong and whether I did not speak to him for his own good and honour.' But the rights and the wrongs of the situation altered nothing. Henri sulked and Louis refused to make the first move. If the two people involved had not been His Most Christian Majesty and his Master of the Horse the whole situation would have bordered on the ludicrous.

On January 8 the King informed the Prime Minister of the

[1] Published document in the Aubery collection.

gravity of the situation. 'Since my quarrel with Monsieur le Grand on the fifth of this month, I have not heard from him. He expects me to go in search of him, which I refuse to do after the way he has used me. Yesterday I observed to his friends that I found it strange that he should make no attempt to speak to me and make peace, hoping that when he heard of this he would wish to do so. It was, however, to no avail; he continues to be as stubborn and aloof as ever. I bring this to your attention now so that if he instructs his friends to tell you otherwise, you will know that all he says or has others say to you is false. I bid you good day.'

An angry Cinq-Mars decided to seize this opportunity to break free, or so historians have claimed. What probably happened, however, was that the princess advised Cinq-Mars to resort to that singularly cunning ruse which Richelieu himself had often used to such good effect. How many times had the Cardinal offered and threatened to leave his master in the knowledge and certainty that he could not possibly do without him! Monsieur le Grand duly wrote to the Prime Minister: 'Monsieur, I am much disturbed to see Your Eminence so frequently taxed with complaints about my person. A remedy must now be sought. I would rather spare myself the pain of giving lengthy and useless accounts of myself and thus I choose to admit full blame for I know not what. I would further entreat His Eminence to show no more of his kind disposition for me and that he should prefer his own peace to furthering my fortunes, and that he should support all that His Majesty's anger might demand. This is not a whim, which I shall later regret. I have given the matter great consideration and have concluded that I shall not fear the outcome providing that I am made exempt from the King's wrath. I take my leave reminding His Eminence that I am, as ever, his most humble and obedient servant.'

He sent another letter to de Noyers saying, 'The extremes to which you see me reduced will give you an indication of the state in which I find myself. I implore you, in the name of the love you bear me, that you consent to help me end this miserable existence of mine. Go to His Eminence and ask him what I must do to break away while safeguarding myself against the King's wrath. This is all that I ask, all that I desire.'

The Cardinal would have been delighted to take the young

man at his word. But the King would not hear of it. The heroic sacrifice of Louise de La Fayette had done him enough violence, and he had no intention of repeating the gesture and losing his 'dear one' four short years after being deprived of his 'beauteous angel'. His whole life was regulated by his terror of being brutally denied the solace of another loved one. Richelieu was put in the invidious position of seeking to mend a rift he would otherwise have welcomed. Thus the young man who had been so viciously upbraided for his follies, and who had been threatened and humiliated and subjected to so many pearls of wisdom, had won a resounding victory. Superficial observers claim that his decline from favour dates from that month of January, when, in fact, the contrary was true. Cinq-Mars, with the help and intelligence of his Egeria, had proved that his very indispensability to the King made him a free agent. Richelieu had used exactly these tactics when Marie de Médici launched her attack on him. The Cardinal, therefore, was not hoodwinked, nor was Arnauld, who wrote to Barillon on January 13, 'Monsieur le Grand is fully reinstated. The quarrel has been a foul and furious one . . . It seems impossible that a real rupture will not eventually occur . . .'

*   *   *

February 7, 1641, marked the apotheosis of the Cardinal-Duke. It was the day when the King signed the marriage contract between the Cardinal's niece Mademoiselle de Brézé—who had the misfortune to be the half-witted twelve-year-old daughter of a totally mad mother—to the Duke d'Enghien, the son of the Prince de Condé, the noblest prince of France. It was a terrible union which the Prince de Condé had negotiated eagerly despite the protests and wishes of his broken-hearted young son who was in love with Mademoiselle de Vigean. The whole court was shocked, but at the same time duly impressed, with the exalted heights attained by the Queen Mother's former chaplain. The court also marvelled at the pomp that surrounded the occasion.

Once the contract had been signed, the Cardinal's palace was transformed into a setting for a spectacle of unparalleled brilliance. A ballet of no less than thirty-six separate parts, each sub-divided into five acts was performed and the great ball that followed it lasted until dawn. 'Never has His Eminence been in better sorts,' remarked Henri Arnauld.

The ill-fated union was to have many dire and unexpected consequences. It ruined the Condé line with Clair-Clémence de Brézé's congenital insanity. It did, however, link the Duc d'Enghien to the Cardinal's faction, and won the future Grand Condé, as he was later known, the command of the French army which won the battle of Rocroi.

Richelieu had his day of triumph, but the more perceptive courtiers had begun to detect signs of some impending peril, a peril which had not threatened his existence thus since his near-fatal Day of Dupes.

Louis's quarrels with his favourite were not his only concern. He knew that the Cardinal was a very sick man and that he would have soon to find a successor to him. Presented with the problem and the prospect of the Cardinal's senility, the King had started to see his favourite in a new light. He noticed that the boy had changed in the past few months, and was surprised by his intelligence, his informed opinions, and his new sterling ambitions. Louis began to wonder whether a suitable period of apprenticeship might not reveal Adonis to have the qualities of a statesman. He was, however, unaware of the princess's influence. It was she who encouraged Henri to ask that he be given serious duties which would mitigate his frivolous reputation. He expressed his desire to enter the Council and the King finally authorized his entry. Richelieu dared not object. Cinq-Mars thus brought himself a step closer to the ministership.

Marie Gonzaga congratulated herself on her achievement. Her 'lover' had climbed the first rung to power.

X

The Widening Rift

The Prime Minister's dissatisfaction with the favourite immediately roused the interests and the hopes of the opposition. Fifteen years of abortive plots, constant court intrigues and futile civil wars had not dulled their militant determination to get rid of the tyrant.

The last serious attempt on the Cardinal's life took place at Amiens in 1636 during the campaign that regained Corbie and repelled the threat of invasion. Gaston d'Orléans and his cousin the Comte de Soissons planned the operation and were helped by Gaston's favourite, Montrésor, and Soissons' factotum Saint-Hibal (or Saint-Ibar). They had intended killing the Cardinal during the commotion of the campaign when he was less protected than usual.

One day, after a council meeting at the Duc de Chaulnes's house and after the King had left they had their chance. Richelieu stayed behind to talk to Soissons. They were in the courtyard of the house and Gaston, Montrésor and Saint-Hibal were present with three other accomplices. The conspirators grouped around the unprotected Richelieu and waited for the signal. Gaston had only to flicker an eyelid and their daggers would have been drawn and the tyrant slain. But His Highness hesitated while the others looked on enquiringly. Gaston finally panicked and ran up the stairs to the first floor of the Hôtel de Chaulnes. Montrésor did not follow his master or persuade him to descend, for the moment had passed. By the time the Prince had regained his self-control the Cardinal had left unscathed and unaware of his escape. Three days later they planned to strike again, but the opportunity never arose. The Cardinal's wary guards had not suspected anything, but Orléans and Soissons gave themselves away when they lost their nerve and fled. Orléans went to Blois and Soissons to Sedan, an independent town controlled by the Duc de Bouillon.

Monsieur eventually made peace with his brother, while the Count remained at Sedan. He was a Bourbon and the head of a cadet branch of the House of Condé. He was a gifted politician and an excellent soldier, and eventually became the leader of a large and powerful anti-Richelieu faction which operated in France and abroad.

Richelieu's exiled victims became a veritable émigré army dangerously in league with France's international enemies. There were many illustrious exiles, such as the Queen Mother and the Duc de Guise, the Duchesse de Chevreuse, the Duc de Vendôme and a host of lesser nobles, all plotting away in Holland, England, Lorraine and Germany. Even the Cardinal's prisoners in the Bastille, men like Marshal de Vitry and Marshal de Bassompierre, conspired against him from behind bars. Then outside the prisons there were those who were kept under close surveillance, and others, who were allowed greater freedom of movement, like the octogenarian Duc d'Epernon and the young Abbé de Gondi de Retz, who were all prepared to take up arms and go into action. The most formidable of these suspects was the Duc de Bouillon, whose citadel in Sedan became the retreat for the exiles and the headquarters for the active opposition.

This dissenting faction never missed an opportunity of asserting the nobility of their intentions, which revolved around their determination to rescue the King from evil counsellors. When France was drawn into the Thirty Years War, her entry gave their cause and motives added weight. The greater nobility were not affected by the people's miserable plight, but the lesser nobility were directly affected by it. Since they derived their income from the revenues yielded by their estates, the peasants' suffering at the hands of requisitioning soldiers and extortionate tax-collectors threatened their very livelihoods. They were therefore forced to plead the peasants' cause and join forces with them. In 1631 Gaston d'Orléans wrote a letter to the King that displays an unusually keen humanitarian concern for the poor. Richelieu could certainly never have written such a letter: 'Less than a third of your subjects eat ordinary bread. Another third eat oatmeal bread and the remaining third are reduced to begging and to such an abject state that some literally die of hunger when they can no longer sustain themselves on a bestial diet of acorns

93

and herbs. Those who survive best are the ones that feed on bran and the blood that trickles down a butcher's gutter.'

By 1641, however, the situation was much worse. The peasants had been in revolt for years; and for years they had suffered ruthless reprisals. Louis XIII and Richelieu sacrificed the country to the interests of a foreign policy bent on making France the most powerful nation in Western Europe. The war was also unpopular among those Catholics who opposed the country's continual alliances with Protestants against the House of Austria, the champion of Catholicism. The conspiratorial opposition thus won support from all sides when it nobly declared that it stood for 'peace among nations and for the relief of the people's miseries'. The leaders dubbed themselves 'Princes of Peace', and their claims and intentions did not fail to move the King, who immediately ordered his Minister to secure an instant and decisive victory and so put an end to the disgraceful situation.

Cinq-Mars was first sounded out as early as 1640, when the Comte de Fiesque approached him on behalf of Soissons. They pointed out that his position was precarious, that the Cardinal was determined to contrive his downfall, and that he would have much to gain from joining forces with the opposition and from helping them to execute a successful conspiracy. He was even offered a royal marriage with Mademoiselle de Longueville, who was Marie Gonzaga's first cousin. At that time Henri had not yet fallen in love with the Duchess of Nevers.

Cinq-Mars asked Fontrailles for his expert conspiratorial advice. Fontrailles proved unusually circumspect. He told Cinq-Mars that it would be 'neither just nor profitable for a favourite to enter into dealings with a prince who was about to take up arms against his King and Minister'. Whereupon Monsieur le Grand spurned his tempters, saying 'it was inconceivable that there be any greater glory or contentment than that of serving his King'. Although Fontrailles was completely devoted to the Prince he considered Monsieur le Grand's participation in Soissons's cause premature, if not unwise.

When the news of the Arras affair reached Sedan, another conspirator, Alexandre de Campion, who was younger but more experienced than Fiesque, went to see Monsieur le Grand. They could not have chosen a better time. Cinq-Mars was furious with the Cardinal for accusing him of cowardice because he had refused

94

to be his spy. He felt he had been humiliated and belittled once too often and was more than ready to entertain treacherous offers from his persecutor's enemies. He was also flattered and relieved to be treated as an influential power. The conspiracy itself and all the dangerous, secret midnight encounters appealed to his adventurous young-daredevil image of himself. On August 20, 1640, Campion wrote to Monsieur le Comte, 'Monsieur le Grand was pleased to receive your compliments and those of Monsieur de Bouillon. He has instructed me to make the best use we can of him and to assure you of his sincerity and loyal service. You can measure the sincerity of his intentions by his conviction that the Cardinal is determined to destroy him . . . No one knows that I am seeing him . . . If his increasing good fortune does not dull the keenness of his conviction I think he may well prove of great service to us. It is, in any case, as well to secure the good faith of the King's intimate friend should you ever be in danger and thus in need of such protection. He has, moreover, a vested interest in helping to bring about the downfall of his dangerous detractor. I know that those who dislike him will accuse him of ingratitude, since the Cardinal has been his bene-factor, but this need not concern you.' A royal prince had come to Cinq-Mars for protection. The compliment was enough to make any young man dizzy with self-importance.

Henri then became infatuated with the Duchess of Nevers. The months passed and Cinq-Mars dreamed of seizing power while Richelieu won victory upon victory. Portugal rebelled against Spain. The Duc de Lorraine asked His Majesty to forgive him for having risen against him and restored a number of territories as a token of his capitulation. The opposition felt it was time to act. In the spring the Duc de Bouillon declared war on Louis as Prince of Sedan. Soissons commanded an army reinforced by 7,000 Imperial troops. His aim was to get to Paris and overthrow the tyrant. Hundreds of Frenchmen began to prepare for this happy eventuality. The Queen and Monsieur were anxiously awaiting the moment when they could reveal their true sympa-thies. The Cardinal was to be replaced by Monsieur le Comte; the King would be put under guard; power would be restored to the nobility; and foreign alliances would be reversed. Cinq-Mars did not actually play a part in these arrangements, but he knew all about them.

Towards the end of May the King went to Abbeville, following his usual route. He stayed for a month and left for Amiens and Corbie. He was in Péronne on July 3. The news from Roussillon was encouraging as was that from Germany, where the Imperial army had been routed at the battle of Wolfenbuttel. But the Eastern prospects were bad. Marshal Chatillon's forces may have been stronger than the rebel army but they were not strong enough to stop Soissons at the Meuse. On July 6 he faced Soissons at La Marfée and was defeated. The Royal Army had never been so completely defeated by a rebel force. Everyone was convinced that a wave of defeats would follow and destroy all that had been accomplished since 1627, returning France to its old feudal structure. Richelieu himself believed all was lost, for he, unlike Louis, always lost the courage of his convictions when he was confronted with a crisis. He had despaired in 1631 when the Spaniards took Corbie, and now he again failed to rise to the occasion.

Cinq-Mars was quick to notice Richelieu's total dejection and he became foolishly benevolent. His saintly reaction to his life-long tormentor's distress was more probably dictated by incredible vanity than by natural goodness. The misused pupil could score off his omnipotent master by offering him his protection. He was so delighted by the prospect of having Richelieu at his feet that he did not stop to consider the possible consequences of such a rash gesture. He went to His Eminence and told him 'to have no fear for he could stop him (Soissons) himself. The Cardinal embraced him and said it would be the greatest service he could possibly render his King.'[1] Cinq-Mars was able to savour his revenge for three joyous hours before a messenger came from La Marfée with news that turned the tables on him and quickly put an end to his folly. Monsieur le Comte had been killed by a pistol shot as he was riding across the battlefield.

The Count's untimely death is still a mystery. The official account holds the prince himself responsible for his own death, claiming that his foolhardy habit of lifting the visor of his helmet with the barrel of his pistol caused the accident. No one, however, believed this explanation. Some were convinced that he had been shot by one of the Cardinal's agents who had ridden along-side him and others preferred the rumour that he had been

[1] Gaspard de Chavagnac, *Mémoires*.

picked off by a straggler from the defeated army. Whatever actually happened, the opposition had to face the fact that a headless conspiracy could not possibly continue. His Eminence was thus saved again. He immediately regained his composure and his omnipotence.

The rift had opened and Monsieur le Grand suddenly found himself on the brink of a catastrophe. He despaired. The promised marriage was indefinitely postponed. Richelieu informed him of this decision as he embraced and thanked him for his concern. Henri regained his lucidity and realized the danger he was in. He cursed himself for his stupidity and wondered how and from where the fatal blow would be dealt.

Fontrailles returned from a long journey to be informed of his friend's mistake. He told Cinq-Mars what he thought of him. He fanned his worst fears and advised him to quit the court. Cinq-Mars, or the Princess, had the good sense to think otherwise and replied 'that if he left there would be no guarantee of any future safety for him; the Cardinal was not a moderate man and leaving would only give him the latitude to destroy him the more easily. He had no other protector than the King and if he remained, he could defend himself to Louis. The Cardinal would find it hard to impugn him since he had not written anything down and there could therefore be no concrete proof against him; witnesses would be far more reticent in his presence than in his absence. He would be willing to entertain the most extreme measures to guard his safety.'[2]

Monsieur le Grand only spoke of entertaining 'the most extreme measures' because he was excited and frightened, but the surprised hunchback listened and took him at his word. Cinq-Mars's convictions might be put to some good use after all. There was no more talk of his leaving court. The conspirator advised him to secure a loyal circle of friends and form a faction of his own.

De Thou immediately approved of the project. 'His disquietude' did not show his usual indecision. He feared for Henri's life and even more for his Queen's. Shortly after this, his mother's cousin, the eighty-seven-year-old Duc d'Epernon, was exiled to Loches despite his advanced age. De Thou sought the old man out and consulted him. The meeting revived conspiratorial instincts and factional hopes in Henry III's aged *mignon*. He had been Henry

[2] Fontrailles, *Mémoires*.

IV's sworn enemy and had always loathed Richelieu. He offered to advise the conspirators and lend them the wisdom of his experience, which extended back to the Wars of Religion. Monsieur le Grand set about seeking support from his father's old friends. This was how he discovered another of the Cardinal's enemies, the Comte de Chavagnac, who 'gave' him his son Gaspard.

In the meantime, the King and Richelieu seized their opportunity. The King took command of the army, recaptured Aisne and proceeded to the Meuse. On July 28 he called a meeting of his council at Mézières. Cinq-Mars was setting out to attend the meeting when a gentleman, Monsieur de Sainction, came to inform him that the Cardinal 'did not approve of the way he saw fit to tread on his toes before the King, nor did he wish him to concern himself with matters which neither required his attention nor presence'. Cinq-Mars was astounded and ran to grumble to de Noyers. But he had scarcely opened his mouth when Richelieu, who had had him followed, rose angrily and silenced him. The Cardinal 'dealt with him with the insulting and authoritarian brutality he might use with his lesser manservants. He disparaged his good fortune; he called him incompetent and worthless and then informed him in the most contemptuous way that the presence of such a man as he was a discredit to the Council as a whole in the eyes of the world. He concluded by forbidding him to enter the Council ever again and dispatched him to the King to see if his master did not concur with this opinion.'[3]

In any other circumstances the favourite would have taken Richelieu at his word. As it was, he had a guilty conscience and feared that Louis would throw his foolish avowals in his face. He burst into tears and again consoled himself with vengeful fantasies.[4]

*　　*　　*

The King crossed the Meuse, stormed Donchery and attacked Sedan. The Duc de Bouillon was disillusioned by Spain's inertia and decided to negotiate for peace. He surrendered on August 5, eight short days after the Mézières incident. Louis had not

---

[3] Fontrailles, *Mémoires*.
[4] Montglat. Fontrailles and Aubery give quite different versions of the incident. It has here been reconstructed in what seems the most probable version.

broached the subject with Cinq-Mars nor had his affections diminished. Cinq-Mars was reassured and was further cheered by the return of François de Thou. It was at this time that Mazarin was writing, 'The Cardinal is paving the way for Monsieur le Grand's downfall.' War had been declared. The favourite was easily persuaded to prepare himself for a surprise attack.

De Thou knew Monsieur de Bouillon very well. When the Duke went to the army headquarters to declare a formal end to his rebellion, the young magistrate took him aside and talked to him. He told him that Monsieur le Grand wished him to know that 'His Majesty was very displeased with the Cardinal and that he did not know how to be rid of him'. Cinq-Mars would send word to the Prince of Sedan when the time came to destroy the Minister. The Duke was surprised and immediately suspected a trap. He sang the Cardinal's praises and refused to believe that His Majesty wanted to be rid of him. In any case, he added, Monsieur le Grand would have to make the first move. Monsieur le Grand then realized he would have to prove the sincerity of his intentions and demonstrate his good faith. He worked on the King to show Bouillon clemency and Bouillon later admitted 'that his good services had been of some use'. The Sedan matter was soon concluded. Sedan became a vassal state of the Crown, in return for which 'His Majesty, who trusted the sincerity of the Duke's repentance, gave him a free pardon which he extended to all those gentlemen who participated in the same crime and might thereafter be identified with it'. The King's usual clemency might have been affected by Cinq-Mars's intervention, but it was more probably the result of his immense relief at the failure of the rebellion. Louis had been really alarmed and he demonstrated this by exacting posthumous revenge on Monsieur le Comte by vilifying his name. Richelieu, who usually enjoyed being merciful when mercy cost him nothing, was reluctant to intercede on behalf of a Bourbon prince even though he was safely dead.

On August 10 the Duc de Bouillon was received by His Majesty and then went on to dine with the Master of the Horse. When Henri was escorting him back he said to Bouillon, 'I was pleased to hear from Monsieur de Thou that you wish to be counted a friend. I assure you that I shall not take advantage of your kindness to me until I have merited it by being of some service.' He did not understand the man, but he admired the

99

unscrupulous and astute Prince. Cinq-Mars 'was more content and at ease' after their meeting.

Fontrailles and de Thou did not allow him to become over-confident. They constantly reminded him that he was committed to contriving the Cardinal's downfall and that if he did not break the Cardinal he would be broken by him. This meant that it was necessary for him to approach the leader of the opposition, Monsieur, and come to an understanding with him. Gaston d'Orléans had suffered a setback at 'Monsieur le Comte's mis-fortune, which had also been his', but he had emerged from the situation unscathed despite the efforts of an *agent provocateur* to entrap him. On August 8 he went to see his brother at Amiens and was given an icy reception. He, too, was furious to find that he had been excluded from the Council. It was at that point that Fontrailles informed him that 'His Highness can count on Mon-sieur le Grand's devotion and service'. The hunchback adventurer and the gallant mystic began hatching a new plot.

De Thou went to Sedan to persuade Monsieur de Bouillon to remain in his citadel and to trust the favourite. He assured Bouillon of Monsieur le Grand's friendship and constancy. The Duke would be kept informed of all that happened at court. Bouillon was delighted that the fires of rebellion had rekindled so quickly. He gave no definite assurances but a note of encour-agement was to be detected in his non-commital attitude. Mean-while Fontrailles arranged a secret meeting between Monsieur and the Master of the Horse at Amiens. This was the first time that the two men had ever exchanged anything other than court pleasantries. Cinq-Mars was thus confronted by the same mirage that had proved fatal to Chalais, Montmorency and so many other conspirators. The formidable hunchback had absolute con-fidence in his capacity to manipulate, control and goad the two equally weak, unstable, impulsive and seductive courtiers. He so manœuvred the conversation as to extract a sighing admission from Monsieur : 'Ah, how happy we would be if the Cardinal were dead.'

'Your Highness has only to make his desire known and many would be pleased to oblige you,' Fontrailles quickly interjected. Contemporaries disagree as to whether it was Gaston or Cinq-Mars who objected to the proposal. In fact they were both terrified of the responsibility of an act which they had both envisaged and desired. The meeting came to an end on this timorous note. 'Monsieur le Grand,' Fontrailles was to write, 'claimed that I was indiscreet and that he feared lest I had shocked Monsieur. I felt obliged to tell him that if that were indeed the case it was well to know from the outset rather than be surprised by it once we had gone too far to turn back.' The incautious Cinq-Mars was further from safety than he imagined.

At the end of September Monsieur de Bouillon met the King at Nesle. He had thought hard about the plot and finally assured Cinq-Mars 'that he would be his friend against Monsieur le Cardinal and would come up to Paris whenever he was needed'.

The war continued for another month. By the time an exhausted Louis retired to his winter quarters victory was assured. He stayed at Chantilly for a short time and then went on to Saint-Germain where he arrived on November 5. Cinq-Mars was reunited with his dearly beloved Marie Gonzaga, whom he kept fully informed of all his various undertakings. She had not allowed their passionate commitment to cool. Not only did she encourage him to pursue his fatal course, but she had also spoken to the Queen about him and his intentions. Anne of Austria had never stopped hating the Cardinal and she continued fearing that he might take her children away from her. She was, therefore, delighted by the new cabal, which would replace the services of Monsieur le Comte. Henri was proud and moved to have his beautiful Queen's confidence. He swore he would serve her and that he would never betray her come what may. Anne of Austria maternally encouraged him to woo and win his princess, who encouraged him with Corneille's enjoinder, 'Battle victoriously for Chimène is the prize'.

XI

The Conspirator's Apprentice

Cinq-Mars's fate was determined between November and the January of 1642. He continued 'sighing at his Princess's feet' but the days of their idyll were numbered. The lyrical romance they had created for themselves was becoming more and more like a real-life reproduction of a Cornelian drama. His life was now entirely governed by his desire to deserve and win his lady. The proud Gonzaga had laid down her conditions, and it remained for him to achieve the goals she prescribed. The lady's motives for participating in this intense relationship are not as transparent. It is difficult to estimate the ratio of genuine emotion to ambition involved in her devotion to Cinq-Mars. They were an incongruous pair: the handsome, headstrong, resolute and dominating young woman, and the graceful but highly strung favourite.

Their relationship was one more festering sore for the Cardinal. Richelieu had changed his mind about Henri after Monsieur le Comte's uprising. He decided to change his tactics and treat him differently. He stopped nagging a naughty boy and assumed his beguiling mask. He sat about fanning and flattering Henri's insatiable vanity. Henri would certainly have fallen victim to these seductive ploys if he had not had his Marie, who was a powerful antidote. One day at Reuil the Cardinal astounded his courtiers by escorting the young man up the steps and saying, 'As you see I show you all the deference due to a great favourite. I am delighted to see you on such good terms with the King. Now that you are in a position to be of help to others, you no longer need my help as peacemaker.'[1]

But no one was fooled by these gestures. Henri Arnauld confided to Barillon that 'there is definitely something gravely amiss between the Cardinal and Monsieur le Grand'.

The real leaders of the cabal were the Princess and Fontrailles. They were not satisfied with the outcome of Cinq-Mars's first

[1] Avnel.

meeting with Monsieur. They wanted to force Monsieur to commit himself to a real alliance. Monsieur went to see his brother at Saint-Germain in November. Louis greeted him as coolly as ever but was not as reticent as usual. He discussed the affairs of state with his brother and told him of some of his worries and enxieties. He complained about the war and the ever-distant prospects of peace. The interview encouraged the Duc d'Orléans to arrange a secret meeting with the Master of the Horse. Henri was thoroughly briefed by his mentors, who persuaded him to express a lot of uncertain assumptions with a great deal of conviction. He insisted to Monsieur that he was at the apex of royal favour and that the King had spent the last eighteen months urging him to found a party and break away from the detested Cardinal. The quarrels they had were staged to allay the Cardinal's suspicions. He also assured Monsieur that the King had sworn to protect him and anyone who would help him negotiate a peace with Spain. Fontrailles was present and substantiated all these claims. Gaston was amazed but he cautiously curbed his natural optimism and asked for greater assurances. 'Have you sounded the King on your proposal to get rid of the Cardinal?'

Henri riposted quickly, 'I wanted to be sure of your protection before approaching the King.'

Monsieur did not haggle. He offered his protection knowing that the favourite would in turn be his protector. He realized he had nothing to lose, for if the plot worked he might gain the throne, and if it failed he would still be the King's brother.

Gaston decided to insure himself completely: he set out to obtain the Queen's support, which would not only safeguard his involvement in the conspiracy but would also minimize the possibility of their rivalry for the regency when the King died. They were still good friends and they still considered themselves victims of the same tyranny. They had been accomplices in the past and their new complicity threw them together again. Anne had a lot of influence over her brother-in-law. She may not have been a very intelligent woman, but her instincts were excellent and she was exceptionally subtle and cunning. She assured Gaston that he could trust Monsieur le Grand and that none of them would take a single step without consulting him. She made him swear not to betray anyone if things went wrong. Anne was fully aware of Monsieur's history of broken promises, but the subtle lady knew that he would have to be discreet and as good as his word on this occasion because he would need her when the regency began. Gaston was so busy concentrating on his own devious ends that he did not realize he was being used to serve hers.

Cinq-Mars thus became the pivot of an enormous faction, composed of a host of warring interests. The complexity, diversity and even the existence of most of these interests were beyond the comprehension of the candid young lover. His friend François de Thou proved himself to be equally naïve. He thought he was serving the interests of his Queen and the desires of his friend. He was in fact being manipulated by both as a a sacrificial pawn. Fontrailles advised Henri to send the young counsellor to Sedan to inform Bouillon of Monsieur's alliance and ask him to come to court. Bouillon was essential to the plot as only he could guarantee them a place of refuge in Sedan if the need arose. Cinq-Mars suspected that 'His disquietude' would raise objections on the grounds of his principles if he understood the implications of his mission. He therefore decided to give de Thou the letter for Bouillon without telling him about the contents. Fontrailles was indignant: 'Monsieur de Thou risks his life and his liberty: He should be informed of the significance of his mission.'

'If I do tell him,' Cinq-Mars answered cynically, 'he will either refuse to go or he will carry out the task with such reluctance and self-disgust that the mission will fail.'

But Fontrailles was persistent. 'He may not want to take an active part in contriving the Cardinal's downfall but he is a loyal and honourable man and you know he would never betray you. He deserves your confidence.'[2]

This discussion would certainly not have taken place had they not intended, as some have argued, to assassinate Richelieu. We have it from Fontrailles that Cinq-Mars finally agreed to tell de Thou all about the mission and that de Thou's reaction was to 'refuse to have anything to do with the plan because he was against bloodshed on principle and he would never be instrumental in causing anyone's death . . . Cinq-Mars let the matter drop.' Fontrailles then claims that he alone persuaded the young man to change his mind. It seems unlikely, however, that de Thou should renounce his principles at the hunchback's behest

[2] Fontrailles, *Mémoires*.

alone. The Queen had learned of the conspirators' ulterior motives from the Duchess of Nevers. When she saw de Thou she did not give away how much she knew, nor did he ask her to explain her reasons for endorsing their plan or for desiring his collaboration. He was satisfied by her assurance that the plot would indeed determine her fate. He did not hesitate a moment longer and was soon galloping through the December snows to the depths of Périgord. Bouillon had left Sedan for Périgord to stay in his château at Limeuil. When he met Bouillon de Thou lost some of his resolution. He could not bear the idea of being mistaken for a hard-bitten professional conspirator. He therefore handed Bouillon the letter, feigning ignorance of its contents. He told the Duke he did not know why the favourite wanted him to go to Paris. He even protested against the way they had misled him. Bouillon's suspicions were aroused and he became defensive. He claimed he could not go to Paris because his wife was about to give birth. He also indicated that the King would regard his unexpected arrival at court as unusual.

'In that case you should not go,' de Thou concluded coolly. Before he left Bouillon he tried to compensate for this deliberate diplomatic failure by lauding Monsieur le Grand and by mentioning the important work being done by some of His Majesty's courtiers.

The Cardinal also made contact with Bouillon. He wrote implying that Bouillon might be given the command of the French army in Italy if he danced to the Cardinal's tune. This put the Duke in the strategic position of intermediary between the Cardinal and his adversaries. He decided to go to Paris and exploit the situation. Shortly after his arrival he accepted an invitation to visit the Master of the Horse. Their meeting was to have far-reaching results. Fontrailles and his friend d'Aubijoux stood guard in the antechamber while Bouillon and Cinq-Mars whispered animatedly in the favourite's bedroom.

Henri felt he was fighting for his love. This obsessive preoccupation of his lent his arguments, or rather Fontrailles's arguments, a convincing ring of urgency. The King, Cinq-Mars explained, was fast declining. He would not live for long. Richelieu was planning to oust the Queen and Monsieur and become regent himself. He had to be stopped at all costs. Monsieur had committed himself 'to work for the Cardinal's downfall', which

H

should convince the Duc de Bouillon to throw in his lot with the rest of them. He could only gain by joining them as everyone knew that His Eminence would eventually find some pretext for punishing him for his collaboration with Monsieur le Comte. The defenders of the Royal Family needed his alliance and his assurance that Sedan would harbour them until the King died if their plans miscarried.

The Duke was frank with Cinq-Mars. He raised no objections but he saw one difficulty : Sedan was not impregnable. At present it was surrounded by three royal armies, one under Monsieur de Guiche, another under Monsieur d'Harcourt and a third under Monsieur de Guébriant. If the Cardinal ever suspected anything the three armies would instantly occupy the hill tops and all the armies in Europe would not be able to allay disaster. Nothing could be done without raising an army, such as they had had at La Marfée, which would be able to repulse any such attack. Of a French army there was no question, for since the death of Montmorency, feudal levies had become impossible to raise. They would have to turn to the King of Spain and come to some agreement with him.

The idea of negotiating an alliance with an enemy country in wartime would be regarded as high treason today. Such ethical considerations were not fashionable in Cinq-Mars's day. In the previous century, the war lords of France had had constant recourse to foreign support in their opposition to the French King. Fidelity was a matter of caste and religion and not of national identity. But a lesser noble, such as an Effiat, who was the son of a loyal servant of the crown, should have experienced a twinge of conscience. Cinq-Mars, however, was ruled by his ambitious passion. He had also learned to see the world through Gonzaga eyes. He had no compunction whatever about accepting Bouillon's treacherous suggestion. He merely said he would refer the proposal to Monsieur. After the meeting Cinq-Mars assured Fontrailles : 'All is well and Monsieur de Bouillon is agreeable to everything.'

François de Brion, the Duc d'Orléans's first equerry, was one of the key figures of the conspiracy. He lodged in the residence of the Venetian Ambassador in the Marais. Cinq-Mars went to see Gaston there and informed him of Bouillon's proposal to negotiate a treaty with Spain. The Prince had consented to many such treaties before and raised no objection to doing so again. Henri was caught up in the drama of the events and was quite unaware of the enormous significance of what he was doing. As far as he was concerned, he wanted to obtain marriage, power and the destruction of his enemy. (The theory that he agreed to the treaty as a way of avoiding the need to assassinate Richelieu is quite unfounded.) He did not think he was in any particular danger. He was blindly gambling away his marriage, his future, his life. Cinq-Mars was oblivious to the wider significance of his actions. In offering Richelieu's enemies their last chance to be rid of him, if his conspiracy succeeded, the course of French history would change; for if the opposition took control France's policies would be reversed. France would lose her grip on Europe, her pre-eminence and her absolute monarchy. She would return to a state of reduced aggression on an international level, but to a state of internal strife and constant faction. She would be open to foreign interference and liable to the sway of the Holy See. Monsieur wanted exactly this. He was delighted by the prospect and went to notify the Queen. Anne gave her approval. She then informed de Thou that she knew all about the conspiracy and heartily endorsed it. Cinq-Mars was also delighted. He was convinced he would triumph. He had become Rodrigue's equal.

*　　*　　*

'You no longer need my help,' Richelieu had said pointedly to Monsieur le Grand. Marie Gonzaga could be proud of her creation. Henri had devoted himself so completely to pleasing her that he had become a very different young man from the unruly youth who had delighted and tormented his King. He now had the manners and the graces of a 'great favourite'. He had become calm, dignified, controlled and discreet and he had learned how to wield his seductive powers with consummate skill. This suited the King, who was worn by a thousand maladies and weakened by his physicians' treatments. He had lost his appetite for maschoistic rows. He, too, had changed. He seemed to need to confide more and more in his favourite. Cinq-Mars would once have tried to avoid shouldering the burden of his master's endless complaints, but he now listened to him with infinite patience and understanding. Their relationship changed. Louis had become an exhausted old man at forty who needed to lean more and more on his chosen confidant. The master-naughty boy relationship had disappeared.

Louis felt increasingly resentful toward the Cardinal. He spent hours complaining bitterly about him to Cinq-Mars. Richelieu was becoming more arbitrary and brutal in his demands on the King. The Cardinal was himself a very sick man and he feared he might die before the completion of his great tasks. He was working feverishly against time and had no patience for anything that might delay or interfere with the conclusion of his work. Louis reacted to the increased pressure by rebelling and denouncing Richelieu to Cinq-Mars as an evil priest who had obtained a dispensation from having to say mass, an upstart who had wrested a vast income of three million[3] for himself, which he lavished on his person to the outrage and dismay of the starving populace, a cantankerous despot, a satrap, a tyrannical persecutor of the royal family and a nasty spy besides. Henri would listen sympathetically and top the list of the Cardinal's vices by referring to Richelieu's stubborn pursuit of a war Louis loathed. He would then leap hypocritically to the wronged Minister's defence, being delighted when Louis recriminated him the more.

After one such series of complaints and calculated defences, Louis exclaimed, 'I would give half my kingdom to rid you of the Cardinal. He has robbed me of all my friends, he even tried to take you away from me.' Cinq-Mars looked pained and indignant, and Louis added, 'Yes, the pressure is unbearable, I should like to see a party rise against him such as rose against Marshal d'Ancre.'

Cinq-Mars was astonished at the King's vehemence. He had never gone so far as to equate Richelieu with Concini, whom Louis had loathed so much when he was a young man, and who was slain on the drawbridge to the Louvre. The Master of the Horse jumped to hasty conclusions. He thought Louis intended to get Richelieu out of the way, which would vitiate the need for the conspiracy. He discussed the situation at length with the Princess and then reopened the matter with the King the following day. When he saw that Louis had not changed his mind, he bravely ventured, 'Sire, since you are master, you could be rid of the Cardinal immediately if you so desired.'

Despite their intimacy, Cinq-Mars did not understand the stoical

[3] Equivalent to several thousand million francs.

aspect of the King's character. At once the King's attitude changed: 'Not so fast, Monsieur, not so fast,' Louis replied curtly. Cinq-Mars never realized how much of himself Louis had sacrificed to his kingship. Long before Henri had come into his life, Louis had resigned himself to serve the interests of his country. Richelieu was a necessary if unpleasant burden, because he had proved to Louis that he could realize Louis's vision of a great and glorious France within their lifetime. Cinq-Mars was only aware of the Royal weaknesses, which gave him a distorted image of his King. Louis, however, realized that his favourite had interpreted his outburst and his sick-man's complaints as a desire to seek a rash way out. 'The Cardinal is the greatest servant the state has ever known,' he said, in his usual formula. 'I should lose everything without him. If he should ever declare himself openly against you, I would not be able to save even you.' He then lectured Henri on the silly impetuousness of youth.

Cinq-Mars crumbled. His enemy remained as omnipotent as ever and he as powerless and insecure. He realized that 'even if the Cardinal died, His Majesty would continue to scorn the capabilities of people of his age. This meant that he might well have to suffer the disgrace of being forever excluded from participating in the affairs of state.'[4]

This incident would have had a sobering and even beneficial effect on most men. But the young Adonis chose to dismiss the warning. He knew Marie would despise him if he withdrew at this stage. He thus decided to keep the incident to himself and to rely on the effect of his charms. The conspiracy which depended heavily on the favourite's influence with the King should have shifted its emphasis at this point. It might even have been wiser if the conspirators had waited for a more favourable turn of events or for the King's death. But Cinq-Mars could not afford to wait. He would have to work on the King and win him round. He did not think it would be hard to dominate a man who had once been a slave to his childish whims. In any case, Louis's bitter fear of Richelieu would also help him. Cinq-Mars, like many, thought that Louis was terrified of his minister and that the 'illustrious slave' would ultimately be grateful to him for liberating him of his scourge. He did not understand his King at all.

[4] Fontrailles, *Mémoires.*

The wheels of the conspiracy were thus set in motion and everything began to happen rapidly. Monsieur and Bouillon, who had fallen out in 1632, were reconciled through the offices of the favourite. One frosty night de Thou agreed to drive Bouillon to the Hôtel de Venise but he refused to enter and have anything to do with the meeting. De Thou continued 'to be involved but not to participate'. This persistent self-deception only served to intensify his risks. That night, Cinq-Mars showed His Highness the draft of a treaty which Bouillon and Cinq-Mars were later to accuse one another of making. The treaty was probably the product of considerably more experience than Cinq-Mars possessed. They did not, however, find the treaty satisfactory, and decided to revise it after the St Anne's Day's festival and then submit it to the Queen.

Anne knew that she was at the crucial stage in her life. Up to this time she had been deprived of happiness and power, but she planned to obtain both. She was determined to become sole regent and to keep her children. Her determination, coupled with her instinct for self-preservation, lent the lovely indolent Spanish princess a Machiavellian grasp of politics. She not only encouraged the conspirators, she also recruited old experts to help them. La Rochefoucauld, whom she had once asked to take her home to Spain with Madame de Chevreuse, wrote in his memoirs that Monsieur de Thou 'came to see me on behalf of the Queen to inform him of her complicity with Monsieur le Grand and of her assurance to him that I could be counted on. Monsieur de Thou also told me that Monsieur le Grand requested my services. These advances had the effect of implicating me in the affairs of a person I had never even seen.' Anne of Austria called her faithful band of supporters into action and lent them to the conspirators' cause.

Once she had committed herself and her friends to the opposition she calmly summoned one of the Cardinal's faithful agents, Father Carré. It was precisely this man whom Richelieu had entrusted with the task of disentangling Mademoiselle de La Fayette from the King. The Queen told the priest that she wanted him to plead Madame de Hautefort's case to the Cardinal. She praised his Eminence and assured him of her good will and intentions. She then proceeded to mention Cinq-Mars and subtly implied that she disapproved of the favourite's rank ingratitude

towards his former protector. 'I do not really like him. If anything were to happen to him I am sure no one would mind,' she
concluded economically. Father Carré wrote off to the Cardinal
and reported the whole conversation in detail. The Queen had
thus betrayed both sides. She then sat back peacefully and waited
for the outbreak of hostilities. However, the King fell seriously
ill and everything remained in suspense.

XII

The Precarious Balance

At the beginning of the year, the efforts of Louis XIII and Richelieu were magnificently rewarded. Alsace and Artois were annexed, and war was carried beyond the borders of France to strike at the heart of the Habsburg Empire. France contained a powerful pro-Spanish party, while the Cardinal's agents were provoking separatist aspirations within the Spanish kingdom. Portugal revolted and asserted its national autonomy under the rule of the Portuguese Don Juan of Braganza. The Catalans followed their example and declared their intention of liberating themselves from the tyranny of Philip IV. In the summer of 1641 their ambassadors had approached the Cardinal and had suggested that Catalonia become a vassal state of France. On September 19 at Péronne they knelt before Louis XIII and swore him allegiance. Louis accepted the title of Count of Barcelona, Roussillon and Cerdagne and promised to liberate those provinces. This meant that Louis could push the frontiers of France as far as the Pyrenees, perhaps further. The next few weeks were spent preparing the great campaign and reinforcing the armies to the north, on the Rhine and in the Alps for the imminent north and westward offensives.

The great plan was on the brink of success when the Cardinal had to face the possibility of complete failure. The King was taken seriously ill and Richelieu knew that if his master's worn constitution did not recover, his work and his life would be at an end. Henri was equally worried and mistakenly so, for had he been endowed with hindsight he would have realized that the King's death was his only hope of salvation. While Louis lay critically ill for ten days, Europe held its breath and waited. Louis's natural resources of strength won through again and a skeletal and waxen King returned to his tasks with redoubled enthusiasm and resolution.

The King threw himself into preparing the Pyrenean expedition. He was delighted at the prospect of 'letting chaos descend on Spain'. Marshal de Brézé, now Viceroy of Catalonia, was pushing on to Barcelona and a strong army was to besiege Perpignan, the key town of Roussillon. The siege was so crucial to the successful completion of the campaign that Richelieu wanted Louis to command it in person. The favourite frowned upon the plan as it would mean leaving Paris and his love. It would be exceedingly difficult to control his conspiracy from such a remote outpost. He was also afraid that the campaign might prematurely kill the ailing King. Thus Henri protested loudly against the trip. His friends set about stirring up public feeling with the argument that the ambitious monster of a minister was ruthlessly risking his King's life. The King, however, dismissed Henri's entreaties and his physical disadvantages as puny deterrents compared to the demands of his royal duties and to the lure of battle. Louis would lead his army.

Richelieu tried to absolve himself of any responsibility for this decision and even make it appear against his better judgement. He made His Majesty sign a solemn declaration, 'I have told my cousin, Cardinal Richelieu, that I would much rather undertake the journey than remain at Saint-Germain . . . he was afraid that I should not have the strength to bear the strain of the campaign. Whereupon I begged him not to concern himself about my person . . . declaring that I had no special preference for dying in one place over another. It is my duty to consider the wisdom of such matters and his to carry out my resolve. I then became more and more convinced that I should indeed undertake the journey since it was sure to bring me glorious rewards and that I should leave Saint-Germain to join my waiting armies.'

Henri was thwarted and refused to conceal his resentment. Louis's illness had made him even more irritable and they soon had a colossal row, in which Henri 'was so harshly reprimanded by the King that even his best friends believed his favour to be on the wane', and his enemies anticipated his downfall. The Master of the Horse tried to quash these rumours. He did not want them to reach the Duc de Bouillon, who had just been made Commander-in-Chief of the French Army in Italy, and who might well change sides if he suspected the rumours to be true. Cinq-Mars invited him to dinner with de Thou, but he was not an accomplished actor. 'He wanted to communicate ease and joy and was extraordinarily lively but his forced high spirits roused suspicion; it is most difficult to talk sensibly when one talks for fear of stopping.'[1]

But it proved to be a minor matter and Louis and his favourite were soon reconciled. Cinq-Mars handled the situation so dexterously that everyone's faith in him was immediately restored. The conspirators decided that time was running short and that they should settle the terms of the treaty as quickly as possible. They gathered together at the house of Monsieur de Mesmes, where Bouillon was staying, and drew up the final text. Monsieur was to receive from his brother-in-law, the Spanish King,[2] an army of 1,200 infantry and 6,000 cavalry and the necessary funds for their upkeep, in addition to which a further 40,000 *écus* would be provided for the levying of troops in France. Philip IV would also provide Sedan with a garrison which he would finance. His Highness would personally receive 150,000 *écus*, and the Duc de Bouillon and the Master of the Horse would each get 40,000 *écus*. The princes had everything to gain from such an agreement. Cinq-Mars agreed to everything. The Spanish army would obey Monsieur's commands and he would keep whatever territories he won for himself. In exchange the King of Spain would have a guarantee that the Duc d'Orléans would secure a 'strong peace' between the two countries and both countries would restore any conquered territories. Monsieur would also renounce France's heretical alliances with Holland, Sweden, and with the German provinces.

The document stated, 'We hereby unanimously declare that we will do nothing prejudicial to His Most Christian Majesty and to the country, to the rights and authority of the Most Christian Reigning Queen; and that all that will be undertaken will be done in their best interest to uphold them.' This hypocritical declaration was a necessary safeguard for the conspirators. It again asserted the nobility of their motives and absolved them in writing of treacherous intentions. On the other hand, homage paid to the Queen and her authority was not extended to the King. Whatever Anne of Austria's apologists may wish to claim, the presence of that clause is conclusive evidence of her complicity.

[1] Bouillon, *Mémories*.
[2] Philip IV had married Elizabeth of France, daughter of Henry IV.

114

The treaty had scarcely been penned when an unexpected incident shook the hopes and confidence of its authors. Guébriant had just crushed an Imperial army at Kempen and taken prisoner its Commander-in-Chief, Lamboy. This upset their plans. A disenchanted Bouillon went to see Monsieur at the Luxembourg Palace and said, 'It was useless to count on the Spanish, for Lamboy's defeat meant that far from contemplating a French offensive, they would be hard put to retain Flanders.'

The setback made them hesitate. They could either forge ahead regardless or wait for more favourable circumstances. Experienced politicians would certainly have waited, especially when the King was in such an unpredictable frame of mind. They had gone so far by that time, however, that they knew that procrastination would mean shelving the plot indefinitely. The inexperienced Cinq-Mars would not hear of it. He was determined to become Constable of France and marry the Duchess of Nevers by the end of the year. Bouillon allowed himself to be persuaded, in spite of having just been given the command of the army in Italy by the King and Richelieu. He did, however, refuse to give Cinq-Mars the letter which would guarantee him free entry into Sedan until he saw the King of Spain's signature on the treaty. Monsieur was his usual confident self. The die was cast.

*   *   *

On January 27 the King left Saint-Germain and spent the night at Chilly, Marshal d'Effiat's enchanted castle. His visit indicated the extent of his favour towards Cinq-Mars, who returned the compliment by preparing a sumptuous welcome for his royal master. Louis retired at his customary early hour, which left Cinq-Mars free to resume his normal activities. He called his friend Gaspard de Chavagnac : 'He asked me to follow him,' he was to write in his memoirs. 'We took a hundred detours and finally reached a door at which he knocked. Monsieur, the King's brother, opened the door to him. He then asked me to stay and guard the entrance. He spent the whole night within.' Fontrailles and d'Aubijoux were there but de Thou was not. It was a veritable hotbed of conspirators.

Cinq-Mars obtained His Highness's consent and requested Fontrailles to leave immediately for Spain with the signed treaty. The hunchback considered the procedure over-hasty. He also took exception to being misled and kept in the dark. Henri was charming and persuasive and Monsieur supported him. Fontrailles wanted to consider the proposition for a while and went into a huddle with d'Aubijoux. The two men whispered away and 'agreed that they were involved in a sorry affair', but that they had gone too far to disentangle themselves. The Cardinal's agents were already suspicious and Richelieu would eventually find something to pin on them and make them pay for the follies of the prince and the favourite. They had therefore no other alternative but to continue.'

Henri was about to resign himself to Fontrailles's refusal when the hunchback told him he had decided to go. 'Henri was visibly delighted.' The Marquis would go on the condition that Monsieur le Grand saw to it that Monsieur and the Duc de Bouillon joined the King at Lyons in order that 'His Highness be present at the attempt on Monsieur le Cardinal's life'.

Henri hesitated. The reality of assassinating the man who had had such a controlling influence on his childhood horrified him. He had learned to accept the idea with Marie's help and had himself wished Richelieu dead every time he had been humiliated by the man. But when it came down to planning the actual fulfilment of this wish he shrank in horror. It was, however, the planning and not the act itself which worried him. Fontrailles had to bully the promise out of him. He pointed out that Bouillon's presence at Lyons was equally indispensable as only he could provide the conspirators with the necessary refuge. The nobility of the Auvergne were hostile to Richelieu and they should also be invited to be in at the kill.

The Master of the Horse finally agreed to all his conditions. He would also instruct Josué de Chavagnac, Gaspard's father, to stir up the Cévennes Protestants and send de Thou as ambassador to the Duc de Mercoeur and Duc de Beaufort, the sons of the exiled Duc de Vendôme. The two young princes were bound to welcome the idea of the Cardinal's downfall after all their father had been made to suffer at his hands. Once they had agreed to these procedures the conspirators set about improvising travelling dress that would conceal the treaty. The three gentlemen unstitched Fontrailles's doublet and carefully sewed the treaty into the lining. They finished at dawn, whereupon Fontrailles said goodbye to his colleagues and set out on his dangerous expedition.

A few hours later the King started out on his own expedition. 'He stayed at Maison Rouge that night and reached Fontaine-bleau the next day where the court remained for five days.' Henri spent most of his time with Marie. She tried to infuse him with her energy and he swore he would return to her victoriously. As always they had to wait until the King had gone to sleep before they could meet secretly. They would sit before an open brazier and express their chaste and legendary love throughout the long winter's night. Louis must have known of the idyll, but there is no evidence that he disapproved of it. He never stopped loathing Marion de Lorme, however. He seems to have preferred compet-ing with his friend's platonic love for a woman who kept him away from his old debauched habits and inspired him with loftier sentiments. Louis's preference was understandable, for an ambitious lady like the Duchess of Nevers would naturally entreat the young man to please his master.

Jealousy, it would seem, was not responsible for the King's curiously unpredictable moods. Louis's treatment of Cinq-Mars would often oscillate between tenderness and fury. One moment he was affectionate and the next he was rebuking him harshly. He would demand his beloved's presence and then send him away impatiently. These changes of mood were sometimes so sudden that Monsieur le Grand was forced to play the fool and laugh the whole thing off. Henri had once enjoyed provoking rows, but he now had to conceal his displeasure and hurt feelings for fear of incurring his Princess's scorn and his partisans' distrust. The King's moods may have appeared groundless and irrational but they could prove disastrous, as Cinq-Mars was to find out. It may have been Louis's illness that was to blame, or Cinq-Mars himself may have inadvertently caused his moods. Louis may have begun to realize that his favourite would never be the talented, gifted, virtuous disciple he had once hoped for and that he would remain a frivolous young man incapable of meriting his exalted status. Ironically it was precisely Cinq-Mars's lack of great ambitions that was to be his ruin : all the boy wanted was to be happy—and happiness was not the patrimony of the great.

*   *   *

The Admiral Marquis de Brézé, the son of Marshal Brézé, in-formed the Cardinal that he had surprised Monsieur and Monsieur le Grand talking together and that His Majesty 'was saying the most diabolical things' about the Cardinal. Richelieu's spies were everywhere. He must have known that something was afoot. One of his ablest agents, Rochefort, watched the favourite very closely and even had a key to a secret back door of the Luxembourg palace, which enabled him to spy on Monsieur as well. When Richelieu heard of this 'liaison' he exclaimed, 'The ungrateful wretch shall perish.' As he had as yet no definite information, no conclusive evidence, he contained himself and began to calculate his next moves. He was determined to avoid another rebellion. Richelieu wearily admitted that the 'four square feet of the King's chamber' really did demand more of his time and attention than all his European political concerns. He cursed the day he ever introduced that dangerous child into the King's chambers.

The Cardinal hoped it was not too late. He tried to ingratiate himself to the Master of the Horse. He was gracious, flattering and even asked the King to give him the governorship of Touraine. The masochistic King gave his consent knowing that he would lose his beloved's presence. Louis offered Henri the honour at Fontainebleau. Henri was struck dumb. Only a few weeks before he would have welcomed the opportunity of stepping closer to his Princess. He had gone to some lengths to make it known that he wanted the post. In the present circumstances, however, he could not leave the King's side even if he wanted to, as he could not extricate himself from the conspiracy which demanded his continued presence. He would have to refuse and the way in which he did so reveals the constructive influence of his Egeria. He thanked His Majesty profusely for his kindness and then said that 'such a reward should be bestowed on those who have won distinction in his armies and that the Comte d'Harcourt merited the post far more than he.' The poor King was astounded by his favourite's selfless consideration and he was pleased that his friend would not leave his side.

Richelieu appreciated the artful parry and worried all the more. He tried to approach his ex-pupil personally. It was Cinq-Mars's turn to enjoy seeing the Cardinal squirm while he coolly stood his ground. The Cardinal was furious. He forgot his usual caution and openly attacked Cinq-Mars. He did, however, choose his day carefully. He waited for February 2, 'thinking that a day devoted to religious contemplation (Candlemas) would find the devout Louis XIII in the right frame of mind to support his indictment of the Master of the Horse. He accused him "of everything that might dispose Louis to send Cinq-Mars off to Touraine or wherever he chose." [3] But the move proved ill-timed. The King happened to be particularly delighted by his favourite and was thus all the more displeased by his minister's untimely interference and his tiresome attempt to escalate hostilities when he would have preferred them to declare a truce. Louis informed Richelieu of his displeasure in no uncertain terms. The Cardinal was shattered by his master's violent reaction. Gasston saw His Eminence coming out of the King's chamber looking pale, crushed and considerably older.

The court was soon agog with the news. The young man whose very beauty was his downfall was at the zenith of his career. It was his finest hour. 'Everything conspired to exalt him. His daily rising ceremony was equal to that of the King and the Cardinal; he had a retinue of two hundred gentlemen, who accompanied him to the King. He outshone every single courtier with the magnificence of his attire, the nobility and charm of his person and the grace of his manners. Women threw themselves at his head and ministers at his feet.'[4]

Monsieur le Grand now had his own party. The gentlemen of his retinue relied on him for advancement and a sizeable part of the army also looked to him. Many of his old comrades from his days in the royal guard were sworn enemies of the Scarlet Courtier and swore him aggressive allegiance. Among these were Monsieur de Tréville and Monsieur de Tilladet, Monsieur La Salle and Monsieur des Essarts. The Master of the Horse was especially fond of these gentlemen, who came to see him every day. Then there were all the well-informed exiles abroad, who wept for joy at the news. The Queen Mother even started planning her return.

In the meantime the Cardinal's external policies continued along their unfaltering course as the precarious balance of internal power continued see-sawing. In the midst of these uncertainties, two sick and shaky men, a King and his Minister, set out on their last and most tragic expedition.

[3] Le Vassor.
[4] Memoirs of Anne Gonzaga, Princess Palatine.

119

XIII

Favourable Circumstances

On February 3 1641 two immense cavalcades set out from Fontainebleau. His Majesty and Richelieu each had such a quantity
of musketeers, light cavalrymen, gentlemen, pages, servants and
guests in their respective trains that they were forced to travel
separately for fear of running out of supplies. The King went
ahead sustained by his usual battle-fire but he was too ill to be
his old energetic self. The Cardinal followed at his own pace,
wincing and groaning at every bump and jolt his carriage made.
They joined forces at the major halts along the way. The procession of mounted soldiers in their blue and red helmets, their
brilliant livery and glinting armour and weapons, the courtiers
in their lavishly worked doublets and lace trimmings all jogged
along in their own clouds of dust.

As they travelled Cinq-Mars commented on the miseries of
the countryside, which were the direct result of the endless war.
The war was a disaster. The battles, the casualties, all the devasta-
tion had achieved little more than an illusion of glory. Peace was
the only answer but the Cardinal would never consent to such a
measure, 'as he would always find a way of deferring a solution
in order to preserve his indispensability'. The unfortunate King
found it hard to repudiate his beloved's sensible argument. Louis
was again extremely anxious. He was terrified of appearing before
his Maker laden with the sin of his dreadful war. But he was not
convinced that Richelieu was acting out of self-interest.

Cinq-Mars did, however, believe just this. One day he said
to Louis, 'There is only one way to find out how the Cardinal
really stands. We should ask a trustworthy person to write
secretly to the King of Spain and find out how the peace negotiations are progressing. The reply will indicate whether or not
the Cardinal is opposed to peace.[1]

[1] Father Griffet.

120

'Whom could one safely ask to carry out such a request?' the King asked, somewhat taken aback.

The favourite hastened to put forward the name of François de Thou, who had originated the idea. The King consented. De Thou was a good lawyer and insisted on a written order from His Majesty. 'The King gave two, one addressed to his favourite and the other to Monsieur de Thou, authorizing them to write to Rome and to Madrid in order to hasten the conclusion of the peace negotiations.'[2] The Counsellor did write but circumstances prevented him from following up the inquiry.

This was the first time the King had tried to trap his Minister. His confidence, which had never wavered in eighteen years, seemed to be doing so now. Cinq-Mars's impetuous friends encouraged him to take advantage of the King's uncertainty. If Richelieu disappeared now, the King would surely not protest. 'Favourable circumstances' presented themselves at the Briare halt when the King's party joined up with the Cardinal's. The Cardinal and Louis worked alone together. The young officers of the guard planned to burst into the room and eliminate the Cardinal before the King's eyes. The King's presence would guarantee their safety. Cinq-Mars refused to consider the plan before he had obtained the King's approval. He suggested 'that the blow should surely be struck at Lyons, where the Duc d'Orléans and the Duc de Bouillon would be present as would the noblemen of the Auvergne'. His cohorts agreed to wait. Cinq-Mars had exactly twelve days in which to extract Louis's consent.

The parties continued their journey through La Charité, Nevers, Saint-Pierre-le-Moustiers and Moulins. Cinq-Mars had never been so gracious and considerate. He even shouldered some of the King's anxieties. The King was delighted and lent a willing ear to the intelligent proposals François de Thou had put in Cinq-Mars's mouth. The favourite was also helped by a minor squabble between the King and his Minister. The incident occurred during one of the halts. Cinq-Mars and Tréville were with the King after the altercation when he started to complain 'of the slavery to which his Minister had reduced him'.

'Then be rid of him,' said Henri.

The King protested that it would not be easy to get rid of such a powerful man. His apparent concern with Richelieu's power

[2] Father Griffet.

suggests that Louis had no intention of carrying his complaints through to their logical conclusion. Cinq-Mars was being presumptuous but not perceptive. Tréville's presence compelled him to press the point and suggest that 'the easiest and surest way to have him [Richelieu] assassinated was to surprise him when he came unguarded to his [the King'] rooms'.[3] According to Montglat, Louis was 'stunned' by the lad's audacity.

The fate of France was once again swaying in the balance. The most significant facets of this dialogue are the emphasis given to certain words and Louis's pregnant silences. Concini's assassination was, after all, the result of such a silence. The absence of objection could thus amount to approval. The King was silent for a long while and then he said, 'He is a priest and a Cardinal. I should be excommunicated.'

Tréville immediately interjected that 'if he had the King's consent he would take it upon himself to do the deed and then go to Rome where he would welcome to be absolved'.[4] Again His Majesty did not answer. It is difficult to ascertain his thought processes. Louis may have been tempted by the idea of unloading his burden once and for all, in which case his silences and mild protestations could be interpreted as positive encouragement. On the other hand, he may have wanted to terminate the dangerous conversation with one of his macabre jokes. Many have chosen to believe the first hypothesis and have then judged his relationship with his favourite in the light of this complicity. The hypothesis seems almost credible when one considers that Louis would almost certainly have arrested his temptors had he disapproved of the assassination. There is, however, another possible interpretation. Louis could have disapproved of the project and even wanted to prevent such a catastrophe but he was loath to punish the object of his passion.

The issue had been raised, however, and doubts remained. Tréville persuaded himself that no such doubts existed and that he had, in fact, obtained the necessary approval. Both Chavagnac and his son, Tilladet and the other young men to whom he related the incident agreed with his interpretation[5] and tried to bring the unconvinced Cinq-Mars round to their way of thinking. They were sure that there was no longer anything to prevent them

[3] Montglat.   [4] Montglat.
[5] Chavagnac.

from 'striking the blow' at Lyons, as Monsieur le Grand had once suggested.

*   *   *

Lyons had the honour of welcoming the King and the Cardinal on February 17. Monsieur de Guenitz, Guébriant's aide-de-camp, brought them a magnificent trophy, the Imperial banners which the army had seized at the victorious battle of Kempen. Richelieu and Louis worked feverishly throughout their brief stay planning the campaign, while the conspiracy took shape around them. After they had extracted the King's supposed consent, the favourite's faction began to call themselves 'Royalists' as opposed to 'Cardinalists'.

Cinq-Mars did his best to postpone the awful moment in the face of constant pressure from his friends. He finally yielded and played the part expected of him; as Chavagnac tells us, he 'assembled us all and informed us that he was on his way to the King and that he would rejoin us shortly'. The young men gathered in the antechamber and waited for Cinq-Mars's order to strike. The Cardinal duly arrived, but he was not alone. His active intelligence network seems to have detected the danger. He was accompanied by de Bar, his Captain of the Guard, who entered the King's chamber with him. As Richelieu went in Louis and Cinq-Mars were whispering excitedly and they both looked distinctly sheepish at the sight of His Eminence. 'They were both so embarrassed that the Cardinal realized they had been discussing something that concerned him.' The favourite was not a cold-blooded assassin; he was not even an experienced conspirator. He lost his nerve in the Cardinal's terrible presence. 'He could suffer Richelieu's presence no longer and left to tell us to go home,' Chavagnac goes on to say. 'Many held him responsible for by-passing the golden opportunity of killing the man. Others have praised him for his prudence. He may have behaved like a good Christian; he was certainly a poor politician.'

The opportunity never presented itself again.

On February 21 the King reviewed his troops in the Place Bellecour. The following day he attended a Te Deum in honour of the victory of Kempen. He then received the Catalan ambassadors, the Geneva delegation, and the Venetian ambassador. On February 23, Royalists and Cardinalists, assassins and victims, Spanish allies and French soldiers all resumed their journey together.

At Valence the King solemnly presented the humble Mazarin with his Cardinal's biretta. Louis reached Narbonne on March 11, and the Cardinal two days later. 'He [Richelieu] had not,' wrote Henri Arnauld to Barillon, 'seen His Majesty for ten or twelve days. This is supposed to demonstrate his lack of anxiety over the current rumours concerning Monsieur le Grand's powers.' The court and the general public at Lyons both sensed that the two rivals had drawn swords but no one knew why. 'Monsieur le Grand's affair puzzles even the most penetrating and experienced of observers,' Arnauld records. Then a week later he repeats, 'The Monsieur le Grand affair continues to baffle the most experienced courtiers . . . He [Cinq-Mars] keeps telling his friends not to worry over him for he has nothing to fear . . .'

Monsieur le Grand's 'popularity grew'. He was glad that he had prevented the assassination. He was sure of his powers, of his charms and of his cohorts. He was also quite confident of his final victory and of the Cardinal's resulting ruin. Modesty and discretion seemed unnecessary in view of such certainty. He openly confessed to Monsieur la Luzerne one day, 'that he was not on good terms with the Cardinal, which affected and concerned him not at all because he had friends who would soon help him to achieve a remarkable feat . . . and that he had so far only hinted at his intentions but that he would shortly be announcing them in full'. La Luzerne reported this statement to his friend le Terrail, who then informed Marshal de Brézé, who passed it on to Chavigny. A coup d'état in Spain's favour was thus desired and feared while other preparations were being made to launch a powerful offensive against Spain.

On March 12 the King sent Marshal de La Meilleraye, the Grand Maître of the Artillery, to take Collioure. The Marshal swiftly besieged the area and occupied Collioure within the week. His Majesty eagerly followed his progress. The King's enthusiasm would have been a revelation to a perceptive observer. But Cinq-Mars had his head in the clouds and noticed nothing. He never understood that Louis may have longed for peace, but he wanted a glorious peace. He was to dictate the conditions of such a peace a few months later. Louis XIII would never have consented to the kind of peace Fontrailles was arranging with Olivares, Philip IV's Prime Minister.

* * *

When Fontrailles left Chilly he galloped as far as Etampes where he caught the post-coach. In his memoirs, Rochefort claims that he was accompanied at a distance 'by a man often used for secret missions'. The Cardinal's agents kept a close watch on this anonymous character, who is supposed to have hailed from Brussels, and who thus, it is presumed, put them inadvertently on the conspirators' track. Rochefort mentions this 'man from Brussels' several times and attributes a great deal of importance to him. When the fellow was captured he promptly poisoned himself, whereupon Rochefort claims that he searched his corpse and found the original Spanish Treaty. There is no factual evidence to corroborate this fantastic story, which is riddled with a number of gross inconsistencies. 'The man from Brussels' was almost certainly a fantasy invented to conceal the real circumstances which brought the treaty to light.

We should therefore imagine Fontrailles and his valet setting off alone. Their journey was not without its dangers and misadventures, however. When Rochefort says that he was ordered 'to find a convenient lookout post from where I was to observe those who entered Spain', he is probably telling the truth. The hunchback reached Limoges and had a meeting with the Duc de Bouillon. Bouillon was in good spirits. 'The Spaniards,' he said, 'will give all that you want and more.'

Fontrailles asked him to be more careful, as all would be lost if the master of Sedan were arrested. The Duke shrugged off the warning and promised he would be cautious.

Fontrailles left Limoges and went to his home in Languedoc where he asked d'Aubijoux to map out a route to Spain. D'Aubijoux proposed several alternatives and Fontrailles finally chose to go via the 'Aspe Valley and the so-called Caucasian port'. Rochefort claims that he actually escorted him as far as Bayonne disguised as a messenger. In any event the conspirator crossed the Pyrenees without more ado. He went to Huesca and then on to Saragossa, where the Viceroy was so angry at his secrecy that he made him leave without his valet at midnight. When he got to Madrid, Monsieur's letter of introduction gave him immediate

125

access to the Count Duke Olivares. This haughty and portly favourite, whose portrait was painted by Velasquez, was an astute statesman, but in the long run he was completely outclassed by the Cardinal.

Fontrailles read him a long memorandum. 'His Most Serene Highness the Duc d'Orléans and those who associate themselves with his cause have agreed to proffer a stronghold protected by a sizeable army which they will use in their defence and in that of His Catholic Majesty should he enter France and need protection and refuge . . . Monsieur le Duc d'Orléans will begin his offensive as soon as His Catholic Majesty's and His Imperial Majesty's armies have crossed the Rhine into France.'

The Marquis was anxious to acquit himself like a skilful statesman and withhold the vital names of Bouillon, Cinq-Mars and Sedan until the clauses of the treaty had been accepted, which explains his arch-convolutions. His efforts intensely irritated the hidalgo. 'We have often been deceived and we will agree to nothing that is not accompanied by full guarantees.'

Fontrailles would not yield and Olivares responded by coolly offering him his pass back to France. Fontrailles was forced to give in. Olivares was pleasantly surprised at the breadth of the conspiracy. His pleasure did not prevent him from haggling over the conditions of the treaty for four whole days. Fontrailles was finally exasperated and proclaimed, 'I am not surprised that your affairs are in such a state. Here you are wasting your time over insignificant details while Perpignan is at stake. If Perpignan falls you will lose Catalonia, too, and forever.' Olivares was amazed at his impertinence but he did accelerate his pace.

The treaty was secretly signed on March 13. Fontrailles was then accorded the singular honour of being presented to His Catholic Majesty. The treaty was resewn into the lining of his doublet along with a letter from Philip IV to Gaston d'Orléans. 'My dear brother, I am most pleased by your proposals for the general good, for the well-being of Christendom, and for the establishment of permanent peace. It is essential that solidarity underline this undertaking and that all parties concerned be prudent and single-minded. I hope that your good intentions and resolve will be enlisted in service of the Lord and the general good, two causes which have been ill-served in our lifetime.'

When Fontrailles reached Huesca, in the company of several

people, he found his Béarn guide, who had conducted him across the mountains, waiting for him. He informed Fontrailles that he had been followed and should not risk returning by the same route as he would probably be arrested. The hunchback made for 'the port of Benasque (Venasque)'. There were no unpleasant incidents and he returned to Languedoc safe and sound. He and d'Aubijoux then set out for Narbonne to report to Monsieur le Grand.

We have no way of knowing how much Richelieu knew by the end of March. One of his agents had trailed Fontrailles as far as the border, but he had not seen him return into France. A letter from the Nuncio in Madrid informed him 'that a certain Frenchman was seen for two or three days in the Count Duke's antechamber and it is known that he had a long meeting with the Minister', but no name was mentioned.

The Cardinal, however, did not act on this information. He may not have known the precise identity of the conspirators' emissary and did not want to hazard his chances on a wild guess. Or he may have been reluctant to cause a scandal at a time when his relations with the King were so poor. There is also the possibility that his agent was unusually incompetent and had failed to recognize Fontrailles and even lost track of his movements.

Fontrailles had a secret meeting with Cinq-Mars in which he informed him of the successful outcome of his trip. He was, however, more terrified than proud of the whole business. He had had the unpleasant sensation of being trailed since he left Huesca. The Master of the Horse was still sure of his lucky star and tried to dissipate Fontrailles's fears. Their roles were ironically reversed. They agreed to send a reliable gentleman, Monsieur de Montmort, to inform Monsieur. D'Aubijoux would then take him the treaty when they were positive that the coast was clear. Fontrailles then requested permission to go to England. He did not dare show his face at Court as he was convinced that 'Monsieur le Cardinal would immediately arrest him on the slightest pretext and, given his complicity and firsthand knowledge, would probably have him tortured. He did not know how he would bear up to such torments and felt he would not be able to answer for his conduct under such pressures.'[6] Cinq-Mars protested, 'He replied that now that I had risked so much, I should follow the

[6] Fontrailles, *Mémoires*.

matter through to the end, but he agreed that it would be better if I did not return to court.'[7]

Fontrailles and d'Aubijoux left for Toulouse. They saw de Thou at Carcassonne, who told them that his mission to Mercoeur and Beaufort had failed. They shared their separate disillusionments, and then parted.

In the midst of all this gloom another 'favourable circumstance' presented itself. A Spanish defeat ironically served the cause of the Spanish allies. At the beginning of April Monsieur de la Mothe-Houdancourt routed the Spanish forces which were to reinforce Collioure, which fell soon afterwards. This victory paved the way for the siege of Perpignan. Louis was eager to conduct the campaign personally. At this vital point Richelieu suffered an attack of malaria and a huge abscess appeared on his right arm, preventing him from accompanying the King and participating in a siege which promised to be as glorious and as crucial as that of La Rochelle had been. Richelieu's indisposition thus left Louis, the campaign and all the glory to his rival. Henri was overjoyed and relished the prospect of having the King to himself while his enemy languished. When they set out from Narbonne, everyone believed in his ultimate triumph.

[7] Fontrailles, *Mémoires*.

XIV

To be Bored a While

Henri was so certain of success that he was not afraid of dropping the mask and declaring himself leader of the party before they left Narbonne. Henri's temerity infuriated Richelieu. The two antagonists started gathering allies in preparation for the trial of strength ahead.

The Cardinal was the first to score. He succeeded in gaining the promotion of two of his loyal supporters, Guébriant and La Mothe-Houdancourt, to marshal. This success was followed by an unexpected reverse which lost him the ground he had won. Marshal de Schomberg, son of the Schomberg who defeated the great Montmorency, was generally regarded as a devotee of the Cardinal. He was given joint command of the French army at Perpignan with La Meilleraye, an honour which offended the Cardinal's nephew La Meilleraye. Schomberg immediately joined the army at the head of five hundred gentlemen and declared himself in favour of Monsieur le Grand. This was a blow to Richelieu and a victory for Cinq-Mars and one which redressed the balance of power. He now had a partisan to share the command of the army with his mortal enemy and brother-in-law La Meilleraye. The Cardinal felt seriously threatened and hurried off an unctuous letter to Marshal Schomberg's wife in an attempt to regain her husband's loyalties.

Richelieu received the bad news on his sickbed and retaliated by asking the King to give Gassion command of the Roussillon army. The King decided to send Gassion to Flanders, which lost Richelieu another point. The letter which the worthy Gassion received from de Noyers at the time is most revealing : 'The time has come for you to declare your loyalties. It is essential that we distinguish friend from foe . . . His Eminence has asked me to write to you and assure you of his good will . . . He is saddened by your absence from his side . . . It would be to your advantage to express your gratitude to him now when one compliment carries the weight of two. Do not take public rumours too seriously. I say this as court gossip seems to be deceiving even the sharpest of wits.'[1] The Army and the court were now expected to choose sides and pledge allegiance to Richelieu or the Master of the Horse. The younger generation declared themselves promptly and aggressively. Twenty-two royal guardsmen were unequivocably Cinq-Mars's men. Cinq-Mars cockily dubbed them 'my Twenty-Two' after Henri III's 'Forty-Five'.

Cinq-Mars continued to recruit supporters. He knew that the Queen's backing would cause a number of valuable people to accrue to him. He would entrust de Thou with the task of approaching Anne. He sent word to de Thou in Paris. De Thou went to see the Comte de Brienne, who was a relative of his and also belonged to Anne's House of Austria. He asked him to obtain blank sheets of paper which bore the Queen's signature. The party would write on these to various officers requesting their support. Brienne was a moderate and cautious man and he was horrified by the demand and so refused. He then reconsidered the proposition because he feared the matter might fall into less trustworthy hands. He approached Anne and to his amazement she immediately agreed. 'I had scarcely broached the subject when Her Majesty consented. I tried to warn her, saying "Her Majesty should be wary of entrusting such papers to anyone, even to me; I know I could not abuse such a privilege but they could fall into dangerous hands." '[2]

Brienne also tried to dissuade de Thou from his complicity with Cinq-Mars whom he regarded as an evil influence. He told him that 'the King was not as fond of Cinq-Mars as he used to be, that he had started having his doubts about him and even found him insufferable of late'. But de Thou did not listen. 'I know,' Brienne continues, 'that my words of warning would not alter his blind devotion. I even went down on my knees to him to show him I meant what I was saying and to emphasize my conviction that his attachment to the Master of the Horse would eventually destroy him.' De Thou was disturbed by Brienne's conviction, but he would not abandon his friend. The Queen dispelled any reservations he may have had. She received him and

---

[1] Archives des Affaires Etrangères.
[2] Brienne, *Mémoires*.

told him that the Spanish Treaty had been signed.[3] Monsieur
had been as good as his word and had informed her as soon as
he had heard. He then sent her a copy of the explosive document.
François was shocked by the news, as it was the first he had
heard of an agreement with the King of Spain. He was worried.

The Cardinal was an excellent propagandist. His agents started
circulating the rumour that Monsieur le Grand had lost the
King's favour. The rumour sounded credible as it was based on
the King's variable moods. But at that juncture, the rumour had
no foundation in fact.

De Thou soon heard the rumour and he did not dismiss it. He
was an anxious sort of man and Brienne's warnings and the
Queen's revelations had shaken his faith. He felt the plot was
being mismanaged and that Cinq-Mars was being too flippant. He
expressed his doubts to the Queen and begged her to be careful.

On his way south he met with Fontrailles, whose recent mission
had drastically reduced his old audacity and confidence. The two
men discussed the whole situation at length. The hunchback was
staggered to learn that Monsieur's orders had been contravened
and that de Thou knew of the treaty. He was doubly shocked
to hear that the Queen had been the informant. These slips
augured ill. Fontrailles decided to take his apprehensions to the
Duc d'Orléans at Chambord.

The Prince was also uneasy. He sent the Comte de Brion to
the King 'begging him to excuse his absence at the Catalonia
victory celebrations for he was unwell'. Brion also took a letter
for Cinq-Mars to hand to the King. The letter was an indictment
of the Cardinal and it was Monsieur's way of evaluating Cinq-
Mars's power. Richelieu quickly reacted to Brion's arrival in spite
of his indisposition. Much to Louis's annoyance, Richelieu had
begun to dispense with his usual formalities towards him. He sent
the King a curt message which Louis complained was little short
of an impertinent order : 'His Majesty will be well advised to disregard Monsieur de Brion and dismiss him as promptly as
possible. I enclose the answer His Majesty should make to Monsieur's letter, the which I have not yet seen.'

There is no way of knowing whether Cinq-Mars withstood
Monsieur's test. The Cardinal continued to maintain publicly
that Cinq-Mars had no power whatever while his actions and

[3] Fontrailles.

131

anxieties proved that he actually believed the contrary to be true. Richelieu was a very worried man. He spent his sleepless nights plotting his course of action. As soon as he received Father Carré's long letter he instructed Baron de Brassac, the Queen's Master of the Household, and his wife, who was a lady in waiting, to watch Anne closely. The Brassacs proved ineffectual spies despite their proximity to the Queen, and they detected nothing unusual in her conduct. Their ignorance convinced Richelieu that the Spanish lady was an artful intriguer, and therefore untrustworthy. In view of the imminent crisis, he thought it impolitic that she should have the future of France in her power. If anything happened to the King she would obviously use her children to bargain for her survival.

Louis suddenly decided to send his wife to Fontainebleau and threatened to remove her children from her keeping. Historians have speculated endlessly on the reasons for Louis's apparently 'inexplicable decision'. They had parted on good terms in February and then in April, on the eve of the Perpignan siege, Louis suddenly attacked her. It is the timing of the incident, rather than the incident itself, which has given rise to the historical confusion. Louis had always toyed with the idea of removing his children from the care of a woman he regarded as worthless. Many have favoured the theory that Cinq-Mars was responsible for Louis's conduct, but this is obviously absurd. Cinq-Mars depended on the Queen's support and could not afford to indulge in such a folly : Anne could easily ruin him.

The Cardinal is the most likely culprit. The tortuousness of the manœuvre is typical of Richelieu's manipulation of people and events for his own ends. The results it bore also indicate his complicity. All Richelieu had to do was to reawaken Louis's own fears and the King would react according to plan. It was Richelieu's way of bringing indirect pressure to bear on Anne, whose security would instantly be threatened. An intimidated Anne played into his hands. On April 30 she wrote Richelieu a panic-stricken letter which said, 'The idea of having my children removed from me at such a tender age is unbearably painful to me . . .' Richelieu did not reply. 'Has Monsieur le Cardinal abandoned me?' Anne cried to Monsieur de Brassac. Anne was left with the shadow of separation hanging over her.

Richelieu won another round and lost no time in securing

132

further success. He acquired the services of the Duc de Bouillon's young brother, the Vicomte de Turenne. He also had the loyalty of the Prince de Condé, who commanded Paris. This removed another worry from the Cardinal's danger list. Richelieu continued to devote himself to his greater tasks while guarding his ailing person against unexpected parries. He was busy drawing in the vast net he had cast over Europe while his health deteriorated steadily. 'My arm is inflamed again,' he wrote to de Noyers. 'The old ulcer which God and Nature opened is suppurating. My physicians try to console me by telling me that it will heal if I subject myself to the knife again. I do not have the courage to face such torment at present. I pray that God will help me obey His Command.' His malady and the resulting feverish restlessness further depleted his failing strength. He became increasingly depressed and dispirited. His two faithful secretaries of state Chavigny and de Noyers were his lifeline to the King, but he realized he was losing his hold over Louis. The King was in the clutches of his rival, and the Cardinal could do nothing to counteract his malevolent influence. He was a powerless spectator and the realization depressed him. He must have felt like the inventor who sees his creation destroyed by inexperienced hands, like the father who witnesses the ruin of his son by a worthless hussy. On the eve of a crucial siege Richelieu's work, welfare, and future depended upon the emotional relationship between a King with one foot in the grave and a boy who was gathering his rosebuds.

*   *   *

The siege of Perpignan is a perfect example of courtly military conduct. Before Louis invaded the area he suggested that the governor ask Philip IV for reinforcements. The governor refused. When the Spaniard ran out of money Louis entreated him not to touch his church treasuries. The governor protested 'that he had never even contemplated such a notion'. These gentlemanly exchanges were punctuated with cannonades and fierce battles. The soldiers flourished on the yields of the fertile lands. Louis installed himself in Jan Pouquet's farm and followed the operations with his usual battle lust. He was constantly surrounded by intrigues and court rivalries. The army had split into two camps, the Royalists and Cardinalists. The King's immediate circle was convinced that the favourite would triumph. Montglat observed that 'they were so certain of his victory that everyone hung about him in such droves that one was crushed by a crowd whenever one tried to get near him'.

Henri was delighted by his popularity, which he encouraged with gifts. He later denied his generosity, but he did relieve himself of a good six hundred pistoles. Monsieur de Campis, a lieutenant-general, received three hundred. Where money failed to buy his allegiance he tried seduction. He had the support of the French guards but there was one captain, Abraham Fabert, whom he had failed to entice. He was therefore particularly eager to establish a relationship with him. Fabert was an excellent soldier whom Louis liked and respected despite his humble origins. One day when the army halted to rest Monsieur le Grand approached Fabert and asked him to join him in a game of quoits. The captain accepted and the two men dismounted and left the company of the royal escort. Cinq-Mars then blurted out his intentions to Fabert. He was so sure of the excellence and universal acceptability of his cause that he thought the upright soldier would instantly come into his camp. But he was to be brutally reproved. 'I have made it my guiding principle to become involved in my friends' interests and in their passions. Any man who insults me by asking me to dishonour myself releases me from bestowing on him the regard and consideration I would otherwise proffer.[4]

Fabert's affront did not really daunt the conceited youth. He was in any case, reassured by another incident. The King had stopped sending a messenger to inquire after his minister's progress, which further upset the Cardinal. Cinq-Mars's friends adopted Richelieu's confidence trick and started circulating the rumour that the Cardinal was finished. Richelieu steeled himself against the inevitable stab in the back. Then the Duc d'Enghien, who had never forgiven the Cardinal for making him his nephew, nor Cinq-Mars for his Arras impertinence, offered to kill the favourite for Richelieu. 'The Marquis de Pienne heard about the proposal and told Ruvigny who, in turn, told Monsieur le Grand and advised him to inform the King. The next day Cinq-Mars told Ruvigny that "The King said, 'Dear friend, take some of my guards for yourself' " . . . Ruvigny looked him in the eye and asked, "Why have you not done so? You are not speaking the

[4] Tallemant.

134

truth." Cinq-Mars blushed, whereupon Ruvigny added, "Why don't you call upon Monsieur le Duc with two or three friends and show him that you are not in the least afraid of him?" ' Henri was piqued but he took his friend's advice. He and Ruvigny paid the Duke a visit and found him playing cards. The young prince either changed his mind or thought the occasion inopportune. He received Monsieur le Grand with manifest delight and was extremely jovial. Cinq-Mars came away from the visit in a triumphant mood.

Cinq-Mars would have been wiser to devote more of his time and energies to his King. Louis was delighted at the chance of enjoying his friend's company without the constant intervention of the Cardinal. He had no intention of supporting any kind of coup d'état but he, like many others, prayed that he would soon be released from his tyrant by his timely death. If Louis had not been so repressed and inscrutable he would have averted a number of misfortunes. If Cinq-Mars had been more patient and perceptive and had dissembled more he would eventually have achieved all his desires. As it was, Louis was uncommunicative and Henri intolerant. Henri had little staying power and little self-control. In Marie's absence he seemed incapable of being all that she had trained him to be. At the very time when he should have been doubly thoughtful, kind and pleasing he relapsed into his capricious, impertinent, freedom-loving ways.

Monsieur le Grand had become the idol of the younger generation. He was also the head of a faction that robbed His Eminence of peace of mind and since this image did not tally with an ingratiating and anxious favourite he rejected his royal duties. Tallemant reports : 'He resumed his former behaviour towards the King. The more the King wished him to be at his side, the more he sought to be away from him. When his friends counselled him to be more loyal to his King he thanked them for their advice and told them he could no longer bear the King's evil-smelling breath . . . nor his ridiculous way of life.' He went out of his way to be as defiant and insolent as possible in spite of the King's disapproval of such behaviour. One day as the short de Noyers approached His Majesty in full military regalia, his sword trailing on the ground, Cinq-Mars rudely burst out laughing. He openly tried to pick a quarrel with La Meilleraye and finally succeeded in having a fierce public slanging match with him on some military question. The King finally broke his silence and said, 'It is very like you to argue with a man who has years of military experience behind him when you have none.'

'But Sire,' protested the impertinent boy, 'one need not have experience if one has good judgement and sharp wit.' Then he fell back on his old trick and sulked. 'In spite of Ruvigny's efforts and advice, he never made any attempt to reconcile himself to the King.'[5]

When de Noyers arrived at court he was surprised by what he found. He immediately informed the Cardinal. 'I arrived yesterday, the twenty-eighth (April) to find that the Pyrenean fogs have settled over the court itself. If only that sun (Richelieu) which has in the past dispelled such gloom and confusion were strong enough to come to the court now and make everything bright and clear.' It is significant that Richelieu was worried by the news. He was so afraid of the favourite that his one concern was to prevent La Meilleraye from falling into disgrace. He wrote back to de Noyers, 'If it is true that Monsieur le Grand and La Meilleraye have quarrelled, see to it that they be reconciled at the King's command and peace restored.'

Henri, however, refused to salvage the situation. He decided to give himself up to a totally debauched life, despite the cautioning words of de Thou and Ruvigny. Marie was farther away than ever. If Henri had been asked to account for his behaviour he would have glibly answered that his former tactics with the King had had good results. Times had changed, however. Louis was engaged in a pathetic struggle against his illness and had no desire to indulge his former masochism. He needed to be comforted and tended with affection. He was in no mood for quarrels and lovers' jealousies. Cinq-Mars was foolhardy enough to ignore the King's displeasure. He prolonged the row and provoked several other unpleasant incidents in the face of the King's mounting exasperation.

Their differences in the past had only been known to a select few. Now they became common knowledge. Fabert was once informing the King on the progress of the siege while Cinq-Mars, who had not forgiven Fabert, kept interrupting him. Louis expressed his resentment viciously. 'Monsieur le Grand, you are in the wrong. You have no experience or qualifications to justify your

[5] Tallemant.

contradicting an experienced soldier. Had you spent the whole night inspecting our fortifications you might be allowed to express an opinion. I know you like to give the impression that you have stayed up helping me plan my campaigns when the truth is that you spend your evenings locked up in my closet reading romances with my valets. You are quite unbearably conceited.'

'Your Majesty will do me the favour of explaining what he means by that,' Cinq-Mars retorted in wounded vanity. He rose and turned to leave, and as he passed Fabert, he snapped, 'Thank you so much, Monsieur Fabert.'

'What was that?' Louis demanded. 'Did I hear him threaten you'?

'No sire,' Fabert replied calmly. 'One does not make threats in your Majesty's presence nor would any be tolerated.'

Louis could not hold his tongue. 'I must tell you, Monsieur Fabert, that no man is more corrupt, vicious and displeasing than he. He is the most ungrateful monster. Do you know that he has kept me waiting whole hours in my carriage while he indulged in some despicable vice. There is no kingdom on earth that could finance his extravagance. He has some three hundred pairs of boots in his wardrobe. I have been sick and tired of him these past six months.'[6]

Now if Louis had really been 'sick and tired' of Cinq-Mars for the last six months all that had happened during that time, Richelieu's panic, the Lyons affair, would be incomprehensible. When Louis spoke thus to Fabert he was exasperated by his favourite's 'despicable vices' and by his rank 'ingratitude'. His anger, his obvious hurt feelings, his scorn ('three hundred pairs of boots') are all indicative of his involved concern. They do not express the waning of an affection which is still patently strong and binding. If he had become indifferent to Henri or even revolted by him, he would have had no compunction whatever about getting rid of him as he had Baradas, Saint-Simon and Marie de Hautefort.

Cinq-Mars was finally shaken. He was so alarmed by the incident that he went to see de Noyers whom he had insulted the previous day. He asked the Secretary of State to be peacemaker but he was refused.

De Noyers immediately wrote to Chavigny, 'N. came to see

[6] Tallemant and Father Barré: *Vie de Fabert.*

me about ten o'clock this evening and spent three-quarters of an hour with me. He was friendly rather than indifferent. He told me that he had suffered three blasting tirades from his Majesty in the past two days and that he had endured them peaceably because of the King's indisposition. If the King were in better health, he assured me he would not tolerate his temper and would speak out. I believe he had his reasons for coming and had hoped I might effect a reconciliation. I did not react to the suggestion for obvious reasons.'[7]

The following day he wrote again. 'It has been a very good day. Everything continues to be as I have already described. It is as cold and unpleasant as it has been for the last six days and there is no sign that warmer days lie ahead.' The old warmth never really returned. The Princess's absence had an enormous effect on Cinq-Mars who needed her strength to carry him over his crisis. As it was, he did not have the courage or stamina to play the part required of him. He refused to do violence to himself and control his impetuousness. He withdrew from the struggle by sulking and bickering. He lost his ground and gave way. Anne of Austria later wrote, 'One wonders what might have happened if Monsieur le Grand had only allowed himself to be bored a while.'

[7] Letter of May 14, *Archives des Affaires Etrangères*.

XV

Two Dying Men and the Queen

'Even the sharpest of wits find they are waiting for something to happen before they can ascertain what the intrigue is all about,' Henri Arnauld wrote to Barillon. In both factions, confusion reigned.

On May 20 Fontrailles finally arrived at Chambord after much to-ing and fro-ing. Gaston d'Orléans was calm and quite confident. The Marquis was still in a state of panic and soon dampened his spirits. He told His Highness that the Cardinal was merely pretending to be dying, that Monsieur le Grand 'had lost the King's favour', that the conspiracy was doomed and that 'it was now necessary to safeguard his person and that of his faithful servants'. Monsieur was alarmed, but he did not lose his nerve. He was concerned that Bouillon had not yet given them their passes into Sedan. D'Aubijoux was dispatched to the Duke to obtain them. When Cinq-Mars gave the signal everyone was to meet. They chose an 'Inn at Moulins where a trustworthy man would be on the constant alert to receive Monsieur le Grand's message'. In the meantime the Prince would make it known that he would soon be going to Bourbon-l'Archambault to take the waters, which would enable him to get to Moulins without rousing anyone's suspicions.

Once he had seen to these arrangements, Fontrailles made for the royal encampment. He had only recently escaped from court and had sworn he would never return; he had gone as far as staging a mock duel in order to banish himself from the scene. Cinq-Mars was engaged in alternating between temerity and depression. He was not the man to change the course of history. The Master of the Horse had some 30,000 francs sent from Paris to a banker in Lyons and carried out a strange transaction with one of his friends, Monsieur de Gué, who was Treasurer of France at Lyons. 'The Messenger will give you a bill of exchange, which I would ask you to cash into Spanish pistoles, since louis are not in current usage down here. I would ask you to keep them for me until I can have them transferred to me safely.' He also sought to safeguard himself with 'fifty gentlemen kept in readiness in the Auvergne'.[1]

While the conspirators thus began to prepare for defeat, the enemy was himself convinced of his own imminent downfall. On May 23 the Cardinal drafted his last will and testament, in which he distributed vast sums of money. He could not even sign it as his right arm was paralysed. He was given two days to live. But the two days elapsed and the steely wizard bounded back and got to work on a counter-offensive. He told de Noyers to approach Father Sirmond, the King's confessor, and ask him to put pressure on the King. Then he sent Daridol, one of Chavigny's adjuncts, to Holland to obtain a pre-worded letter from the Prince of Orange. The Prince was asked to write 'that his confidence in my (the Cardinal's) capacities is what binds him to France and her interests and dissuades him from accepting the overtures made him by Spain'. Father Sirmond agreed immediately but the Prince of Orange kept a discreet silence.[2] Richelieu must have thought he was in great danger to humiliate himself before a prince whom he already subsidized heavily.

He used very different tactics with the Queen. He saw through her motives and knew where her sympathies were. François de Thou was away and Anne had no way of knowing what was happening. Brassac was ordered to aggravate her anxieties about her children.

These manœuvres were no solace to the worried minister. He could not decide whether there was a plot to kill him or whether the opposition was merely frightening him and intimidating him as he was Anne. At the root of all his anxieties was his obsession that he was being threatened with extermination, a fear which he communicated to his entourage.

His niece, the Duchesse d'Aiguillon, received an anonymous letter in Paris which said, 'You would be wise to warn His Eminence to be very careful because his enemies are trying to persuade the King to have him arrested as soon as he is well and will stop at nothing short of this.' The Duchess alerted Chavigny.

The Cardinal no longer felt safe. He instructed his doctors to

[1] Henri Arnauld.
[2] He answered on July 18 when circumstances had changed.

inform Louis that the climate of Narbonne was detrimental to his health. Louis did not object to his departure. Richelieu left immediately but Montglat is wrong when he says that 'he departed without taking leave of the King and without any particular destination'. The Cardinal had, in fact, decided to go to the fortress at Tarascon, where he could protect himself against an attack. He did not rule out the possibility of being forced to withdraw to the papal refuge at Avignon as the last resort. He took a thousand precautions and wrote as many missives before leaving Narbonne. His mind was incredibly active and sharp for such a very sick man. First of all he wrote a carefully worded letter to the King. 'I am following Your Majesty's counsel, which cannot but be excellent and good coming as it does from a good master, and I am leaving . . . with the help of God's grace I shall accept whatever change He may give my malady. I shall be constantly cheered by news of Your Majesty's well-being and of his victorious progress at Perpignan.'

He handed his Secretaries of State a volume of instructions which mapped out the positions they were to take and the lines they should adopt. 'I am certain now that my innocence is under attack. Silence is not the best policy in these circumstances as it would be used by connivers as a weapon against me. We will use the most innocent means of defence to prevail upon the King to undo the evil that is being done . . .

'The Brussels and Cologne newspapers, the Queen Mother's preparations to terminate her exile, all the puchases of vehicles and transport mules, Madame de Chevreuse's revealing communications, all the secret exchanges traversing the whole country, all the reports from every court in Italy, the rumours that stir the armies, the hopes nourished by the Spaniards . . . Monsieur's decision to stay away despite his promises, all indicate that something catastrophic is afoot . . . and have persuaded me to inform the King about it all so that he may restore such order as pleases him and counteract the rumours which are fast destroying his affairs.

'. . . Monsieur de Thou and Monsieur de Chavagnac must be sent away. Monsieur de Chavigny and Monsieur de Noyers should be frank with Monsieur de Schomberg when he approaches them, and should tell him that he must declare himself openly and dissipate his ambiguous public position.'

When Richelieu had finished giving many more such instructions he addressed a moving exhortation to the King. 'Had the Lord chosen to take my life, Your Majesty would now be calculating his loss. The loss would be the greater if my life were taken at your behest as Your Majesty would then himself lose all the trust and confidence that he has won.'

Chavigny's and de Noyer's blind devotion to their protector had already made Louis wary of them both. Richelieu began to look for a spokesman who could double as informer and was not suspected of blind partiality to him. He was fortunate in finding such a man in the First Gentleman of the Bedchamber, Gabriel de Rochechouart, Marquis de Mortemart (father of the future Madame de Montespan), whom Richelieu always called 'the faithful Mortemart'. Louis was fond of him.

He was certain he had provided for all contingencies and foreseen all possible combinations, and yet he was as anxious as ever when he set off on his great purple litter. His friends in Paris, however, the Prince de Condé, Chancellor Séguier, the Duchesse d'Aiguillon appeared calm and confident and spread the news of His Eminence'c excellent relations with the King, of his ease and contentment, and of his restored health and energies. Richelieu was nonetheless fleeing. The formidable Cardinal, the universally dreaded and admired Minister of France had been routed by a love-sick youngster. He was a shattered, insecure, and anxious man who trembled in anticipation of the future.

*　　*　　*

On May 27, torrential rain pelted down on Perpignan, severing communications and toppling the French army's tents. The rain lasted three days and an attack was feared. But the besieged city was paralysed by famine. According to one prisoner the Governor was seen to share a cat with his noble guests. The King was suffering from haemorrhoids and his health was affected by the rains. It was rumoured that Monsieur le Grand was going to take him back to Saint-Germain or Fontainebleau. The Cardinal was on his way to Béziers, Agde and Saint-Privas, when he heard the disturbing news. Louis's departure would remove him from his sphere of influence and leave the field open to the favourite. The Minister wrote to the King every day. He tried to elicit the King's sympathy. 'I do not need evidence,' he wrote on June 4, 'of His Majesty's affection because it has always been constant, even when great efforts were made to remove it.'[3] Louis reacted to the entreaty by reverting to his past reassuring manner. 'Despite the groundless rumours that are abroad, I am devoted to you more than ever. We have been together too long ever to be separated.'

The King was still furious with Monsieur le Grand. Henri missed his Princess and he began to detest Louis. Henri would finish their unpleasant scenes by wishing for his freedom. He knew he would only be free if his tyrannical benefactor died. Someone asked him how the King was and he replied, 'Oh, he is dragging along.' Louis sensed Henri's revulsion and felt humiliated by the realization that he was nothing more than a tottering old man for the magnificent youth. He would dearly have loved to be able to dazzle him with reports of his prowess. He was no longer the hero of 1629 who turned to his defeated generals and proudly said, 'I will not send my soldiers to the slaughter, but I will lead them myself.'[4]

On June 4, the Cardinal sent His Majesty a sentimental letter. Chavigny had just arrived at the camp and the Duc d'Enghien wrote, 'Monsieur de Chavigny has returned and has not as much as mentioned Monsieur le Grand to the King. He has found everything so much in accord with his desires that he has not had to say anything. The King and Monsieur le Grand are at odds and the King is well disposed and even indescribably tender towards the Cardinal.'

Louis was ill on June 4-8, and kept to his rooms. Henri could easily have reinstated himself in Louis's affections with as little as a single word, a mere gesture, or a smile. But he seems not to have wanted to do so. He may have found himself incapable of doing such violence to his instincts. Or he may have nourished the hope that Louis would soon die. Louis seemed to recover on June 8, but then two days later he felt 'somewhat unwell again'. His doctors ordered him to take the waters. He decided to leave the encampment and go to Narbonne which he reached on the evening of June 11. Cinq-Mars met Fontrailles there, who had a message from Gaston. Fontrailles informed him of Gaston's arrangements. He also received a letter from Marie, which said, 'All your plans are as much common knowledge here in Paris

[3] Archives des Affaires Etrangères.
[4] Spoken at the Battle of the Pas de Suze, when the Cavalry attacked the enemy's cannon.

as it is that the Seine passes beneath the Pont-Neuf.' When Fontrailles read this he panicked and told the favourite to withdraw
immediately to Sedan. Henri hesitated. 'I thought I had settled
the matter,' the hunchback wrote later, 'when he turned and asked
if I had informed Monsieur that he would soon be joining him,
to which I answered that I had not done so since he had not asked
me to.'

'In that case,' Cinq-Mars said, 'I shall send Montmort to get
him to set a date when we can arrive in Sedan together.'

Fontrailles begged him 'not to risk his life for the sake of appear-
ances'. But the Master of the Horse would not listen. This time
he was not wrong to ignore the advice. If he had arrived at Sedan
alone he would have become a common fugitive, losing all hope of
success and his princess as well. If, however, he arrived in the
company of the King's brother his position would be vastly different. He knew he could not afford to act precipitately at this
juncture. In any case Marie Gonzaga knew nothing of the Spanish
Treaty because Henri had been considerate enough not to involve
her in such a dangerous secret.[5] This meant that the 'plans' she
referred to were his plans against the Cardinal. His greater plans
still had a chance of success if Richelieu or Louis XIII died or
if he tried to make amends with the King. Henri still believed he
held the trump card and it never occurred to him that news of the
treaty had leaked. He sat down and wrote a reassuring letter to
his beloved. It was to be his last letter to her.

*   *   *

The Baron de Brassac understood the importance of his mission
and his every action proves his constancy and devotion to the
Cardinal. He continued to fan Anne of Austria's anxieties. By the
beginning of June Anne was convinced by his insinuations and by
the King's and the Cardinal's silence that her children were
about to be taken away from her. The conspiracy seemed to
be marking time and the Perpignan campaign was drawing
to a successful conclusion. Richelieu was obviously not as slow
and weak as his enemies claimed. Anne was disappointed by the
conspiracy, which had shown no results whatever. She began to
think that the restoration of the half-dead Minister might well
avoid a catastrophe, might save her position and would certainly

[5] Avenel.

win her a little time. These considerations were of paramount importance to the vigorous woman who had so much to gain from the two invalids, whose inheritance she intended to receive. In these circumstances it is not surprising that she wasted no sleep over her friendship and loyalty for Marie Gonzaga, de Thou and Monsieur. She could not afford to have a conscience. The princes of the time, whatever their religious convictions, placed themselves above the moral considerations of mere mortals.

On June 7 the Queen told Brassac to inform the Cardinal that she would 'give him her support, knowing that His Eminence would return the compliment and not abandon her'. Brassac's next letter to Richelieu the following day informs him that 'Her Majesty has sent word to Chavigny through Monsieur de Gras'. The Queen's precise message is unknown, but it seems likely that she told him of the existence of the conspiracy and even sent him the text of the Spanish treaty. We know from Madame de Motteville that several copies of the treaty were in circulation at the time.

All manner of attempts were immediately made to conceal the identity of the real informant. The names of Schomberg, Béthune, Abbé de La Rivière, who was Monsieur's confidant, and the Duchesse de Chevreuse, an enemy of Bouillon, were bandied about. Tallemant, whose authority we do not question any more than Avenel's,[6] was not, however, taken in. 'They claim,' writes Tallemant, 'that a messenger who missed him [Richelieu] at Narbonne arrived with a packet from Marshal de Brézé, Viceroy of Catalonia, who briefly informed him that they had found Monsieur le Grand's or rather Monsieur's treaty with Spain on a shipwrecked vessel along the coast, and that he enclosed it. This is a rumour which most people seem over-eager to accept but it is quite false.'

There is another theory that an obscure French agent in Madrid, a certain Pujols, was the man who sent the document, or so Monsieur de Termes claims. But the anonymous commentator of Monsieur de Termes's memoirs then writes, 'I remember that in 1659 when Monsieur de Fabert was talking about this matter he said, "I should like to be able to reveal the identity of the person who gave Cinq-Mars's treaty to the Cardinal, but I cannot satisfy you until two persons have died." ' The following

⁶Cf. Antoine Adam.

year Gaston d'Orléans died and the commentator reports, 'Fabert told me on another occasion, "Only one person has to die now before I can tell you who it was that handed in the treaty." And I believe that person was Queen Anne of Austria.'

Voiture once tried to make Chavigny confess, ' "You insist on the safeguarding of this secret, yet Monsieur le Prince has whispered it abroad." "Monsieur does not share it," said Chavigny, "and when he does he will never dare reveal it." '[7]

Brienne is enigmatic: 'Monsieur was not betrayed, as everyone knows, and yet the mystery was revealed by a totally unexpected source.' Even La Rochefoucauld, who was so devoted to the Queen, does not rush to exonerate her, 'It seems best,' he says, 'to give credence to the most harmless opinion and believe that the treaty was truly found in the Spanish courier's bag, which is usually searched when couriers pass through Paris.'

There may be no formal proof, but there is little doubt that the culprit was in fact Anne of Austria. She believed she was in a trap and saved herself by sacrificing the friends whom she had encouraged to undertake the dangerous conspiracy. These ruthless sacrifices enabled her to keep her children and prepare for her regency. It is interesting to speculate whether the devout Spanish matron lived to regret her actions and whether they were included in the self-reproach that seized her towards the end of her life and finally killed her.

[7] Tallemant.

XVI

The Great Discoveries

Paris was in a state of anxiety. The French army had been defeated at Honnecourt and there was fear of another invasion. This fear was aggravated by new troop levies and by the order issued to civil militia colonels to have their companies ready. There is, however, some evidence that suggests that these emergency measures were not taken against the Spanish advance but against a threatened coup d'état.

Richelieu had entrusted the capital to the care of completely reliable men who saw to it that no disquieting news was released and that optimistic opinions were disseminated. The public did however, have an inkling of the Cardinal's illness, of the precariousness of his position and of some of the favourite's activities. A thousand incredible tales were common currency and there was a general feeling that nothing was impossible : the King and the Minister might die; there could well be a civil war or an enemy invasion. People woke up surprised to find that nothing remarkable had happened during the night. Everyone was frightened and wary of the uncertain prospects.

The Cardinal was no less fearful when he arrived at Arles. His physical maladies continued to exacerbate his torment and he felt everything was lost. He was in one of his lethal depressions when a saviour presented himself. Historians have been unable to identify this mysterious guardian angel, but we believe him to be Monsieur le Gras. Gras left the Queen on June 7 to deliver a message from her to Chavigny and it is known that he was carrying a crucial document. Whatever the document may or may not have been the Cardinal miraculously recovered his strength at the sight of the paper. He had no sooner read it than he dismissed everyone from his presence except for Charpentier, his first secretary, whom he then asked, 'Bring me an enema, for I am upset.' Charpentier brought him the enema and bolted the door behind him. He was amazed to see His Eminence throwing his arms up and shouting for joy, 'Dear Lord, thank you for watching over the Kingdom and my person.' Then he added more calmly, 'Read this and make copies of it.'

The sick man, who had recently lain on his deathbed, now proceeded to exhaust his staff, for throughout the next two days he ceaselessly dictated dispatches to inform the King and to destroy his enemies. He had to tread cautiously for he knew that all the quarrels that had affected the King's affection for his 'dear one' had in no way destroyed the suspicious King's incredibly strong attachment. Richelieu did not interrupt his journey. He still felt the need to be surrounded by the stout walls of Tarascon. He carried out his enormous labours as he travelled. Chavigny joined him at Tarascon and was promptly dispatched to His Majesty with the papers that determined France's fate.

'Master Youthful,' as he was affectionately known, left by coach on June 11 for Narbonne, as the Cardinal wrote to de Noyers, 'The purpose of Monsieur de Chavigny's journey will astound you. God has come to the King's aid with wonderful discoveries.' The rest of the letter deals with a host of different matters. 'His constant lucidity reflects the orderliness of his mind, or rather his incredible capacity to appear calm even when subject to the most violent emotions.'[1]

On June 12 Chavigny reached Narbonne at dawn. The King had arrived the previous day. Chavigny went straight to de Noyers and they prepared a plan of action. They then attended the King's awakening. Louis, ever a conscientious servant of his country, immediately agreed to withdraw to the adjacent room. Cinq-Mars started to follow him but Chavigny barred his way. 'Monsieur le Grand, I have something to tell the King.' Whereupon 'the other, like a good boy, left them alone together'.[2] But the incident frightened him and he hurried off in search of Fontrailles. They both waited nervously for Chavigny to emerge and were further perturbed that de Noyers had been summoned in to the closed meeting. Their wait was a long one.

When Fontrailles realized that Cinq-Mars was being excluded from the discussion he panicked. 'We are undone. We must withdraw' (to Sedan). But Henri would not hear of it. The hunchback lost his temper and snapped, 'You have no cause for concern, I suppose, for you will still be head and shoulders above me even

[1] Avenel.   [2] Tallemant.

when they sever the one from the other, but I am too small to risk my neck.' Then he changed his tone and became thoughtful. 'It is a pity that I shan't ever see you again.' He turned on his heel and left. He donned his Capuchin habit, which had disguised him on his journey to Spain, and vanished. Had Henri followed him he would certainly have prolonged his life span. A Maltese astrologer had once predicted that if he survived his twenty-second year he would be the happiest man alive. But pride or indolence or his blind confidence in his power over the King or a combination of all three made him linger and face his fate.

*   *   *

Louis was completely taken aback by the shattering revelation of Cinq-Mars's treachery. His violent reaction to the news refutes many claims that his passion for his favourite had died long before. He was beside himself with rage. He ranted and he raved that it was another of the Cardinal's inventions and that he was not going to be taken in. Chavigny and de Noyers remained un-daunted as Richelieu had prepared them for this reaction. 'The King will tell you that it is all untrue, but you must persuade him to have Cinq-Mars arrested, as we can easily prove his complicity if he is safely in prison. It will be harder to destroy him once he has taken refuge.' The two ministers found their task very diffi-cult. The luckless King was once again forced into a tragic Cornelian dilemma. His whole life seemed to be dogged by the conflict between his sense of duty and his personal inclinations. He had already had to sacrifice his mother, Louise de La Fayette and many others to his royal duties. And now his greedy political Moloch demanded his cruel, impossible, but adored boy. He was being asked to renounce his last joy on earth.

Another king might have rebelled and even executed the bearers of such unhappy news as the ancient kings had done. The expos-ure of Cinq-Mars need not have been such a serious revelation. The danger was now over and if he forgave him Cinq-Mars would be eternally indebted to him and finally submissive to Louis's will. But Jeanne d'Albret's grandson never considered such a com-promise. His rigid principles were outraged by what he read : 'It is agreed that neither of the contracting parties shall approach the French crown without the consent of both parties . . . After the war, Spain shall recover all the strongholds, provinces and kingdoms which His Most Christian Majesty has already seized or which he shall have seized.' There were no two ways about it. The Master of the Horse had committed high treason. Louis felt disgusted and despondent. He finally mastered his immense sorrow and resigned himself to his bereavement. When the Lord's anointed, the guardian of France, accepted the news, he submitted totally to the Minister's demands: Messieurs de Cinq-Mars, de Thou, de Chavagnac the elder, the Duc de Bouillon's father d'Ossonville were to be arrested and Monsieur de Castelan was to be sent to Casal to arrange the arrest of the Duc de Bouillon, who was surrounded by his troops. Louis also agreed to the Cardinal's Machiavellian plan to deal with Monsieur.

As soon as the Secretaries of State emerged from the royal chambers at ten o'clock that morning they sent a triumphant message back to Richelieu.

'Monsieur de Chavigny arrived this morning an hour before the King's rising. He and Monsieur de Noyers conferred together and then went to see His Majesty to give him a detailed account of the matter. His Majesty duly read all the relative documents. Everything has complied with His Eminence's wish. Orders will be dispatched this evening without fail. His Majesty has agreed that Monsieur de Castelan should go to Piedmont.'

Signed: 'Chavigny-de Noyers'.

*   *   *

The matter was kept secret and nothing happened that day. Chavagnac claims that the favourite was warned, but it seems unlikely. Fontrailles had fled and if Cinq-Mars had really known that he had been exposed he would certainly not have dined so calmly with Monsieur de Beaumont, Governor of Saint-Germain, who was his guest that evening. The dinner took place at an inn called The Three Nurses because of the caryatids that decorated its façade. One of the King's valets interrupted the dinner to inform him that His Majesty 'was retiring'. Protocol required that the Master of the Horse be present at the King's retirement, which was unusually late this evening. According to his statement at his trial, Henri left the inn immediately and hurried to the Archbishop's palace where the King was staying. When he arrived he was accosted by an unknown character who handed him a note.

'What is it?' Cinq-Mars asked.

'Read it,' came the reply from the vanishing messenger.

Henri deciphered the hastily written scrawl in the doorway of the Archbishop's palace. It read: 'You are in danger.'

He retraced his steps in a state of agitation, wondering who had sent the message. Some historians claim that it was a ruse of Chavigny's because he later declared that 'Monsieur le Grand's flight proved his guilt'. But the claim lacks substance. It was unlike 'Master Youthful' to play such risky games. He would have incurred Richelieu's fury if he had put his principal victim to flight. Nor would de Noyers have exposed himself to such a danger. On the other hand there were only three people who knew of the decision to arrest Cinq-Mars.

The third person was, of course, Louis. If he was the informant, it was the first and last time he allowed personal sentiment to take precedence over the interests of state. The man who had exiled his own mother would be giving a treacherous but beloved conspirator a last chance.

Henri hesitated for a moment and then made for one of the gates, but the gates were closed. The precise whereabouts of his place of refuge are not known. He may have gone to the house of Burgos, whose daughter he knew, or to that of one of his valet's mistresses, or to that of the goldsmith who lived opposite the garden of the Archbishop's palace. The most convincing suggestion is that he took cover at Monsieur Siouzac's in Rue du Tribunal. He is said to have had an affair with Madame Siouzac during his first visit to Narbonne. The lady would not have turned him away if he asked her help.

While Cinq-Mars was busy seeking shelter the King ordered the Comte de Charost to arrest the plotters. Charost first called on Monsieur le Grand. He arrested his servants, seized his papers and his caskets, which Monsieur des Yveteaux was instructed to open.

' "Heavens above," exclaimed a valet to the military gentlemen, "you will be surprised to find what you are not looking for."

'They were letters from his mistress.'[3]

Ceton, a lieutenant in the Scottish Guard, arrested de Thou and gallantly allowed him to burn his papers.

Charost went to tell his Majesty that the bird had flown. The

[3] Tallemant.

King ordered the consuls of Narbonne to shut the city gates and instructed Charost to search every single house in the city as from dawn. The King somehow learned of his friend's whereabouts. The honest Father Griffet writes, 'At three in the morning a valet whom he [Cinq-Mars] did not recognize knocked at the door of the house where he was staying and informed him of the King's order.' Henri's reaction was to turn jovially to his valet Belet and say, 'Go and see if there is any way out of the city.'

One of the city gates had in fact been left open to allow La Meilleraye's retinue to enter the city that night. The King must have known about this and probably hoped that Cinq-Mars would slip away unnoticed. Unfortunately, however, Belet was as imperceptive and negligent as his master. He was so convinced that all the gates would be closed that he did not take the trouble to check.

The King awoke at his usual early hour and asked for news of Monsieur le Grand. When he heard that there was none he thought Cinq-Mars was at a safe distance. He therefore continued to act out his part and brazenly ordered the public pronouncement of the death penalty for anyone who attempted to hide him. He then set off for Béziers without waiting for any results.

Claude de Rébé, Archbishop of Narbonne, and an agent of Cardinal, hastened to reinforce the King's commands by offering a reward of two thousand *écus* to anyone who handed over Monsieur le Grand. When Madame Siouzac heard the town heralds broadcast the offer and the order she panicked. She told her husband 'that a nice young gentleman had asked her for shelter and that she had taken pity on him and not turned him away'. Siouzac did not hesitate. Cinq-Mars had drifted off into a troubled sleep and was lying fully dressed on a bed with the poster curtains drawn when the armed troops invaded the house. He rose and 'calmly and resolutely' presented himself to the soldiers. Ricardelle, Charost's lieutenant, asked for his sword. Cinq-Mars 'asked permission to keep his sword as he did not want to walk through the streets bereft of great coat and sword like a common criminal'. The permission was granted.

Chavagnac's father was also arrested. His son and Cinq-Mars's other friends ran to the rescue. They talked to Cinq-Mars at the Archbishop's palace and planned an escape. Their plans were foiled by Jean Ceton's arrival at the head of forty Scottish Guardsmen. Ceton's guards were soon reinforced by the Champagne Regiment. Richelieu was obviously taking no risks. The Master of the Horse still had a great many friends. Richelieu was particularly afraid of what Tréville, Ruvigny and Chavagnac's son might do. Ruvigny nobly announced to La Meilleraye, 'I am loyal to Monsieur le Grand and even if I were to see the Spanish treaty with my own eyes I should not believe in it.'

Henri was taken to Montpellier prison. He was sobered by his solitude and by the loss of his princess's moral support. He soon came to realize the folly of his ways. As he crossed the drawbridge to the fortress he was heard to say, 'Must I really die at twenty-two? It is a shame that I committed treason at such an early age.'

* * *

The King was consumed with anger towards Monsieur, who was responsible for the Spanish treaty, as it could never have existed without his participation. He raised no objection whatever to Richelieu's cunning trap. On June 13 he sent Monsieur two letters from Béziers. The first one announced the arrest of the Master of the Horse for fictitious reasons. 'His excessive insolence towards me,' he wrote, 'has forced my hand. I am certain that you will approve of the punishment meted out to those who do not pay us due respect.' The second letter appointed the Duc d'Orléans commander-in-Chief of the Army in Champagne. The army had recently been defeated at Honnecourt and it was now being hastily reformed to repulse the threatened invasion. The King was thus making Gaston defend the frontier against his secret allies, the Spaniards. The Cardinal calculated that Monsieur would need superhuman nerve to resist the temptation of fleeing to the enemy camp.

Gaston was amazed but he did not see the trap. On June 17 he wrote the Cardinal a letter which really debases the son of Henri IV. 'Dear Cousin, my master and King has done me the honour of writing to tell me of the consequences of Monsieur le Grand's preposterously ungrateful behaviour. He must be the most contemptible man alive. He has persisted in displeasing you who have done so much for him. The King's favouritism has always made me wary of him and of his artful ways ... you, dear cousin, have always had and continue to have my regard and

L

sincere friendship.' The prince was anxious to demonstrate his gratitude for the honour bestowed on him. He spent so much time trying to ingratiate himself that he lost his last chance to escape. He had fallen into Richelieu's trap.

Louis XIII had decided to go to the Montfrin spa and stop on his way at Tarascon. The conspiracy and Cinq-Mars's arrest had exhausted him. He performed his duties like a robot and travelled from one town to the next in the company of Chavigny and de Noyers. His thoughts returned constantly to the prisoner whom he had tried to save without failing his duty. On June 15, de Noyers showed him the document which had been attached to the original treaty. It contained a list of the plotters and when the King read Cinq-Mars's name he queried miserably, 'Could it not be that his name was put there in place of another?' De Noyers was upset by the suggestion and dismissed it sharply. His Majesty withdrew into a 'distracted mood'. De Noyers sought to shake him out of his dejection by referring to a number of state affairs. But Louis turned a deaf ear and continued to muse. He then cried out plaintively, 'Monsieur le Grand really leapt into the darkness. Yes, he really did,' and he kept repeating his lament.

'Yes, he did,' said de Noyers. 'A disloyal subject is doomed to darkness.'

Louis refused to listen to these words. He had always accepted such pronouncements as sacred and he now realized that his compliance had invariably brought him misery and isolation. How could this shrivelled little man understand his feelings? He was only the tool of a man who was a genius at reaping personal vengeance in the holy name of the state. He knew that de Noyers's sole concern was to prevent Louis the Just from choosing happiness over cruel justice, from pardoning a guilty child whom he longed to clasp once again. But Louis did not need to be coerced. He was too ruthless with himself to yield to any such temptations. Cinq-Mars was not entitled to gentler treatment than Montmorency, the idol of the Languedoc, or than Marillac, the valiant old soldier, had received, simply because he loved Cinq-Mars. He could not afford to throw away all the positive results of his iron rule with one weak gesture. To save Cinq-Mars would be to capitulate and to unleash a series of similar rebellions. He could not be permissive. He could only die of chagrin.

De Noyers did, however, understand Louis's internal conflict.

He described the incident to Richelieu in two long letters. 'I think
Monsieur le Cardinal Mazarin should join the King immediately.
His Majesty is truly in need of consolation, for he is heart-broken.'
But Richelieu had other plans for Mazarin. He left the restora-
tion of the King's spirits to the wily Marquis de Mortemart.

The King's health deteriorated and this worried His Eminence.
His letters are full of concern. 'I beseech Your Majesty to take
great care of your person, for the welfare of France and perhaps
of all Christendom depends upon your well-being. I also entreat
you not to torment yourself . . . I again beg Your Majesty to take
care of your health and not to torture yourself with all the weighty
problems which have once again assailed you. I can assure you
that as long as you are of good health you will be victorious.'

Shortly after this the Cardinal learnt that Louis had burned
a good many letters since Cinq-Mars's arrest. We cannot know
what these letters contained nor what secrets Adonis and the
Stoic shared. Richelieu was concerned and ordered his agents
'to impress upon the King that he should never tell anyone he
burned the papers'. Other documents continued to disappear in
the same way, however.

On the night of June 17, a messenger from the Duc d'Enghien
informed Marie Gonzaga of what had happened at Narbonne.
The princess was shaken, but immediately thought of the 'terrible
quantity of incriminating letters' which must have been seized
from Cinq-Mars's apartment. She ran to ask her friend Mademoiselle de Rambouillet to approach the Duchess d'Aiguillon,
Richelieu's much-cherished niece. The Duchess was staying at
the Cardinal's palace in order to guarantee her own security.
Mademoiselle de Rambouillet called on her and then took Marie
to her. The proud Gonzaga fully confessed her worries and no
doubt her regrets. She hastened to add 'that the letters only dealt
with their marriage'.

The former Madame de Combalet was the widow of a minor
gentleman, and she had once suffered the degrading experience
of being chased away from the court by the jealous Marie de
Médicis. She was therefore delighted at the opportunity of having
the Duchess of Nevers at her feet. 'She received her in the kindest
way, and immediately had all her letters returned to her.'[4] As
these letters were immediately destroyed we have no firsthand

[4] Tallemant.

155

account of Cinq-Mars's fatal love affair nor of those aspects of his relations with Louis XIII which were concealed from Richelieu. If ashes could speak history might be very different.[5]

The announcement of the discovery of the plot in Renaudot's *Gazette* of June 21 dejected most of the court, the Hôtel de Rambouillet and the Marais. Marion, who was still called Madame la Grande, wept bitter tears. Many a sensitive soul, most of Richelieu's enemies, and a number of eminently sane and distinguished individuals who took exception to the Cardinal's political conduct were genuinely distressed. One person really was delighted. The Queen at Saint-Germain had been rewarded with 'the thing she most desired'. The King had written an almost affectionate letter on June 15, asking her to keep the children with her. Brassac informed the Cardinal of Her Majesty's gratitude and assured him of her loyalty as if any such assurances from her carried any weight. 'Nothing will ever change her.' Anne of Austria had taken a decisive step towards reaching the goal she was to attain the following year when she became regent.

[5] The history of Louis XIV's reign would have to be rewritten if we had Madame de Maintenon's voluminous correspondence.

XVII

The Word of Honour of a Son of France

Monsieur had no idea that his sister-in-law had won such a resounding victory. His suspicions were not even aroused when Chavigny came to see him at Moulins and presented him with the proof of his treason. 'Master Youthful's' voice wavered as he concluded his mission. 'Your Highness's crime is so great that you are beyond His Eminence's help. Your life is in jeopardy, for you have committed an unpardonable crime.'

The Prince finally broke down. 'Chavigny, I must find a way out of this dilemma. You have twice before interceded on my behalf with His Eminence. I assure you that this will be the last time I shall ever make such a request.'

'Your only hope is to confess the full extent of your crime.'

Gaston understood that what Richelieu wanted of him was enough material evidence to discredit him and hang Cinq-Mars. Before he committed himself, he sent his favourite, who knew nothing of the Spanish Treaty, to the King and the Cardinal to see how serious the situation really was. The Abbé de La Rivière was the 'most infamous, wealthiest and best paid traitor in the kingdom, who fully appreciated his Master's value, having sold him on countless occasions.' This time, however, the Abbé was loyal. When Richelieu knew of his departure he sent Louis strict instructions on how to deal with him. Louis passively acquiesced. His despair had made him indifferent to everything and his inertia was now neutralized by his congenital resentment towards his brother.

Louis was slowly approaching Tarascon where Richelieu was waiting to upbraid him for failing in his duties. Louis dreaded the encounter as he dreaded his mentor's justified self-righteousness. Before he reached Tarascon he learned of the Duc de Bouillon's arrest at Casal.

The ruler of Sedan had suffered the indignity of being surprised in the middle of a tumble in a barn. Louis revealed his true sympathies when he said that 'Monsieur de Bouillon has perverted

157

him [Cinq-Mars] and that it was he alone that should die'. But the Cardinal had no such sympathies. At this stage he was less concerned with eliminating pernicious traitors, who had in any case ceased to represent any real danger, than with avenging himself personally on the youth he had forced out of obscurity only to escape being his victim by a hair's breadth. After his earlier physical and political recovery, his body once again rebelled against the resulting over-excitement and overwork. He was forced back to his sickbed from where he directed the capture of his enemies and the Thirty Years War. Several floors beneath his sick-room, de Thou and Chavagnac patiently awaited their fates.

The King was in no better health than the Cardinal. His extreme grief and depression, his inertia and anxiety all indicate that he was, in fact, verging on a real breakdown. The sudden news that Marie de Médicis was seriously ill at Cologne aggravated his condition. He had not seen his mother for eleven years and he still winced at her exile. 'No son ever honoured his mother more,' he once wrote her, which was true despite the fact that he had never managed to move the hard-hearted woman. She never once embraced her son in the seven years of her regency. Louis had been forced to spend his life fighting her while he yearned to demonstrate his unworthy affection for her. He was now faced with the torment of letting the Queen Mother die an ignominious death in exile bereft of the past-obliterating blessing he longed to bestow on her.

On June 28 the Marquis de Brézé's fleet defeated Ciudad-Real's Spanish fleet. France was thus supreme master of the Mediterranean, which robbed Perpignan of its last hope. The King arrived at Tarascon on the day of the sea victory. The Cardinal dreaded their meeting after three tragic months just as much as the King. Neither had the energy to see the other immediately. The two collaborators, whose first serious misunderstanding had nearly changed the course of history, finally met stretched out on their respective litters like two invalid travellers who were nearing the end of their life. The two litters draped with rugs were placed side by side in a beautiful room overlooking the Rhône that lapped peacefully at the walls of the fortress. To their mutual relief there were no recriminations, no bitter undertones. Their conversation inevitably revolved around all the unhappy incidents they had to discuss but there were no explosions. The Cardinal

158

was too clever to complain. He thanked His Majesty for not endorsing the adverse rumours that had circulated about him. Louis was reassured by the Cardinal's consideration and treated him with his old deference. His meeting with the implacable genius whom he still admired, hated and to whom he was so indebted had the effect of calming him and removing his persecuting demons. He regained his self-confidence, and his doubts, if not his pain, began to dissipate. At one point in their conversation, the exhausted King's thoughts started to stray. 'Dear Cousin,' he said, 'the Rhône is so near that I can hear the sad sound of the waves lapping beneath us.'

They came to no decisions before they parted, but Richelieu had won. He had regained the King's confidence, which alone enabled him to rule France for eighteen years against her people's will. The following day, the King set out for Lyons and sent Richelieu a reassuring note. 'I never fail to benefit by seeing you. I feel much better since yesterday . . . I hope that, God willing, all will be well.' He was tired, however, of sitting in judgement over his fellow men and of executing justice. He wanted to see the end of the whole unpleasant business and withdraw to his beloved refuge in the forests of the Ile de France. He longed to go out hunting again and to regain his will to live. From Bagnol he gave the Cardinal full legal powers and appointed Richelieu to deal with the conspiracy as he thought best and to arrange the conquest of Roussillon. He had shifted the burden, but it did not have the desired effect of reducing his torments.

*   *   *

Rebuffed by the Cardinal, the Abbé de La Rivière dashed off to the King, who received him rudely. 'Do not tell me of my brother's fidelity, for everyone knows he never had any,' said the King, and he then showed the Abbé a copy of the treaty. La Rivière was ruffled but he controlled himself sufficiently to plead his master's cause by shifting the blame on to others. The King asked him to put his imputations down in writing, which the Abbé bravely refused to do. Louis was taken aback and concluded the interview with an attempt to intimidate La Rivière. 'Those who led my brother astray will receive their just deserts. If my brother agrees to give me a complete account of all his actions he will benefit from my customary goodness towards him.'

159

As soon as he left the King's audience, the Abbé was seized by Chavigny, who threatened to have him arrested. The luckless emissary 'was so terrified that he fainted and then proceeded to throw a nervous fit which was only cured by reassurances'. The Minister reassured him and then suggested that 'he undertake to persuade Monsieur to submit a full written confession to the King. Then once he had given his confession he would be well advised to leave the country for a time.'

Richelieu then invited the Abbé to see him, and put extra pressure on him. Richelieu was less confident than he seemed. If Monsieur refused to release the original treaty his efforts might well prove useless. A duplicate of the treaty would not have the effect of the original at a trial. 'Monsieur's actions are unworthy of a Son of France,' the Cardinal declared. 'He deserves to be put to death. If, however, he obeys His Majesty's commands he will be given leave to withdraw to Venice.' He gave the Abbé a letter for Monsieur in which he urged him once again to 'agree to submit a full and honest confession.' Richelieu was still uneasy, but Chavigny reassured him once the Abbé had left, 'Fear is the most likely agent to persuade Monsieur to agree.'

Fear did in fact persuade Gaston and his collaborators to give themselves away. Vincent Voiture wrote to Mademoiselle de Rambouillet, 'Monsieur is ruined and so are all of his friends and their ruin is inevitable and definite.' The prince's servants did not acquit themselves very well. 'If you could see the anger and despair which has seized his household you would be sorry for him,' wrote Du Boulay, one of the less cowardly, to Chavigny. Gaston feared arrest and took refuge in the mountains of the Auvergne, 'and kept on the move to avoid the realization of his worst fears'. Richelieu grew impatient. Cinq-Mars and de Thou had both resolutely denied everything during their preliminary interrogations. The Cardinal instructed Chavigny to offer Henry IV's son as much money as would buy a confession from him. But this financial persuasion proved unnecessary. Gaston's fear of exile and his friend's encouragement spared Monsieur the supreme dishonour of selling his friends for money. On July 7, he wrote to Richelieu from Aigueperse in the Auvergne, expressing his 'extreme regret at his past relations and dealings with his [Richelieu's] enemies', and swearing innocence of any plot to assassinate him. 'I would rather have died than lend an ear to anything that might have caused Your Eminence harm.' There followed a long 'declaration to the King' in which Monsieur revealed 'all that he had been a guilty party to', which in fact did reveal a good part of the conspiracy. He did not mention the Queen and defended de Thou : 'He never mentioned the Spanish matter in the two conversations I had with him . . . I know he condemned it to the Comte de Brion, whom he told that he would rather go to Rome than become involved.' He vented all his anger on the favourite, whom he accused of tricking him, despite his solemn word to Cinq-Mars that he would never expose him. Henri had given his word in return to Monsieur and when he learned of Monsieur's betrayal he exclaimed, 'If I must die, I shall die an honourable man and shall betray no one.' But the Son of France did not attach such sanctity to his own word of honour. He begged Chavigny to spare him having 'to leave the country', and added, 'there is nothing I will refuse to do to avoid this'. A hundred and fifty years later another Duc d'Orléans was to comment after voting for Louis XVI's death, 'I could but do what I have done.' Gaston was not being asked to commit regicide, he was merely sending a foolish youngster who believed in a prince's word of honour to the scaffold.

*   *   *

The Marquis de Montemart had succeeded in becoming Louis XIII's confidant, as Richelieu had wished. Louis needed a confidant. The stoic may have resigned himself to being unhappy but he had to communicate his miseries. Mortemart took enormous advantage of his position, aided and abetted as he was by the Duc d'Enghien and other gentlemen who wanted to dissociate themselves from the Master of the Horse. They never passed up a single opportunity of reminding the King of his prisoner's insolence, faults, indiscreet love affairs. Louis was being prepared for the blow that would eventually be dealt by the Cardinal and his agents. Mortemart repeated the heartless quip Cinq-Mars had given an inquirer after the King's health, 'Oh, he is dragging along.' The unhappy King was cut to the quick. Louis nourished the very normal hope that despite everything the object of his love felt something for him, even if it was only friendship. The man whom Louis had loved more than anyone else and who had, albeit briefly, taken precedence over his royal duty, had wished him dead for the sake of a silly conspiracy and an evil woman. Louis had a nagging suspicion that he had wished to rid himself of the unpleasant company of an invalid who revolted him.

Louis's future reactions would be hard to explain unless we give this revelation its real importance. His affections refused to dwindle despite all his anger, humiliation and grief. He did everything he could to lessen his attachment and overcome a weakness he despised. He tried to force himself to hate Cinq-Mars. He took to repeating 'The loathsome wretch wished me dead' ten times a day. He talked of nothing else and he encouraged everyone to express their loathing of 'the worst villain and traitor that has ever lived'. One day, when two Jesuits reported the hopes nurtured by the Protestants because the conspirator Chavagnac was a Protestant, Louis exclaimed to de Noyers, 'I am sure Monsieur le Grand would have been capable of becoming a Huguenot!'

'He would have become a Turk,' the little man replied, 'if it would have enabled him to wrest the crown from God's chosen monarch.'

'I am sure he would,' was Louis's incredible reply.

One evening he summoned Fabert to discuss his only topic of conversation—Monsieur le Grand. 'He was so incredibly extravagant,' he exclaimed, 'that he has forty-three suits. He had a German cabinet made for him in Paris worked with gold and gems, which cost him a hundred thousand *livres*. His extravagance leads me to suspect that he had other sources of income besides myself, for I know how much I gave him in the last two years, which could not possibly have covered his expenditures. Now that I have seen the Spanish treaty I know that my suspicions were fully justified.'

The King, however, knew that Henri was hopelessly in debt and did not really believe that he had received bribes. He may have thought Fabert could give him some evidence that would convince him. But Fabert, who was no particular friend of Cinq-Mars's, said nothing.

On July 6, Chavigny wrote to the Cardinal, 'His Majesty is so incensed with the traitor that he is less likely to be clement than ruthless.' Then another part of the plot was revealed by a number of people who were directly or indirectly involved with the conspiracy and had decided to buy their safety. The attempt on the Cardinal's life at Lyons took the Cardinal by surprise.

When Cinq-Mars was questioned about the attempt he declared that 'he had done nothing which the King had not approved'. Richelieu was really horrified. It had never occurred to him that Louis would ever consent to his assassination. He had, at the time, explained away Tréville's presence in the royal antechamber as part of his guard duties. He dealt with the matter in a consummately cunning way. He told Mortemart to ask His Majesty about the whole thing as if it had only just been brought to his attention and as if the Cardinal did not yet know about it. It was Louis's turn to be shocked. What had he really meant by his ambiguous opposition to Cinq-Mars and by his silence to Tréville's rash suggestion? Had he ever realized what had happened when Cinq-Mars decided against taking advantage of that occasion? He could understand how his manner might have been interpreted as it was and he shuddered to think what might have happened as a result of his ambiguousness. His detractors have accused him of cowardice and compared him to his brother. But the comparison is odious. They could not have been more dissimilar. The one was a dedicated king, a martyr to his duty, and the other an unprincipled prince who thought nothing of sacrificing his friends to save himself from a distasteful exile. Louis feared the outcome of such a revelation and resented Cinq-Mars all the more for implicating him. This hardened him and made him all the crueller towards his 'dear one'. But he was not afraid of his minister whom he could strip of power with a single word. On the contrary, it was Richelieu who feared his King, as the deviousness of his tactics demonstrates. At a time when victory was about to reward all his years of personal and official sacrifice, Louis was loath to publicize his brief flirtation with a notion which would certainly have jeopardized his and his country's chances of success. His mother had just died and he could not afford the luxury of superfluous and dangerous gestures. He was too upset to be wily and simply trusted Mortemart to play a simple-minded trick on Richelieu and inform him of the horrible plot which had fortunately miscarried.

The King was being naïve, and Richelieu kept up the pretence by writing him a naïve letter: 'Monsieur de Chavigny has informed me of the latest discovery concerning Monsieur le Grand's plot against me at Lyons and of His Majesty's indignation, for which I am extremely grateful. I confess that Monsieur le Grand could easily have executed his plan on my unsuspecting person. I would never have believed he was capable of sullying himself with the blood of a Cardinal who, by the grace of God, has had the good fortune of serving his master for twenty-five years and would gladly serve him a thousand more if he had them to live. The more evil that miserable soul reveals the greater appears His Majesty's goodness. Reason demands that Kings protect those who serve them but His Majesty has always protected me with his innate natural goodness.'

This letter reveals the Cardinal's extraordinary cunning, his hypocrisy and his belief in the necessity of flattering the injured King. Richelieu did not even consider verifying the facts of the case. His fever helped convince him that he had narrowly escaped the fate of a Concini and that the King had, in fact, given the Master of the Horse his consent to kill him. He began to resent the King. His hatred and his fear of Louis were to dominate the last weeks of his life. His conviction is attested by his coded letter to Chavigny dated July 14 : 'The darkest mysteries are slowly coming to light. The traitor [Cinq-Mars] would not confess to plotting against the life of Monsieur Amadeau [Richelieu], but he has confessed that his plans were known to du Chesne [the King] and had his consent . . . now that Monsieur Amadeau knows of du Chesne's consent he will never trust anyone again and will certainly be wary of walking abroad to those places where he would be in danger of succumbing to that which he once narrowly escaped, especially when such people who were present at the attempt [Tréville] are still abroad.'

Even if Louis forgave Cinq-Mars for wishing him dead he could no longer afford to be interested in his welfare. Many historians have criticized him for doing away with his 'loved one' after inciting him to do the same to Richelieu. But the King had no choice but to endure his martyrdom stoically. His leniency would be taken as proof of his complicity and would doubtless have had the effect of encouraging the Master of the Horse's accomplices to renew the attempt. He had no desire to discuss the dangerous topic and dismissed it with a declaration that 'Cinq-Mars was the worst liar in the world' and that 'he must be made to submit to the full rigours of justice'. He ordered that Cinq-Mars be locked up in his cell to prevent him from escaping and asked His Eminence 'to reinforce his guard'. He constantly dwelt on the 'enormity of the conspirators' crime and on the punishments that would be meted out to them. He declared that 'Sedan should get a reprieve,[1] but that he would never pardon Monsieur le Grand'. He eventually dispatched two letters to the magistrates ordering them to condemn to death the boy to whom he had 'given his heart' and sworn 'to share it with none other'.

* * *

On July 13, the King wrote to his brother before leaving Lyons for Fontainebleau. The Cardinal was not satisfied with Gaston's 'Declaration' and wanted to arrange a confrontation between Monsieur and his accomplices. Richelieu's letter to his ministers, in which he expresses his intention, is a masterpiece of duplicity and provokes our pity for a totally worthless and unsympathetic individual. The meeting was to be suggested to the Duc d'Orléans as an 'act of virtue by a Prince trying to save those who have served him'. The meeting was the price set for Monsieur's reprieve from exile. They should be careful not to let him suspect that he would then be deprived of all his rights and privileges.

Gaston had managed to reach his sister, the Duchess of Savoy. She was alarmed by his tiresome visit. He continued to excuse and lower himself in Richelieu's eyes. He was base enough to write, 'If you could only feel the extent of my sincerity, I know that you would not be reluctant to add to your glory the further glory of helping a needy Son of France.' But he refused to agree to the meeting. 'I much regret that I cannot consent to the King's expressed desires. You know what a toll my actions have already borne upon my honour and I could never live with myself or show my face to the world again if I did consent to this as well.' Gaston was more afraid of appearing before his victims than he was of incurring the Cardinal's anger. He appeared indignant and refused to 'act as accuser or witness against a man who had undertaken to act as he had because he had received his [Monsieur's] word of honour that he would not be betrayed'.

Mazarin decided to be far-sighted and intervened on Gaston's behalf. Chancellor Séguier discovered that in 1574 the Duc d'Alençon had not been confronted with the condemned La Mole and Coconnas. This precedent made Richelieu relent. He wrote to Gaston and expressed his pleasure at seeing him choose 'the

[1] He wished to show mercy to Bouillon.

only way out of his miseries and malpractices'. They both signed an agreement which offered Monsieur his privileges in exchange for his confirmation of the conspiracy and of the Spanish treaty. He had burned the original, but he agreed to certify a copy. He would also make a solemn deposition before the Chancellor of France.

Gaston was forced to submit to another indignity. He was asked to change his evidence and state that although de Thou had not actively participated in the plot he had known of the 'agreement between Monsieur le Grand and Monsieur de Bouillon and of the proposed escape to Sedan'. But the Cardinal was not satisfied. He persecuted the Councillor with inexplicable hatred. He was hard put, however, to find any real evidence with which to prosecute. He even set a spy on his heels, the agent Crombis, but to no avail. The Cardinal tried to extract a confession from the Duc de Beaufort, who defended himself brilliantly, but nonetheless decided to join his father, who had taken refuge in England.

Mazarin was asked to work on the Duc de Bouillon, who agreed to co-operate. 'He handled Monsieur de Bouillon, so adroitly that our evidence is complete,' the Cardinal exclaimed triumphantly. The Duke felt the dismal proximity of the scaffold and broke his word of honour just as Gaston d'Orléans had done. Richelieu and Mazarin instructed him to deny being party to the Spanish treaty and maintain that he had only promised Monsieur free entry into Sedan 'in the event of the King's death'. The full blame for the entire conspiracy was pushed on to the shoulders of Monsieur le Grand, who had been its moving force. It was further established that Monsieur de Thou had known nothing. Bouillon saved his own life, but he lost Sedan. Thus did the two mortal enemies conclude their monstrous agreement to transform a misguided child into a vile and dangerous criminal while whitewashing the real villains of the piece. And thus did Orléans and Bouillon preserve all their deadly and dangerous strength intact.

XVIII

Montpellier Fortress

Cinq-Mars had fallen from the splendour of a court favourite to the miserable condition of a convict. He pined away in Montpellier prison, veering between despair and fear, resignation and rebellion. He would 'rant and rave' and then become touchingly docile. At first he banked on the King's affection, but then he realized that he could expect nothing of him, that he had, in fact, been abandoned and betrayed by everyone. He became a disillusioned and embittered man. He was also suddenly overtaken by grief. He had always been sure that he had never loved the King whom he had treated like a toy with total disregard to his wounded sensibilities. He had ever scorned and deprecated his jealous, cantankerous, sententious tyrant, whose trying inconsistencies had bored and exasperated him. He was sure that he had never felt anything and yet the residual effects of Louis's passion for him lingered. The King's attachment had left its mark on him. Henri suddenly discovered how accustomed he had become to Louis's smothering affections and how much he had unwittingly come to depend on the King for help and support. His three years of involvement in the King's emotional life had made Louis an essential component of his own life. He was so grieved and indignant at his rejection that one would think he had shared those feelings he had so often rejected. He blamed the King for his plight. He maintained that he had been far too young and inexperienced to know that Louis had only wanted to confide his frustration in him and had never wanted him to remove the source of his anxieties.

Father Robert, the chaplain of the fortress, tried to calm him and persuade him to resign himself to his fate. Henri was greatly comforted by the priest, who soon began to feel sorry for him. 'He [Father Robert] could not extol his virtues and qualities enough.'[1]

[1] Guiraud, *Notre-Dame de Montaigu à Montpellier.*

The eminently seductive captive also managed to charm his gaoler, who was that rough and ready lieutenant of the Scottish Guard, Ceton. Ceton was sixty-six years old and a totally reliable, loyal and obedient servant of the Crown. This bull of a man was so affected by his prisoner's plight that he actually shed tears over him while discussing him with the President of the Grenoble Parliament. He allowed Henri to take short walks and to buy books. He was as lenient as he could afford to be. But once the Master of the Horse had been imprudent enough to mention the 'evil designs' which 'the King had approved', the Cardinal ordered that he be put in solitary confinement.

Father Robert's comforting and Ceton's leniency did not, however, make prison life acceptable. Cinq-Mars decided to escape. He was still permitted visits by his bootmaker and his launderer, through whom he made contact with Prugues and Siougeac, two of his more constant and loyal friends. He then set about winning over several of his guards. Prugues and Siougeac rounded up a handful of reliable men. The plan was that the accommodating guards would let the prisoner out one night. Monsieur le Grand would then slide down the bastions into the moat, meet his friends beyond and ride away with them. Unfortunately a letter was intercepted on the eve of the escape and the plot was exposed. When the news reached the Cardinal he flew into a rage. He scolded Ceton, whom he did not replace because he knew him to be exceptionally dutiful. Fifty soldiers were sent to reinforce the Montpellier garrison and Monsieur le Grand's friends were proscribed. Siougeac managed to escape but Prugues was captured. Rodes, the bootmaker, and Carpentier, the launderer, were promptly hanged. Cinq-Mars was put 'in a dungeon where he could scarcely see the light of day'.[2] He stayed there for two dark, silent and stifling summer months. Ceton naïvely sought to persuade him to save himself by making a full confession.

Henri would say, 'I once knew a song that went "I would rather die than say". They have no proof against me, you see, so what they want me to do is give myself away.'

'But you must confess the truth,' the old officer would repeat tirelessly.

To which Cinq-Mars would reply, 'Do you really not know that one is hanged for telling the truth? If they guaranteed me my

[2] Vittorio Siri.

freedom I would then tell them what I would not otherwise tell. I have been asked to confess but I have not been given any assurances.'

Thus did the two pathetically naïve men argue day after day. Ceton really believed that a display of sincere repentance would win him a pardon. Cinq-Mars was positive that his princes would be true to him and that they would never obtain substantial evidence against him. He therefore tried to obtain what could only be false assurances of his future safety.

'If they would only pardon me,' he once said when he was feeling particularly sorry for himself, 'I would be happy to be spared and should ask for nothing more. I would gladly submit to all manner of deprivations if I were left a life to lead.'

He rebelled against the idea of dying before he had had the chance to live.

Ceton was shocked by the humility of his desire and snapped, 'If all you want is to save your life you deserve to lose it.' Then he added, 'Everyone is talking about your crimes and you are fully aware of what you have done, so why not confess?'

The old soldier was touched when Cinq-Mars said, 'I shall say nothing and I shall accuse no one. If I must die, I shall die an honourable man.'

Ceton decided to set caution and discretion aside when he suggested, 'Monsieur may well have confessed everything to His Majesty, you know.' Cinq-Mars refused to believe him. 'I have a great respect for Monsieur but should he accuse me of anything I shall contradict his claims to his face and to that of all my detractors with the exception of His Majesty.' These futile dialogues continued for weeks. We know of them from Ceton's statement at the trial. The officer continued to urge Cinq-Mars to seek a royal pardon and he would answer with the same refrain, 'I have been asked to confess but I have been given no assurances.' Henri's living conditions, his inconsolable grief and the loss of his beloved broke his health. He dwelt morbidly on his approaching death, but he retained his confidence that his guilt and complicity could never be proved.

Richelieu was still toiling away on the completion of his great tasks but he found the time and energy to devote himself feverishly to the preparation of the trial which would remove his former protégé. A letter of Henri Arnauld's indicates how he spent

M

his time. 'He works and dictates from seven o'clock [in the morning] until eight o'clock. From eight until nine his health is attended to. From nine to ten he gives audiences to those who have come to see him on business matters. From ten until eleven he works again. He then hears mass and dines and talks with Monsieur le Cardinal Mazarin and others until two o'clock. Then from two to four he works and then he gives further audiences.'

The Cardinal was determined to take no chances over the outcome of the trial. The dishonourable measures he resorted to were unworthy of a man in his position. He chose Police Superintendent Chazé to conduct the interrogation of Cinq-Mars and tested him out on de Thou. 'If Monsieur de Chazé proves efficient,' he wrote to Chavigny, 'we will give him the President of the Grenoble Parliament, who is biased in our favour, as assistant in order to make the proceedings seem authentic . . . It is essential that the case be dealt with by favourably disposed officials as we all know [the Cardinal, Chavigny and de Noyers] that the traitor will say a good many things which will have to be suppressed.'

The interrogation began on July 22. Henri obstinately denied everything. He kept his word of honour to the Duc d'Orléans and to the Duc de Bouillon and refused to say what had transpired between them. Richelieu was annoyed but he saw that there was some advantage in Cinq-Mars's reticence. 'Monsieur le Grand's silence over Monsieur will not prevent him from making any serious accusation against him later on.'

He was worried to hear from the President of Grenoble that Ceton was so well-disposed toward his prisoner. Mazarin and La Vrillère were asked to inspect Montpellier. Mazarin confirmed Ceton's 'genuine affection'. Ceton at first refused to repeat any of the conversations he had had with the Master of the Horse. Mazarin then used his Italian wiles to trick him into divulging parts of their exchanges. He managed to find out about Ceton's ill-advised reference to Monsieur's confession. Mazarin reproached him for his indiscretion and Ceton objected to the reproof. The ingenuous officer then thought to help his protégé by saying, 'If Monsieur le Grand were guaranteed his freedom and his position I think he would speak. If you instructed me to give him such assurances he would speak.'

On August 6 at Fontainebleau the King signed a long declaration to Parliament, to the Commanders of the Armies and to the guilds. It was an account of recent events and an indictment of Cinq-Mars. The document was something of a humiliation, as Louis had to admit to giving his favourite great freedom of speech and action in order to discover the true extent of the evil designs which his 'erring and godless soul' had nurtured.

Richelieu expended a good deal of energy on the conviction of de Thou, whom he wanted out of the way. He interrogated de Thou himself on the pretext that the King had asked him to proceed with the peace negotiations with Spain. De Thou saw the trap, however, and said that he had been ordered by the King to see to the negotiations and that the signed documents were in safe keeping until such time as they were required. The Cardinal preferred not to dwell on this aspect as it constituted the one and only crucial breach of confidence between Richelieu and Louis. The young counsellor kept his head and effectively thwarted the spy Crombis and all the commissioners who were ordered to make him speak. Monsieur de Thou had never suspected his friends Cinq-Mars and Fontrailles of any involvement in reprehensible plots. He gave irrefutable explanations and alibis for all his trips. He had never heard any mention of conspiracies or any particular plots. De Thou had other reasons than his own safety and loyalty to his friends. He knew a great deal about the Queen and would have endured the worst tortures rather than expose her. He would have been deeply shocked had he known that his idol had been the first to speak, but he was never disillusioned.

The Cardinal decided that his presence at the trial at Lyons was essential as it would intimidate the judges in his favour. He wanted Monsieur Séguier, the Chancellor of France, to conduct the trial in person. He asked the King for his consent and Louis wrote, 'Dear Cousin, I have ordered the Chancellor to go to Lyons to advise and assist you with his knowledge and long experience of such matters, which may help achieve the outcome I desire. You should both examine everything that can be justly done, and do anything which you believe will benefit my person. I shall leave the whole matter eventually to your judgement. I have always been so content with the results that my unreserved confidence in you has brought that I give you full powers in this matter.'

Louis wrote Richelieu this empowering letter from Fontainebleau. He was at a sufficient distance from his mentor at Tarascon

171

not to have been pressured into such an arrogation of power. Louis had finally succeeded in controlling his own impulses. He had sacrificed his friend for the great political scheme which leniency would have endangered.

On August 17 Richelieu felt well enough to leave Tarascon. His illness and the constant fear of assassination made the journey troublesome. He took special precautions. The people were only allowed to admire his enormous escort from a safe distance. He travelled down the Rhône on a sumptuous barge. His cabin was hung with crimson and gold brocade silk and he never left his bed, which was covered in purple silk. He was preceded by a frigate and another ship manned by arquebusiers. De Thou, twelve guards and a guards officer were towed behind his barge in a closed boat. There were also barges for bishops, abbots and gentlemen and cargo boats bearing His Eminence's treasury and silver.

A philosopher might have mused at the spectacle of this dying man proceeding, so elaborately protected against a violent death himself, to put another mortal to such a dreadful end.

*　　*　　*

A few days later Monsieur le Grand was also conducted to Lyons. He made a last attempt to stay the executioner's hand. An officer at the fortress, a Monsieur de La Bonaudière admired Cinq-Mars in the way that young people admire famous men. He jumped enthusiastically at the opportunity of risking his life for his glamorous prisoner. He bribed a guard and a fresh escape was planned. The plan was a daring and dangerous one, but appeared not to be beyond the abilities of the twenty-two-year-old adventurer. On the chosen night, La Bonaudière opened the window of Cinq-Mars's cell and helped him along to a chimney ledge which served as a rampart. Henri 'was then to hang over the edge of the slate roof from his hands which would leave him suspended five or six feet above his landing step. He was then to descend nine or ten steps and inch along twelve or fifteen paces before reaching the parapet where a rope ladder had previously been attached with thick knots on which to rest his hands and feet. Had he had the self-confidence to do all this he would have been saved. His path of escape had been made easier since

172

the only sentry that could possibly have detected his movements had been bribed. His only limitation was time.'[3]

Speed was in fact essential. Father Robert saw a man pass overhead and ran to rouse the warden while one of the guards, who had not been bribed, discovered the empty cell and sounded the alarm. A second later the citadel was alive with shouts and clanging. Cinq-Mars had a few minutes' grace in which to get himself down to the steps and reach the parapet. A vigorous and determined man could have made it, but his dungeon existence had not only affected his health but undermined his mental stamina. At the crucial moment of his drop, his strength and his will deserted him. He clung miserably to the chimney ledge paralysed by the glare which suddenly illuminated the fortress and by the din of the search. He was soon discovered. La Bon-audière was thrown into a cell and Henri was returned to his, where he was locked in all the more securely. All he could then do was suffer his irreparable misfortune. Shortly afterwards he was put into a heavily guarded carriage and taken to Lyons. He was given an enormous escort of four armed bodyguards inside the carriage with him, a hundred of the Cardinal's own guards and five hundred other guards, including two hundred Catalans. His carriage was left open throughout the journey and as they approached Lyons Cinq-Mars asked that it be closed, but Ceton refused. The former fashion-setter of France was allowed, how-ever, to wear his finest clothes. He chose to face the worst ordeal of his life as a beautifully dressed dandy. The citizens of Lyons were not disappointed. Monsieur le Grand wore a musk-coloured Dutch doublet covered in gold lace and a scarlet cape trimmed with large silver buttons. He decided to make the most of the occasion and looked more like a prince visiting one of his cities amid his guards than a convict on trial. He smiled continually, nodded to those he recognized, and even greeted them by name or leaned out of the carriage to exchange a few friendly words. It was a very long ride and onlookers kept penetrating the escort and delaying their progress. During one of the halts, a Catalan footman threw him a little wax ball. Henri opened it and found Princess Marie's last message to him.

He was feeling dejected when the carriage finally halted before the formidable castle of Pierre-Encise. He thought they would

---

[3] Delort, *Mémoires sur Montpellier*.

first take him to the forests of Vincennes where he hoped they would let him go hunting one last time. But he was ordered to get out of the carriage and enter the castle on horseback.

'This, then,' he sighed, 'is my last ride.'

He was given a room at the foot of the castle's great tower which had two tiny windows overlooking a garden. Ceton and four guards shared the room with him and the garden was crammed with a host of guards. The precautions were so extensive as to make it almost appear that the fate of France depended on the security of this ailing youth.

Henri was still ill. He suffered from a 'looseness of the bowels' which had not had time to heal. The intense heat and the lack of sleep imposed by his close quarters with five other men aggravated his ill-health. When Richelieu's brother, the Cardinal of Lyons, visited him the following day, he found a 'pallid and weak' young man lying in bed under a pink damask spread.

'I have been sent to distract you. I hope you do not mind my coming,' His Eminence said.

'I should be delighted were it not that I thought myself unworthy of such attentions.'

Father Malavette, a Jesuit paid him a good deal of attention and managed to 'touch the soul of the boy'. Henri asked for this confessor every morning and night during his brief stay at Pierre Encize. Richelieu had wanted the Jesuit to spy on Cinq-Mars, but he turned out to be Monsieur le Grand's last and only consolation.

XIX

'The More Dead, the Fewer Foes'

Lebrun's portrait of Nicolas Séguier, Chancellor of France, is one of the finest paintings of the 'realist' school. The gold-clad Chancellor walks under a parasol in Queen Maria-Theresa's retinue. His sharp, astute eyes, the ironical curl of his lips, his calm, almost contemptuous self-confidence, reveal the cool and clever lawyer beneath his magnificent attire. Ever since Richelieu's rise to power Séguier had suppressed the arrogant and frivolous sides of his nature to suit the weight of his office. He looks the man he was : a courtier and an opportunist supremely indifferent to everything that did not advance his own fortunes. This was the parliamentarian who had sent thousands to their deaths at his superior's orders, who had seen to the slaughter of the Norman rebels, and who had once dared search the Queen of France's corsage for a compromising document. Now the Cardinal required this man to handle Cinq-Mars's case.

Séguier was a personal friend of François de Thou and he felt eager to protect the interests of one of his subordinate counsellors of state. He wrote to Richelieu 'that it will be difficult to condemn him to death, as the circumstantial evidence we have against him is insufficient to convict him'. But his effort was in vain. Richelieu merely responded, 'Say what you will, Monsieur de Thou must die.' Séguier could not disobey. He left Paris on August 28, accompanied by six counsellors or examining magistrates : Messieurs de Laubardemont, de Miromesnil, de Marca, de Chazé, de Paris, de Champigny. They arrived at Villefranche-en-Beaujolais on the following day, where they interrogated Gaston d'Orléans at length and made him sign a twenty-nine-article Declaration embracing the whole of the conspiracy, which compromised everyone, including his intimate friends Brion and d'Aubijoux. Anne of Austria was spared by omission. He also certified the copy of the treaty. Monsieur was so unperturbed by his actions and their inevitable consequences that he boisterously

175

threw a lavish dinner to celebrate the occasion, the guests including the Chancellor and his judges.

Séguier left Villefranche for Lyons, where he proceeded to
examine the Duc de Bouillon on August 31. Bouillon knew his
lines and the interrogation was soon concluded. The Cardinal
joined them with vengeance in his heart. There is something distinctly unpleasant about the avid determination of this distinguished Prince of the Church to send the two young men to
death when he knew he would soon be dead himself. Séguier
made another bid for de Thou's life and was foiled by his colleague
Laubardemont. The over-zealous courtier, magistrate and opportunist found an accommodating precedent from Louis XI's reign,
which Richelieu brandished at Séguier. 'Whosoever has known of
any conspiracy,' read the old ordinance, 'shall suffer the same
punishment as the principal conspirators if he does not immediately make his intelligence known to the King or to the judges
of the country in which he is resident.' Séguier was thwarted and
defended himself saying 'that it [the ordinance] had never arisen
or been used in the Parliament at Paris where he had always
practised'. It was now his duty to obtain proof that François
had known about the conspiracy in order to condemn him and
satisfy the Cardinal.

On September 6 there was a dramatic confrontation between
the Duc de Bouillon and the Master of the Horse. One of the
magistrates read the Duke's statement and that of Monsieur le
Grand and Monsieur's certified copy of the treaty was produced.
Henri was stunned. The conspiracy was revealed in its entirety.
The two princes had ignominiously betrayed him and broken
their sacred word of honour. Cinq-Mars reacted violently. He
lashed out at Bouillon, 'I should never have suspected a nobleman
praised for his courage and generosity capable of such baseness
after so many noble promises and assurances. I would sooner
be tortured to death than betray a friend. Now that you have
broken faith so easily I have no desire to quibble vainly over my
life.' But his instinct of self-preservation and his concern for de
Thou soon returned. His outburst amounted to a confession which
he then tried to deny. His friendship for the Duc de Bouillon had
not been motivated by any desire to harm His Majesty. Monsieur's declaration was 'false to the last article', and 'as he had
not had any part in it (the treaty) and had never seen the original,

he could not know whether the copy was accurate or forged'. They were unable to drag any more out of him. The lawyers would not have had a case if Orléans and Bouillon had not been cowards.

The following day de Thou was summoned. Séguier reminded him of his oath as counsellor of state and asked him, 'If he did not feel he had committed the crime of omission when he failed to inform the King about the treaty with Spain and their lordships' plans to take refuge in Sedan'. De Thou protested that he had never known about either project. He was then confronted by Bouillon and by his statement. This confrontation differed vastly from the earlier one with Cinq-Mars as the Duke was no match for the trained lawyer who ran legal circles round him. De Thou stood his ground and forced Bouillon to declare 'that he had never spoken of any conspiracy to Monsieur de Thou'.

The investigation was not proceeding to Richelieu's satisfaction. Then a letter from the King altered the whole complexion of the trial. The supreme Judge of France lowered himself before his chancellor in order to facilitate the conviction of his former favourite. It is difficult to understand what induced the proud and angry monarch to write such a letter. He may have had a guilty conscience over his part in the Lyons affair; or he may have thought it a convenient way of proving to the powers-that-be that he no longer loved Cinq-Mars. But these suppositions seem insufficient motives for such an action. If, on the other hand, Louis feared that certain intimate secrets, which had no direct bearing on the matter in question, were in danger of being revealed to his detriment, then the humiliation would make sense.

'Monsieur le Chancelier,' wrote His Majesty, 'I learned from Monsieur de Ceton and from Monsieur du Repaire and his brother the Abbé that Monsieur de Cinq-Mars pretends, insinuates and maintains that his wicked designs on Cardinal Richelieu's life were known and approved by myself. I am sending you this letter to inform you that I have long known Monsieur de Cinq-Mars to be a vile impostor, liar and slanderer, as many have often heard me say. I would also warn you that he believes this conduct to be just and that he will defend his lies with conviction. Monsieur de Cinq-Mars has indeed heard me express dissatisfaction with my cousin Cardinal Richelieu when I learned that he would prevent me from conducting the siege of Perpignan in person or persuade me to return from the front because of my health and other similar complaints. But Monsieur de Cinq-Mars should not forget all his efforts to antagonize me against my cousin which I tolerated until he surpassed the bounds of moderation by proposing to rid me of my cousin himself. I was horrified by this evil notion, which I rejected. If my word is insufficient proof of this rejection one need only consider that had Monsieur le Grand indeed won my consent to his evil notion he would not have sought the King of Spain's alliance against my person and my government, for fear of not accomplishing his designs. I want you to convey this intelligence to your subordinates that they may be advised of the truth of these matters.'

When Séguier read this he exclaimed, 'The Cinq-Mars case is clear and closed . . . But Monsieur de Thou's is not.' Richelieu felt the letter was doubly incriminating, for he interpreted the King's protestations as proof of his complicity. The Cardinal began to hate his master.

* * *

The Chancellor and the young favourite had once been friends and Henri had done Séguier a number of favours. When the Cardinal ordered him 'to do absolutely everything to induce Monsieur le Grand to confess his guilt and name his accomplices', Séguier decided to use their former friendship as an instrument of persuasion. He visited Cinq-Mars alone and told him that he had come as a friend and not as a magistrate, but Henri would not divulge anything. Séguier then assured him that there would be no transcript of the conversation, therefore it could not be used against him. Cinq-Mars's defences began to tumble before Séguier's benign paternalism. The Magistrate pressed his advantage. 'The King loves you too dearly to let you die, but you must merit his mercy by complying with his and the Cardinal's wishes. Confess all and you will never regret it.'[1] Henri was ill and confused and he was tempted to trust his false friend. The Chancellor's deceptive reassurances worked on Henri's impulsive nature. He made Séguier promise that his confidences be respected and not go beyond the Cardinal's ears. Séguier agreed and Cinq-Mars complied. He recounted the entire story from the very first day that his protector became his enemy. He described all the ill-treatment and all the painful humiliations to which Richelieu had

[1] Father Griffet.

subjected him and confessed 'that he had conceived an aversion for him which he had been unable to control'. Séguier asked if de Thou shared this aversion and Henri 'was indiscreet enough to reply that he [de Thou] hated the Cardinal personally and that if he were ever released from prison he would have to be watched'. He withheld nothing except the Queen's participation. That remote deity escaped again. He also admitted that de Thou knew about the treaty. The trusting boy was naïve enough to think that the same man he had just denounced as a villanous tyrant, the man who had exterminated Chalais and Boutteville, would stop at knowing the truth and reward him with his life and liberty.

Richelieu never stopped short of final solutions. He angrily dismissed the confession as useless, as it would prove nothing in court and also revealed nothing new. The Cardinal grumbled that he would have to see to the matter himself and lower himself to perform the functions of a magistrate in order to ensure that his interests would be adequately represented at every level of the proceedings.

'It was inded a strange situation. Europe's foremost statesman, who held the fate of nations in his hands, who fought and was defeating Spain and the Empire with diplomacy and war . . . who was busy rearranging Europe and drafting his great Peace of Westphalia, which Mazarin would conclude according to his dictates . . . was here dividing his precious time between the crucial duties of a statesman and the base trivia of a gaoler.'[2]

Séguier tried to appease His Eminence by suggesting that Cinq-Mars, who only a few hours previously had responded to his affectionate assurances, be put to torture. Richelieu dismissed this suggestion angrily. He would have been delighted to torture Cinq-Mars but he was afraid of the King's reactions to his friend's mutilation. He may also have feared that Cinq-Mars would say too much.

The Attorney-General demanded that 'Monsieur le Grand be found guilty in fact and in law of the crime of high treason and that prior to execution he be subjected to thorough interrogation in order to learn the identity of his accomplices and that any further action against Messieurs de Bouillon and de Thou be suspended until such a time'. Richelieu ignored the procedure

---

[2] Avenel.

and proceeded to give Séguier his orders as if the trial did not exist. When Richelieu had achieved his ends and Cinq-Mars had been condemned he coolly informed the King that 'Monsieur le Chancelier and I decided two days before Monsieur le Grand's conviction to declare that he would suffer torture when he would only be subjected to the declaration and not to the fact.' They also decided on capital punishment and ordered the erection of a scaffold on September 11.

By this date, however, they did not have enough evidence to convict de Thou. Mazarin doubted that the counsellor had known of the treaty and had written, 'No one worked more tirelessly for His Eminence's ruin than he, but he had never been given to violence.' This was why the Attorney-General had sought to suspend further action against his young colleague. Séguier wrote to Chavigny, 'Tomorrow, Friday, the trial should produce a conviction but the trials of Messieurs de Bouillon and de Thou will be deferred. I shall have to remain here until the conclusion of the trials and do not expect I shall leave until the beginning of next month.'

But Richelieu knew his own days were numbered and had no intention of extending those of his enemies. He had no compunction about resorting to tricks that defiled his holy office, his reputation and even his life's work. He lost patience with his incompetent chancellor and summoned Laubardemont, who agreed to play the dastardly trick which was to sully his name and reputation forever. Laubardemont's sartorial elegance, officious manners and courtly pomp disguised an unscrupulous opportunist. He went to see Cinq-Mars on September 10, and came straight to the point. 'In your present situation you have no alternative but to make a full confession if you wish to be pardoned for Monsieur de Thou has revealed all. You would be foolish to persist in protecting a man who has betrayed you at the expense of your own life. Your avowals to the chancellor are legally ineffectual. The King and the Cardinal require you to make a legitimate written declaration. If you continue to refuse you will not only die but be subjected to interrogation and torture. If you declare the whole truth, however, you will spare yourself both calamities.' He then added, 'I give you my word of honour as a gentleman and magistrate that you will come to no harm if you do this.'

Laubardemont played his role to perfection. Henri was pre-

sented with the most gruesome facts and prospects. His friend had
betrayed him and torture and death awaited him if he rejected
the offer of a certain pardon. He was confused, heartbroken and
terrified. A more experienced and self-confident man would have
sensed the trap and recalled the innumerable times that judges
resorted to such tactics in the execution of their disreputable
duties, and that Richelieu was not a compassionate soul. But
Cinq-Mars was too young, too impetuous, and even too generous
to harbour such suspicions. 'He repeated everything he had told
the Chancellor and promised to make a full and honest declaration at his interrogation.' He had successfully acquitted himself
as an honourable and loyal gentleman for months only to yield
to the temptation of venting all his anger and disillusion with his
real betrayers on his innocent friend. Laubardemont rushed off a
transcript which Cinq-Mars duly signed.

Laubardemont left Cinq-Mars' company a triumphant but
dishonoured man. 'A judge villainously betrays his duty,' Father
Griffet wrote, 'when he makes promises to an accused which he
cannot keep. The trick is the more despicable when the promise
is false.' De Thou had said nothing and Richelieu never considered clemency.

There seems to be no satisfactory explanation for Richelieu's
excessive dislike of de Thou. The obsession was so great that he
was prepared to lessen his own renown in order to see the man
die. Avenel rejects a number of hypothetical explanations, and
suggests that Chavigny's formula solves the mystery: 'The more
dead, the fewer foes'.

*　　*　　*

The trial opened at Lyons High Court of Justice at seven o'clock
on the morning of September 11 1641. Laubardemont read the
'trial brief', which the Prime Minister himself had written. 'The
Cardinal's style and personality were very much in evidence,'
noted Father Griffet. The passage that refers to de Thou is particularly revealing. 'The crime of high treason, be it but known
through conclusive conjecture, is nonetheless justly punishable.
I say this with conviction as its legality has been authorized by
several eminent doctors in law who have based the assertion on
the reasoning that the State, which must at all costs be preserved
and constantly guarded, would be endangered and destroyed if

181

crimes aimed against her safety required definite evidence to substantiate individual details and thus ruled out the possibility of averting such dangers by not convicting such criminals on conclusive conjecture.' The twentieth century has reinstated this notion, which was then regarded as outrageously untenable. 'Monsieur le Grand,' the brief continues, 'has been charged not only as an accomplice to this conspiracy but as its originator and its promoter. Monsieur le Grand is guilty of having poisoned the mind of Monsieur with fabrications and illusory fears. This in itself is a crime. Then in order to make these fears come true he persuaded Monsieur to form a factional party within the State. This is his second crime. He encouraged him to side with Spain; this is his third. He induced him to contrive Monsieur le Cardinal's ruin and removal from office, which is a fourth. He tried to make him rise up against France during the siege of Perpignan to weaken the defences of the state, and that is the fifth. He then drafted the Treaty with Spain. That is a sixth. He suggested that Monsieur send Fontrailles and Monsieur le Comte d'Aubijoux to Spain with the Treaty. The consequences of this mission combine all the previous crimes and are considered to constitute a seventh crime. All seven crimes are those of high treason.'

The indictment wrongly imputes the betrayal of Monsieur and Bouillon to Cinq-Mars. Cinq-Mars was indeed politically guilty and fully deserved to die in spite of Laubardemont's promises to the contrary. Historical hindsight condemns his enterprises, which would seriously have threatened France's expansionism and unity. But if a humane and dispassionate court were confronted with this confused twenty-two-year-old it would surely plead extenuating circumstances.

Henri d'Effiat was forcibly drawn out of adolescence and thrust unprepared into the midst of court intrigues. Against his will he was made the object of the immoderate affections of a neurotic and inscrutable King. He incurred the hatred of his protector for refusing to spy on the friend who had been foisted upon him. He was made to pay the price for the King's favours, which he never wanted and which he always wished he could refuse. He was led to believe that his master would always help him. Then he fell in love, which confused his sense of values. His values were still those of an adolescent. Despite his many faults, Cinq-Mars deserved greater clemency than most hardened conspirators. Nor was his death indispensable to the 'preservation of the state'. The Cardinal's enemies had proliferated and continued to conspire undeterred by the probability of punishment for eighteen years, and a lovesick boy was unlikely to change the course of history now that he had fallen from favour. But the implacable Cardinal had no time for such considerations. He left Lyons on his scarlet litter just as the judges began their examination. The incorrigible schemer who had once exulted at turning Cinq-Mars's handsome head to his advantage, now revelled at the certainty of its imminent separation from its body.

XX

Justice and Vengeance

The gentleman of the watch fetched Monsieur le Grand at eight o'clock in the morning. 'He [Cinq-Mars] was pale, drawn and ill, but he waved to the crowds that gathered to see him pass through the streets.'[1] When he arrived at the courthouse he asked where he was going and then climbed the steps 'with resolution and dignity'. He entered the courtroom, and leaned over to whisper to Séguier. We do not know what exactly he had to say to the chancellor, but we presume that he reminded him of Laubardemont's promises. Richelieu, however, claims that he leaned over to 'mention his master, whereupon the Chancellor silenced him and made him sit down'. The reprimand did not worry Cinq-Mars because he was so confident of receiving the promised pardon. He answered all the questions fired at him 'in the unruffled manner of a true gentleman'.[2]

When he was called to indicate his supposedly treacherous friend he was calm and candid. 'He was asked if Monsieur de Thou had known about his Spanish treaty and about the relationship between Monsieur and the Duc de Bouillon, and he answered that Monsieur de Thou had known of both the relationship and the Treaty . . . He was asked who had told Monsieur de Thou about the negotiations and when he had first learned of them, and he answered that the King himself had once informed Monsieur de Thou, and that he knew of the decision to approach the King of Spain.' The judges let the matter drop and the Queen was again saved by omission.

The only accusation Cinq-Mars persistently denied was his intention to assassinate Richelieu. He maintained that Fontrailles had often suggested arranging such a plot to him 'and that he had always rejected the proposal as heinous and unworthy'. The Chancellor did not press the charge as he had more than sufficient evidence to condemn him to death. His main concern

---

[1] Report.   [2] Tallemant.

was to satisfy the Cardinal's demand that de Thou be found guilty and condemned.

Cinq-Mars's stomach was giving him a good deal of trouble. He asked to be given leave to return to Pierre-Encise 'to take the medicine that had been prescribed for him'. He was so elated by his belief 'that he had been acquitted that when he was offered breakfast . . . he said "I do not wish to eat. I want to feel purged and to take the pills I have been given." '³ He was exasperated by the long adjournment and paced about the courtroom impatiently. At one point he made for an antechamber which gave on to the Saone, but his terrified guards stopped him before he reached its riverside windows. If Henri had looked out of these windows he would have witnessed the magnificent spectacle of the Cardinal's departure from Lyons. The man who had thrown him into historical relief was peacefully drifting away from the trial that would condemn his creation to death. 'My God, this is a lengthy business,' he complained.

De Thou arrived at about half-past nine and Cinq-Mars was taken into a small side room. Séguier asked him about the treaty and François again denied all knowledge of its existence. Henri was summoned into the courtroom. The Chancellor turned to de Thou and said, 'Have you any reproaches to make to Monsieur le Grand?'

'I have none. I know Monsieur le Grand to be a gentleman of incontestable honesty and sincerity.'

Cinq-Mars's face fell. Then de Thou turned to Henri and blurted out, 'Is it really true that you told them all I have just had to read?'

Henri was crestfallen and confused. He began to mutter, 'No, please, listen . . . I can explain . . .'

De Thou cut him short because 'he was afraid that he might say something which would further endanger his friends'—that is, the Queen. 'Sirs,' he said to the Magistrates, 'I shall give you a brief but honest summary of my involvement in this affair which may well prove clearer than the Master of the Horse's account.'

Cinq-Mars realized he had been the victim of a dreadful trick. François proceeded to admit his complicity. He also asked 'Monsieur le Grand to verify that he had entreated him daily to desist from participation in the Treaty. Monsieur de Thou explained

³ Tallemant.

that he had not admitted this previously because he had not felt in a position to do so.' This account of the trial may have been 'cooked'. Such a practice was traditional and has given his statement the heroic dignity of Plutarch.

'Gentlemen,' the young magistrate is supposed to have stated, 'the only proof you have of my guilt is Monsieur le Grand's testimony. I have never written or talked about [the conspiracy] to anyone. Now, as we all know, an accused man's accusations of another are legally invalid. The death sentence demands the testimony of two irreproachable witnesses. Therefore I know that I can either save my life or choose to condemn myself with my own words. In this knowledge, gentlemen, I admit my complicity and my acquaintance with the conspiracy. I have two reasons for confessing this now. My three months of imprisonment have accustomed me to the idea of death and have convinced me that death is a sweeter alternative than the continued deprivations of life imprisonment. . . . I am strong enough to face and choose death now, but I know that I may later weaken and change my mind. I therefore take the opportunity of my present health and perfect faculties to confess and condemn myself. My crime may be capital, but it is neither heinous nor grave. I admit that I knew of the conspiracy, but I also maintain that I did all in my power to deter Monsieur de Cinq-Mars. He considered me his one and only faithful friend and I did not wish to betray him. This is why I deserve to die and this is why I am condemning myself to death.'

Richelieu's enemies insisted on the validity of this sublime statement. The account may be sublime but it has its inconsistencies. It was precisely de Thou who originally persuaded Cinq-Mars to rebel against his protector. Cinq-Mars's consequent rebellion inevitably drew him into the conspiracy that de Thou so vehemently repudiated. We also know that de Thou had his motives for confessing when he did as he later declared that he would much rather die than suffer torture and life imprisonment.

The proceedings were adjourned while Séguier and Du Faure, the Attorney-General, argued. Du Faure doubted whether they could find de Thou guilty of a capital crime.

'See to your summing up and leave the rest to me,' snapped the Chancellor. Séguier set about 'arranging the judges in order to bias the court in his favour'. Monsieur de Miromesnil was known to be partial to de Thou and was seated 'in such a way as to be the last to pass judgement so as to prevent him from influencing any of the other judges with his eloquence'.

The Attorney-General asked the court 'to consider the two accused men guilty of the crime of high treason'. The Chancellor turned to the judges for their verdict. Cinq-Mars was unanimously condemned to death and to a 'thorough interrogation prior to execution.' De Thou was condemned to death without torture by eleven out of thirteen judges. Monsieur de Sautereau suggested he be sent to the galleys for life and Monsieur de Miromesnil defended his young colleague so eloquently that he disrupted the proceedings. Séguier leapt to his feet to tilt the scales back against de Thou. He resorted to a weighted, if not altogether judicial, argument. 'Gentlemen,' cried the Lord Chief Justice of France, 'I ask you to consider how the King will judge you for sending his very own confidant, his very own favourite to his death and for saving the life of a colleague in law.' François Auguste de Thou's fate was sealed.

The verdict was agreed, pronounced and hastily signed by Séguier, who dispatched it immediately to the Cardinal. The courier Picaut handed his Eminence the document at Lentilly near Lyons. The Minister was delighted at the news, which capped a series of crucial victories. He had just heard that the Spanish troops had withdrawn from Perpignan on September 9 following the formal capitulation of the province on August 29. The Duc d'Enghien was now occupying the defeated city. Thus did Richelieu cut down his enemies while endowing France with a new province. He was particularly pleased with de Thou's sentence. 'The good Chancellor has delivered me of a great burden,' he exulted. His glee was suddenly cut short by the awful recollection that the Lyons executioner had recently broken his leg. He scowled at the messenger and said, 'But, Picaut, there is no executioner.' 'The courier assured him that they would find a replacement.'

The same inconvenient mishap had befallen Chalais's execution and the poor man had been butchered to death. But Richelieu did not choose to remember the gory precedent. He dismissed the detail and wrote Chavigny a quick note full of predatory satisfaction. 'This brief missive is to inform you that Perpignan is in

187

the King's hands and that Messieurs le Grand and de Thou are on their way to the next world where I hope they will find joy.' Then according to Father Griffet, he briefed the King, 'Sire, your enemies are dead and Perpignan is yours.' Richelieu, however, was not that succinct or that kind. His letter to Louis reads, 'I have the pleasure of informing Your Majesty of two different but successful operations. The first is that the rich and beautiful Perpignan has been won for France. The other is the condemnation and execution of Monsieur le Grand and Monsieur de Thou. (They had not yet, in fact, been executed.) Their guilt was so great that the judges found no difficulty in unanimously condemning them to death [which was not true in de Thou's case]. These two successes prove how well God loves Your Majesty.' This was undoubtedly Richelieu's cruellest thrust at the King.

*   *   *

The Chancellor also chose to be viciously ironical. He ordered Counsellor Saint-Germain and Laubardemont himself to inform the two condemned men of their sentence in person and to dispose them 'to prepare themselves for a Christian death'. Only Shakespeare could describe such a bitterly ironical scene. The indignant magistrate had to face the very victim of his felony and inform him of his impending death. Cinq-Mars took the news heroically despite his previous hopes. 'It was a harsh and unexpected blow, but he did not show the least surprise.'[4]

He could not, however, forgive himself for betraying his friend. His guilt made him look upon death as a form of deliverance. De Thou was no less gallant and heroic. He turned to Henri and 'gently' said, 'Ah well, dear friend, I could complain that you have accused and killed me but God knows that I love you dearly. Let us die bravely and meet again in heaven.' Cinq-Mars threw his arms around him. 'They embraced tenderly and agreed that they would find great comfort in dying side by side after so many years of happy friendship.'

Pallerue, the clerk of the court, interrupted their exchanges to read the final verdicts. He asked the prisoners to kneel and hear their sentences. 'Dear friend,' cried Cinq-Mars to his companion, 'you have no need to worry.' De Thou knelt and heard some verses from the Bible. The Master of the Horse knelt on one knee

[4] Tallemant.

and clasped his hat to his breast with his left hand 'in the cavalier fashion'. Pallerue began to read and de Thou objected to the words 'conspiracies' and 'adventures' : 'These words do not apply to me or to my actions,' he protested. Henri subsequently learned of the 'thorough interrogations' he was supposed to undergo. He could not know that it was only to be a mock torture. He was horrified.

'Is there no mercy in this world?' he pleaded. When he had regained his self-control he turned to the Magistrates and said, 'Gentlemen, I think this is too brutal. A person of my age and station should not be subjected to such treatment . . . I have said everything I can possibly say and I am willing to do so again. I am prepared to meet my death in my own way and think the rest unnecessary. I know my weaknesses and beg that I be spared such treatment.'

The Magistrates may have felt tempted to reassure him, but they had been sworn to secrecy. The night before the trial Séguier had taken the precaution of writing to Chavigny, 'I am informing you of the mock torture trial to enable you to tell the King the truth should he hear to the contrary.' Cinq-Mars was not to be tortured but the Cardinal wanted to make him go through the agony of expectancy. He also hoped that this would frighten Cinq-Mars into proffering the names of those officers who had conspired to assassinate him at Lyons. Henri feared for his soul as much as for his body because he knew that the condemned were forbidden confession and absolution before undergoing 'thorough interrogations'. He dreaded dying unabsolved in the throes of torture. Richelieu later tried to scare Louis XIII by claiming that Cinq-Mars had actually threatened 'to spare no one if he were pressed beyond endurance'. Cinq-Mars confided his spiritual fears in Father Malavette, whom he was allowed to see when the judges withdrew. Father Malavette rushed off to the magistrates to plead for mercy. Two of the magistrates told him the truth and begged him not to share their confidence. The priest ignored their request and returned to Cinq-Mars. 'Are you capable of keeping a secret?' he asked.

'Father, I assure you that I have never broken faith with anyone, save God.'

'Well, you are not to be tortured. I shall accompany you to the chamber to remind you of your promise.'

But Henri was not prepared to believe him after all the lies and false promises he had endured. He bravely faced Ceton, who came to escort them to Thomé, the Provost-Marshal of Lyons. As they were leaving Cinq-Mars turned to de Thou and excused himself again. 'Dear friend, we are both going to die but I am less fortunate than you in that I am going to have to suffer torture as well as death.'

Ceton was unable to conceal his grief. The guards in attendance were also weeping. Monsieur le Grand tried to comfort them. 'I beg you not to cry over me for I am not afraid of death. Goodbye, my friends, and pray for me.'

He may not have been afraid of death but torture was another matter. Laubardemont and the clerk of the court led him to the interrogation. The sometime royal favourite was led past the reeking dungeons crammed with rotting peasant prisoners. He discovered the existence of a horrible underworld he never knew existed. 'My God, where are you taking me? What is this evil-smelling hole?'

The 'torture chamber' was a small cell lit by three candles. Laubardemont conducted the interrogation amidst the horrifying apparatus of torture. Cinq-Mars was questioned 'on his conspiracy to assassinate the Cardinal'. Henri was astonishingly self-possessed and controlled for a man on the verge of fainting away from fear. He insisted 'that he had always refused to consider the so-called attempted assassination as anything other than a preposterous fantasy'.

'You will not receive absolution if you withhold the name of your accomplices,' thundered Laubardemont. 'You should consider the salvation of your soul and not your worldly reputation which will be of little use to you when you are gone.'

The condemned man retorted, 'I would rather spend whatever time I have left in preparation for God's grace and mercy than waste it on these futile speculations.'

Laubardemont ordered him to be put on 'the interrogation rack'. The Queen, Tréville and his companions were suddenly in danger. Cinq-Mars overcame his fears and mastered his reflexes. He declared that he had already said as much as he had to say and that all the tortures in Christendom and beyond would not persuade him to divulge any more.[5] Laubardemont had him un-

[5] Father Griffet.

190

strapped and returned him to the courtroom, where they exchanged a few words. When Laubardemont left him he had tears in his eyes. Cinq-Mars and François de Thou fell into each other's arms.

'Dear friend, how much I regret your death,' wept Henri.

'We are lucky to be dying the same death and together,' comforted de Thou.

De Thou then went to his confessor, Father Mambrun. Cinq-Mars objected to the presence of so many guards and was allowed the privacy of a separate room for his confession to Father Malavette. Malavette had just obtained special permission for Cinq-Mars to mount the scaffold with his arms untied. Henri confessed for over an hour and then fainted from hunger. He had not eaten anything all day long. Father Malavette called for some eggs and wine but he 'merely rinsed his mouth and swallowed nothing.' He told Father Malavette 'that what he found hardest to bear was the painful realization that he had been abandoned and betrayed by every single friend'.

'Such is the way of the world,' replied his confessor.

According to Vittorio Siri, Henri wrote the King a letter which was intercepted and never reached him. There is, however, no substantial evidence of a letter of farewell. We do know that Cinq-Mars wrote to his mother, who certainly played a part in his tragic misadventure. Richelieu allowed Madame d'Effiat to receive the letter 'as His Majesty had expressed total indifference as to whether she did or not receive it'.

'Dear Madame and most honoured mother, as I am unable to pay my respects to you in person I am writing to ask you to favour me by granting a few last requests. I beg you to pray for my soul and my salvation. Then I would ask you to obtain from the King the price and value of my post as Master of the Horse, which I would have received had I lived to sell it. Should you be refused the sum I entreat you to settle with my creditors. I know that this request may be distasteful to you, Madame,[6] because I am acutely aware of the value of worldly considerations being so near to losing them and life itself. I bid you farewell and beg that you will forgive me for my past disrespect and disobedience, assuring you that I shall die your very humble and obedient servant,

Henri d'Effiat.'

[6] He fully appreciated his mother's avarice.

Richelieu vehemently opposed surrendering the proceeds from the sale of the Master of the Horse's office to settle the debts of his dead rival. Louis XIII personally paid thirty or forty thousand *écus* owed by his 'dear one'.

De Thou feverishly prepared to meet his death. He was in a state of religious excitement. He felt so close to his Judge and Master that he was terrified of harbouring the minutest trace of worldly vanity. He did all he could to humble himself. 'When I die I want everyone to say that I was a vile coward and an ill-mannered hot-head who did not know how to live. As I stand naked before my Maker I see that I am indeed a guilty, base and worthless creature.'

De Thou wrote to Monsieur Dupuy, his cousin, and to the woman that had caused him so much suffering, the Princess of Guéméné: 'Madame, never in my life have I felt so attached to you as I do now that I am about to lose my life. I am almost glad to quit a life you have rendered so distressing . . . I beg you to forgive me, Madame, for everything I have done to displease you and all those I came to hate because of you. I assure you, dear lady, that, aside from my love for God, I die your most absolutely devoted, humble and obedient servant.'

Richelieu did not allow the princess to read this bitter message. 'I have done with my worldly attachments now,' de Thou said when he had finished writing. 'Let us now turn our thoughts to heaven.' He started intoning the *Miserere* with such ardour that his body shook and twitched violently. One felt that he was about to levitate and leave his body and this world.'

The Place des Terreaux, which was about eighty yards square, began to fill with the thousand soldiers who took up their positions in readiness for the execution. A seven-foot high scaffold was erected in the middle of the square and a small stepladder was placed against the ample platform. An enormous crowd 'from every walk of life and of both sexes' converged on the square and pressed in behind the deep formation of the guards. Hundreds of others clambered on to the surrounding roof-tops and hung out of every window to watch the fabled royal favourite's pretty head roll.

XXI

'My God, What a World!'

The former leader of fashion revived his dandy habits for his last parade. His suit was brown trimmed with yards of golden lace; his shoes were green silk tied with a wide white ribbon; from his shoulders swung a great scarlet cloak with large silver buttons, and he wore a black hat cocked in the latest Catalan style.

At about five in the evening he was with his confessor when the officers arrived to escort him to the scaffold. He was suddenly in a hurry.

'They have come to fetch us,' he said. 'Let us be off for it will soon be over.'

He met François de Thou in the courtyard. De Thou was sombrely dressed in a black suit of Spanish cloth with a short coat.

'Come, Monsieur, let us be off,' he said. 'Our time has come.'

They descended the marble staircase. Monsieur le Grand went first holding Father Malavalette's hand. Cinq-Mars bowed low and graciously to the crowd that lined the steps and many were moved to tears. At the foot of the stairs he faced his judges and thanked them—perhaps ironically—'for the kindness they had shown him'.

An enourmous throng had gathered outside. The two young men 'bowed long and low' as if they were at the Louvre and drove off in the waiting carriage.

'Messieurs,' de Thou cried out, 'how very good and kind of you to let two guilty convicts ride to their death in a carriage when they deserve to be carted off, nay dragged through the mire like the son of God, who was so reviled before he died for all of us.'

The proximity of death seems to have shaken his reason somewhat. He chattered compulsively, recited prayers, psalms 'and other such pious invocations'. He called upon the martyrs, he begged Cinq-Mars's pardon throughout their last slow journey. Cinq-Mars forgave him and de Thou embraced him and thanked heaven for allowing them 'to eradicate all their sins with a little infamy and to conquer heaven with a little shame'. He urged his friend not to regret his life and cried, 'I regard our death as an infallible sign of our predestination. We must thank God for the revelation as for our lives themselves.'

The unfortunate Henri found it hard to preserve his equanimity and withhold his tears under this verbal torrent. He stuck his head out of the carriage window and asked the people for their prayers and blessings. A cluster of young girls wailed and screamed and Father Malavette was moved to tears.

'Dear Father, you seem to be more put out by my misfortune than I am myself,' Cinq-Mars said. 'I beg you not to make us sad, for we need your strength and your support.'

The carriage inched slowly through the jostling crowds. The executioner followed behind on foot. He was an ageing porter who was sometimes called to lend a hand with the torturing of prisoners. He had been chosen to do a job he had never done before because no executioner was available.

Henri said he wanted to go first because he had been tried first and was the guiltier of the two. 'I would only die twice if I went last.'

Monsieur de Thou objected on the grounds of his greater age.

Father Malavette intervened, 'You are indeed older but you are also the more generous.'

'That he is,' cried Henri.

'Ah well, you will open the gates of heaven to us,' François returned.

Father Malavette settled the question of precedence by deciding that Monsieur le Grand would have his way.

When they caught sight of the scaffold de Thou became very excited. 'Dear friend, behold the stairway to heaven. Why has fortune favoured such a miserable wretch as me with today's blessed promise of happiness?'

The carriage finally came to a halt. Henri embraced his frantic friend who proceeded to deliver a lengthy oration; 'We are about to be physically separated only to be spiritually united . . . Come . . . We shall only be apart for a few minutes and then we shall be together again for ever before our Lord and Maker . . .

194

You have achieved greatness in your life but you will win infinite glory and grandeur in your life to come . . . Show them all that you know how to die.'

Cinq-Mars leapt out of the carriage. 'He held his head high and wore a smiling countenance.' The trumpets sounded three blasts and Pallerue read the sentence again on horseback. Henri flourished a courtly bow, donned his hat and started up the stepladder. He was stopped on the second rung by Lenfray, the guard, who picked off Henri's hat and said, 'You should be more modest, Monsieur!' Henri wheeled round and treated the insolent fellow with his old haughtiness, 'You will return that hat instantly, Sir.'

Malavette put the guard in his place and returned it to the angry dandy. Henri continued up the stairs 'with the valiance of a soldier hurling himself into the fray'. When he reached the platform he faced the crowd to savour his popularity and magnetize his audience with his seductive powers for the last time. He raised his left hand to his chest and bowed low in the manner of a court dandy. He repeated this gracious gesture three times as he walked round the scaffold. The crowd acclaimed him with desolate cries, to which he answered as he had to Father Malavette, 'Dear friends, you seem to be more put out by my misfortune than I am myself.' He then threw himself into his confessor's arms and whispered urgently in his ear. Richelieu later claimed that Henri was telling Malavette that he wanted to rebel against his silence and make a public pronouncement about the King and that Malavette had difficulty in dissuading him. In any case Malavette persuaded him to kneel and receive absolution. Henri was surprised to find that there was no proper executioner's block and that he was expected to lay his head down on a make-shift tree stump. He bent forward to test it and was then asked to remove his doublet. As he did so he handed Father Malavette a diamond-studded box. 'Inside the box is the portrait of the lady I loved, which I wish you to burn. Give the box to charity.' He snatched the executioner's scissors from his hands and trimmed off a couple of his brown curls which he handed to Malavette to burn with the portrait. He may have hoped that the priest would give these relics to Princess Marie. We do not know if he ever did. Henri requested that Father Malavette's assistant and not the executioner should cut his hair off. As his hair fell about his shoulders and on to the floor Cinq-Mars sighed, 'My God, what a world.'

After praying for a few minutes he turned to his executioner and snapped, 'What do you think you are doing? What are you waiting for?'

The man removed from a sack an axe 'that looked like a meat cleaver only larger and squarer'.

'All right, then,' Cinq-Mars whispered. 'It's time to die. God rest my soul.'

He was not made to wear a blindfold. Monsieur le Grand placed his head squarely on the stump and faced the front of the scaffold. He hugged the stump tightly, shut his eyes, clenched his teeth and waited for the blow. The executioner stood on his victim's left, clasped the axe in both hands, raising it into the air and letting it fall slowly. The heavy thud was accompanied by an 'Ah!' that was drowned in a flood of blood. Cinq-Mars's knees jerked up as if he were about to stand, then knelt back again. The blow did not sever the head completely. The executioner stepped over him and grabbed his hair in his right hand and chopped at the unsevered tracheal artery and the piece of skin that held his neck on.'[1]

The charming head which had won so many hearts rolled across the length of the scaffold to drop into the crowd below. 'The cries of horror and the groans were terrible to hear.' Henri's body was removed with great difficulty, for his arms remained locked round the awful stump. The executioner covered the head and body with a cloth.

It was then François de Thou's turn. The counsellor sought to allay his terror by making solemn speeches. He jumped from the carriage and 'bounded up the scaffold, cheerfully discarded his cloak, threw open his arms and kissed his executioner saying, "Dear friend and brother, I love you. I embrace you because you are going to bestow eternal happiness on me this day." '

He bowed to the crowd and demonstrated excessive piety, humility and resignation. But as soon as he saw his friend's blood and covered body he stopped play-acting and said soberly, 'Gentlemen, I confess that I am a coward. I am afraid to die. If I appear at all brave it is God's effort to save me.' He turned to the executioner and said, 'You will have to bind my eyes.'

[1] Report,

'Monsieur,' answered the brute, 'I have no blindfold.'

De Thou turned to the crowd. 'I am but a man and I am afraid to die. This thing [Cinq-Mars's body] frightens me. I ask you to take pity on me and give me something to bind my eyes.' Two handkerchiefs were thrown up at him. He caught one and said, 'Your reward will be in heaven.'

The hideous preparations lasted a long time. De Thou finally put his head on the stump and said his last *Maria, mater gratiae, mater misericordiae . . . In manus tuas . . .* 'His arms began to shake as he waited for the blow, which fell too near his head to cut more than halfway through his neck. The blow threw him sideways and so turned his face to the executioner and the sky beyond. His legs twitched and struggled and he weakly tried to raise his hands. The executioner wanted to turn him to his original position but the crowd was so angry and threatening that he hastened to finish his butchery. He frantically swung down on de Thou's upturned throat and severed the head at the third or fourth blow. The head dropped off but did not roll away.'

The horrified Lyons crowd pressed on the scaffold and all but lynched the clumsy executioner. The bodies were quickly bundled into the carriage and the executioner followed with the open-eyed and almost living heads.

*   *   *

Madame de Pontac, François de Thou's sister, had his body exhumed and buried in the family graveyard at Saint-André-des-Arts. No one went to such lengths for the former favourite's remains. His friends and relatives were terrified of incurring the Cardinal's persecution. Monsieur du Guay, Treasurer of the Lyons region, was so moved by Cinq-Mars's untimely end that he had his body interred before the high altar of the Church of the Feuillants. The city of Lyons was similarly moved, as was the rest of the kingdom. The two young men won their greatest political victory by dying as they did. The French nation felt no gratitude whatever to the minister, who had that year given them Roussillon and Catalonia in spite of ill-health and his near ruin. His success in no way mitigated the public fury at the sacrifice of two gallant young men on the altar of that insatiable Minotaur.

The Cardinal slowly wound his way back to Paris. The returning procession was so opulent as to require the widening of city gates and the ransacking of private houses for supplies. Resentful, hate-filled eyes watched the progress of the enormous scarlet litter with its twenty-four porters and its army of guards. But Richelieu was too satisfied and pleased with his recent achievements to give a thought to popular resentments, as his letter to Chavigny of September 15 shows. The humiliations imposed by the little favourite's threats to his work, existence and the future of France had been very grave indeed. 'Monsieur le Grand,' he wrote to Chavigny, 'was his haughty self to the end . . . Everyone who saw him die said he did so more bravely and resolutely than Monsieur de Montmorency and Monsieur de Saint-Preuil, but I am sure that they died a more Christian death. I think the Abbé d'Effiat should be demoted for his warped wits do not suit a minister of the Lord. The King should remove him from the Mont Saint Michel Abbey (which Louis XIII had given his friend's brother despite the Minister's objections) . . . Madame d'Effiat should be allowed three or four weeks more at Chilly where she is staying to settle her son's debts, which I very much doubt she will, and then she should be sent to Touraine . . . It is as well to keep such people at a safe distance from Paris.' The Cardinal did not in the least feel guilty in persecuting the innocent family of his faithful friend Marshal d'Effiat. The towers of Cinq-Mars's castle were torn down and the forests felled 'to the level of his infamy'. The Cardinal was truly obsessed by the affair. He wrote a long memorandum in which he again enumerated and exaggerated the crimes of 'that miserable, damned hell-bent devil'.[2] He asked Séguier for the names of the two judges who had resisted sentencing de Thou to death. Richelieu was also obsessed by the continued existence of those whom he had not succeeded in condemning to death. After the execution, Bouillon took to his heels and abandoned Sedan, which Mazarin occupied in the name of the crown. He had been promised a pardon, but the Cardinal was only biding his time before he pounced again. Monsieur had taken refuge at Blois. He spent his time 'trying to dispel the gloom that had settled over him in Savoy'. He felt safe enough until Richelieu presented him with the abrogation of his rights to succession.

Richelieu's revenge seemed to have no bounds. He was eaten away by the realization that the whole affair would have been

[2] Archives des Affaires Etrangères.

impossible without Louis XIII's acquiescence. The Cardinal had a short memory. He could dismiss Marshal d'Effiat's loyalty as conveniently as he could dismiss his own sizeable share of the blame. It was, after all, he who had forced Cinq-Mars on his reluctant master. He nonetheless decided to make the King pay dearly for all his partially self-induced humiliations and for the whole tragic episode.

* * *

His Majesty arrived at Fontainebleau on July 23, where the Queen joined him the following day. Louis suspected her complicity and thus 'received her with cold fury'. His mother's death depressed him as much as the sinister trial. The court went into mourning for Marie de Médicis, which helped conceal grief at the double bereavement. The mournful King hunted out his sorrow from Fontainebleau to Saint-Germain, from Versailles to Chantilly, from Nanteuil to Monceaux. He heard about the sentence and execution when he was at the beautiful Château at Monceaux which had once belonged to Belle Gabrielle. Louis still talked about Cinq-Mars. He mentioned him in anger as if to justify his horrible death with memories of his friend's desire to hasten his. He was reticent with his courtiers and refused to confide his sorrows. There is a tale which claims that on the day of the execution he looked at his watch and said, 'In an hour's time Monsieur le Grand will wear a very different look.' There is an even more gruesome version of the story. He worked himself into a state of false hatred, just as de Thou had become overexcited and overpious, and interrupted a game of chess with a vicious, 'I should like to see Monsieur le Grand's new look now.' These stories are not very convincing, as it is almost certain that he learned of the deaths and the fall of Perpignan from Richelieu's letter, which arrived several days later.

He returned to Paris on September 17 to attend a Te Deum in honour of his victories. Louis XIII offered thanks for the glories that God had bestowed on his reign and he may have felt a twinge of regret for the price he had been made to pay for them all.

XXII

The Dead Bury the Dead

Richelieu reached Fontainebleau from Bourbon Lancy on October 13, and moved into the Albret palace. He did not go to see the King, who had taken to working at his Minister's offices to lessen the risk of assassination. Richelieu was terrified that he would meet the same end as his ex-patron Concini now that he had reconstructed the Lyons attempt on his life. He even knew the names of his near-assassins, Tréville, des Essarts, Tilladet and La Salle. These men would continue to be a real danger to him as long as they remained in their posts in Louis's royal guard. Louis reversed etiquette and called on Richelieu at the Albret Palace. Chavigny and de Noyers helped the Cardinal to his feet and the two men embraced theatrically but with little genuine enthusiasm. Those who witnessed the scene were surprised by the coldness of their encounter and by the stony silence that followed. The King finally dismissed everyone from their presence.

It was only the second time they had met since the discovery of the conspiracy and this occasion differed greatly from the previous one four months before. Richelieu had then feared Cinq-Mars and the King's attachment to him and he had not known of the King's probable complicity in a plot on his life. He had been anxious to win over his equivocal king and to restore their old confidence. Now, however, Henri d'Effiat was safely underground and Richelieu's awful knowledge poisoned their relationship and ruled out any possibility of confidence. Louis was an embittered and lonely man who could never forgive the scarlet courtier for sacrificing his friend.

The ghost of the decapitated favourite haunted the three-hour conference. We have some idea of what occurred between them because Richelieu always put down their important conversations on paper and then submitted a summary to the King. His account of the Fontainebleau interview is full of daring reproaches, refuted accusations and thinly veiled sarcasms.

'Monsieur le Grand played on the King's jealous nature to persuade him that my renown dimmed His Majesty's glory and that the authority he had given me detracted from his own. This was utterly false as everyone knows that I have always considered it a great honour to walk in my master's shadow . . . Monsieur le Grand played on the King's suspicious nature to cast doubt on all my actions . . . His Majesty has won many great victories, not the least of which are those he has won over himself. For two years His Majesty had to contend with the ploys of a young man who maliciously tried to alter his government and reverse his policies. The King's decision to conquer this inclination was one of his finest victories. It was no easy matter to convince His Majesty of the evil consequences of these designs and of his evil influence on His Royal Highness and on his affairs, but God took compassion on us all and revealed the truth and helped His Majesty overcome his inclination and revive his good opinion of his old and faithful servants.'[1]

The King and his Minister were far less happy and satisfied by the outcome of this encounter than by their last one. The old magic, the absolute trust that had weathered so many trials had finally disappeared. They had nothing left with which to mend their disputes. Their relationship, their fellow feeling and their mutual confidence had been severed on the scaffold at Lyons.

The two men's proximity to death did not help reconciliation. They both anxiously prepared for the other's disappearance and replacement. The Cardinal, on the one hand, had no intention of leaving the state to the Queen and Monsieur. He aspired to the position of regent himself and set about accelerating the Duc d'Orléans's dispossession. He was also concerned by the immediate future. He had not yet routed Cinq-Mars completely. The memory of his dead rival alone was a serious menace. The King had not recovered from the affair and Tréville and others made it their business to keep his memory alive. Their constant defence of their hero made Louis bitterly resent his Minister and regret the loss of his friend.

Richelieu went to Paris on October 13, determined to have done with the constant danger once and for all, even if it meant forcing Louis's hand as he had never dared to do before. Richelieu

---

[1] Avenel, *Letters of Cardinal Richelieu.*

had punctilicously demonstrated his respect for his superiors. He had swallowed his pride and had done all manner of violence to his feelings. But he had always been respectful. When, however, the Queen did him the honour of coming to see him at his Palace, he did not rise to greet her. 'I presume that Your Majesty will not object to me sitting in her presence as I know she is well acquainted with these "privileges of Spanish Cardinals." '

Anne of Austria retorted quickly, 'I should not object had I not become a Frenchwoman.'

They weighed each other up while they exchanged formal pleasantries. Anne had enabled the dying Minister to score a great victory and he now intended to use his regained supremacy to dispossess her. But Richelieu's frailties were Anne's strengths. She was young and she was healthy. Anne's betrayal of the ill-conceived conspiracy had given her time to multiply her chances. De Thou would have died more readily if he had known he was being of such service.

Richelieu behaved as if he had his whole life before him. On October 27 he threatened the King with his conditional resignation. 'Monsieur le Grand used every possible argument and artifice to persuade a number of people that the King was tired of his Cardinal and displeased with his services. Despite the worthlessness of an impostor's false judgements, I do not feel that I can serve Your Majesty justly amid a court that gives credence to such utterances because the King has not seen fit to disprove them. I therefore beg leave to withdraw myself and my services.' Having proffered his resignation he proceeds to enumerate his 'five conditions'. If the King agreed to satisfy his impertinent demands he would reconsider his decision : 'First, His Majesty should never have another favourite and be content to occupy his time and mind with the affairs of state'; the King should trust and confide in his ministers alone 'and conceal nothing from them that is said to their detriment'; he should keep the proceedings of his council to himself and not violate their secret nature';' he should order his council to be free with him and speak their minds'; 'he should occasionally purge his court of evil influences, and banish them rather than let them grow to be infamous, and to choke others with their fatal influence (as happened in Monsieur le Grand's case)'.

Louis was shocked and surprised. Richelieu had renounced

his subtle intimidation techniques for direct blackmail. He had never before taken Louis to task like this nor had he ever dared order the hero of the Pas de Suze to submit to his will and command. Louis might well have accepted his resignation if he had not been in such a state of confusion. His insolent 'valet', as Marie de Médicis used to call him, had timed his thrust perfectly. The Roussillon campaign planned for 1643 made him indispensable to the King. If Louis dropped his pilot now he would have to admit that Cinq-Mars had died in vain. Louis played for time; he acknowledged receipt of the memorandum but made no reply. Richelieu waited for nine anxious days, which aggravated his illness. The King may have played on his nerves in the hope that the strain would accelerate his death and so save him the humiliation of submitting to Richelieu. But he had not allowed for Richelieu's immense reserves of energy. Richelieu launched another attack.

The Cardinal's memorandum to the King of November 5 is unadulterated blackmail. 'God has not chosen to make the impossible possible and I find it impossible to continue executing services and duties which are deemed inadequate. It is every man's duty to himself to preserve his person when it is threatened. It is my duty therefore to remove myself now that I am in danger. I would have Your Majesty know that I learned a good deal from Monsieur le Grand and that I have so far withheld my valuable information. Monsieur de Cinq-Mars was not submitted to a thorough interrogation for fear that he would reveal publicly what we know in private. He had threatened to do so and spare no one if he were pressed beyond endurance. His confessor also had to restrain him from making such declarations from the very scaffold.'

Chavigny was entrusted with the menacing letter and with the task of repeating verbally all that Monsieur le Grand had told the Chancellor on the Lyons affair. Louis was infuriated by Richelieu's tactics and retorted that 'he would have preferred the Chancellor to have allowed him [Cinq-Mars] to say all he wanted against him as that would have conclusively damned the ungrateful wretch in everyone's eyes'.

Poor Louis. He had elevated his Minister to incredible heights and was rewarded by humiliations and ultimatums. He had exalted and loved Cinq-Mars who turned on him, wished him dead, betrayed him and remained loyal to his treacherous Queen. Louis had good cause to feel bitter and disillusioned.

On November 5 and 6 Chavigny pressed Louis for a reply, but Louis still held out. Then on November 7 he brought Louis an incredible message. If the King refused to dismiss his suspect officers 'he would have to submit to the Cardinal's guards bearing arm in his presence in order to ensure His Eminence's safety against the insults of the King's men'.

'Does the Cardinal have any more right to dictate the conduct of my men than I have of his?' demanded the King furiously.

'If His Eminence thought that His Majesty disapproved of anyone in his retinue he would dismiss him instantly,' Chavigny assured him. Whereupon the King snapped, 'He would have to dismiss you then, because I find you insufferable.' Chavigny was undaunted.

On November 8 Chavigny showed the King a letter which Richelieu had written to him. The letter dealt largely with state matters. 'There are those who begin to suspect a rift between the King and myself. The suspicion is deleterious to my health and certainly detrimental to the King's interests.' Louis was unmoved and Richelieu's health continued to deteriorate.

On November 13 the Cardinal made his final bid. He sent the King a third memorandum in which he summarily repeated his previous demands and hinted that the conclusion of the peace negotiations might amply compensate the King for his capitulation. 'I beg Your Majesty to state your intentions at the foot of this Memorandum . . . and to inform me of the conditions you wish to put forward for the peace.' His Eminence had thrust home. Cinq-Mars's pretty face could never have threatened French politics if Louis had not passionately desired to put an end to the war and to conclude a lasting peace and if the King had not also doubted his Minister's peaceable intentions. The King pondered the offer for twenty-four hours. The treaty would not only give him peace of mind and a clear conscience, it would also put an end to his people's sufferings. But capitulation was still a bitter pill. Chavigny wrote to Richelieu on November 14, 'The King clearly stated that he wished to comply with Monseigneur's wishes on the condition that his honour was not made to suffer. I reassured him as best I could. I shall press him for an early reply.'

Six days were to elapse before Louis gave in. He wrote his reply at the foot of Richelieu's memorandum. He again sullied the memory of the man he secretly mourned. 'I have duly read the above and have nothing to add except what my cousin Cardinal Richelieu already knows : that Monsieur de Cinq-Mars was too great an imposter and a liar for anyone to give credence to his slanderous imputations on my cousin's good character and on our mutual friendship and esteem.' He then copied down the Cardinal's conditions and surrendered unreservedly. The terms of his capitulation would justify Madame de Motteville's trite opinion that 'the greatest king in the world' were no more than a humble slave if one omitted to read the peace terms that followed. The son of Henry IV was not prepared to buy peace by total defeat. His conditions were those of a highly skilled statesman who intends to achieve a glorious peace without significant concessions. 'I am not prepared to become the laughing stock of Europe or leave myself open to a renewal of hostilities from my enemies who would certainly be debarred from such folly if they were made to pay for the war they have forced me to wage. There must therefore be no question of conceding Lorraine, Arras, Hesdin, Bapaume, Perpignan, Roussillon, Brisach or the Alsatian territories that border on Lorraine. Pignerol is mine by birthright and I will never surrender it to anyone. My nephew the Duke of Savoy should be returned to his kingdom or I will not consider any peace settlement. These are my conditions. If they are accepted I shall be agreeable to whatever schemes are deemed necessary to hasten the conclusion of a general peace which will bind me to my allies.'

This document demonstrates conclusively that Richelieu's policies really were those of Louis XIII. These postscripts are dated November 20. The two old colleagues were reconciled just in time to make their final bows to history but too late for the Cardinal, whose last energies had been spent on their most mortal battle. While the King instructed Monsieur de Guitant to banish his four compromised guards officers, and dispatched the dispossession papers to Monsieur, Richelieu began to complain of a pain in his side which the doctors diagnosed as pleurisy.

*　　*　　*

On December 2 Louis learned that the Cardinal was spitting blood and that his physicians were concerned. He left Saint-Germain and went to the Cardinal's palace. He saw Richelieu at two o'clock. The sick man turned to him and said, 'Sire, this is our last farewell. I will take my leave of Your Majesty in the knowledge that I have made your kingdom greater than it has ever been before . . .' And he could not refrain from adding, 'and, moreover, free of enemies.' Richelieu was not boasting. In 1624 France was a chaotic state. On Richelieu's death the French Bourbon line was the strongest in Europe. Louis and Richelieu had checkmated the Habsburg dream of European domination. During Richelieu's ministry France had acquired an army and a navy, Artois, Alsace, Roussillon. She had occupied Lorraine and Savoy. She had colonized Canada, the Antilles, Madagascar and Senegal. The Protestant threat had been eliminated and Protestants had not been persecuted but absorbed into the nation state. The provinces of France had been united under the single authority of the crown.

Nonetheless, Richelieu died too soon. His immense external achievements paved the way for further expansion. His foreign policies were absolutely irreversible. But he would have needed a good hundred years more to achieve the royal revolution of the country's internal policies. The crown was not to find a man capable of changing and reorganizing the crumbling foundations of the old order (the fiscal system, the venality of parliamentary procedure) and breaching the dangerous rifts that continued to widen till they finally submerged the country in total revolution. Richelieu could not possibly have achieved all this in one lifetime. He might, however, have lived a few years longer had he not been worn down by the fears and anxieties that dogged him throughout 1642 and which undoubtedly precipitated his end. He could blame no one but himself for this calamity. He was originally responsible for throwing two equally reluctant men together. He must have regretted his self-destructive plan to his dying hour.

The Cardinal recommended his three ministerial aides, de Noyers, Chavigny, and Mazarin to the King's service. He asked Louis to execute his will and testament and to favour his relatives and heirs. He left them his vast fortune, but was wise or grateful enough to bequeath his Palace and a large share of his furniture and jewellery to the King. Louis might have been delighted at

Richelieu's impending death but he gave no evidence of such pleasure. He appeared 'tender' and solicitous when Richelieu was brought two egg yolks and Louis insisted on giving them to him himself.

When he left Richelieu's bedside he strolled a while along the galleries of the Cardinal's magnificent palace that was soon to be his. His own Louvre next door seemed old-fashioned and comfortless by comparison. He laughed 'while he was looking at some paintings' and many interpreted this as an expression of acquisitive glee. But it seems unlikely that Louis, who seldom laughed, should have been tickled by the thought of gaining so much for so little. It would be more in character if Louis was laughing at one of his morbid private jokes: Cinq-Mars's executioner was himself expiring less than three months after his victim.

Louis stayed at the Louvre for he was reluctant to leave Paris 'before knowing the outcome of the malady'. That night the Cardinal received the last sacrament before a large audience. When Monsieur Le Tonnelier, the curate of Saint Eustache, asked him whether he had forgiven his enemies, he proudly delivered the famous statement: 'I have had none other than those of the state.' Many a pious witness was shocked by his lie. Cinq-Mars was just one example of such a non-political enemy. He began to hate Henri when he had refused to become his spy, which pre-dated the conspiracy by a long time.

The King returned to the Cardinal's palace on December 3. He looked sad and stayed with the dying but lucid man for an hour. That evening his household left Paris. The separation that had so often been expected, desired and feared throughout their eighteen years together finally took place. Richelieu died at midday on December 4. As soon as the King heard the news he assured Chavigny, de Noyers and Mazarin and Richelieu's family of his good will and favour. Before he left Saint-Germain he made a public declaration that 'many might think the day was lost or won but in fact nothing had changed or was going to change. His policies would be maintained even more rigorously if that were possible than they had been in Monsieur le Cardinal's lifetime.[2]

Louis did not attend the Cardinal's impressive commemorative

[2] Letter from Le Duchat to his brother quoted by Gabriel Hanotaux and the Duc de la Force.

service the following month. The sadness which had assailed him during the last few months seemed to vanish. He seemed almost relieved. He must have welcomed the dissipation of the guilt he had felt since the discovery of the conspiracy. According to Montglat, 'He was delighted at the bereavement and did not deny this to his close friends.'

The young Scarron gives us an idea of how the public took the Cardinal's departure:

> My plans and not my services
> Made me King and not a vassal.
> My deeds for good and those for ill
> Found numerous accomplices.
> So did I profit from heaven and hell
> For both did make me Cardinal.
> The son I crowned, the mother killed
> And had he lived Monsieur I'd chilled.
>
> .   .   .
>
> My foes in life had not a chance.
> To trick old Spain I ruined France,
> And wonder still if I did ill.

*   *   *

The day after Richelieu's death, Parliament registered Monsieur's dispossession and Cardinal Mazarin entered the council as its president.

In fact, nothing had changed. Richelieu's political machine continued to function normally. The 'slave' was a freer man and could follow his own bent, if that had ever differed from Richelieu's. Louis was determined never to allow another man to take such liberties with him again. Many historians have closed Louis XIII's political career with Richelieu's death. They have not given him the credit for making one of the most important decisions since his election of Richelieu as minister. He now chose Mazarin to follow in his master's footsteps. He chose to make the Italian grandson of a humble fisherman of possible Jewish origin the guardian of the future Louis XIV.

Louis had always been suspicious of foreigners, especially of his mother's countrymen, but he had come to admire and respect the one-time double agent who had evolved into a suave Cardinal. Louis welcomed the fact that Mazarin had not been involved in the Cinq-Mars affair, as had his two colleagues. His Cardinal's purple was not stained with blood, nor with unhappy memories. Louis was also persuaded to favour Mazarin because of his growing concern for his salvation, and Mazarin proved an excellent saviour. He counselled the King to be clement as Corneille had done before him in his *Cinna*. In January Monsieur was returned to court and restored to his rights and privileges. He was 'so gay that one would have thought nothing had befallen Monsieur le Grand and Monsieur de Thou', his daughter the Grande Mademoiselle was to write. He was quickly followed by all the other exiles,[3] who even included Fontrailles. Had Richelieu died a little sooner Cinq-Mars would undoubtedly have won back Louis's favour and the King might well have lived a little longer.

Cinq-Mars's fate hastened Louis's death as his life had Richelieu's. The King could not bear to think of his friend's handsome head rolling across the scaffold. His grief exacerbated his chronic condition. He had had pneumo-intestinal tuberculosis for twenty years but he no longer had the strength or the desire to keep it in check. The three protagonists of the tragedy were each succumbing to their individual fates in the true classical manner. From February 21 the King was bed-ridden at Saint-Germain, where he remained until his death. On March 27 he ordered Bouvard to reveal the extent of his illness. The physician dared not answer, whereupon Louis sighed, 'Your silence is eloquent. I must die.' He then added, 'God knows I have never found much joy in life and shall not be sorry to quit it.'

Anne of Austria was a model of conjugal solicitude. She did not leave her husband's bedside, where she wept copiously and constantly. She asked his confessor to persuade him to renounce his conviction that she had been a party in the Chalais attempt on his life. Louis answered, 'In the present circumstances I cannot but forgive the lady but I am sure I am not obliged to believe her.' He may have forgiven her that complicity but not her last and doubly treacherous one. He intended to deprive her of all power, but Mazarin intervened. He convinced the King that the dispossession of the future King's mother would not only be ineffectual but dangerous. He suggested a clever alternative, the

---

[3] Except for Châteauneuf, Madame de Chevreuse and Madame de Hautefort. Louis could not bring himself to forgive the first two and Madame de Hautefort would have revived too many sad memories.

creation of a regency council of able and responsible men who would run the state and deal with all crucial decisions. Anne could then bask in the glory of her title but she would not have effective powers. Louis was persuaded. Mazarin then convinced the Queen of his loyal services and obedience. He assured her that she would be sole regent and that she would reign supreme as Marie de Médicis had done before her. Anne believed him, admired his skill. She even felt grateful and tender towards her failing husband.

On April 20 Monsieur de La Vrillière read 'His Majesty's declaration on the government of His Estates', which proclaimed one of history's only constant laws. 'France now knows that united she stands invincible and that divided she falls. The country's greatness depends upon her continued unity.'

The Dauphin was baptized the next day. Once the King settled his worldly affairs he turned his thoughts to heaven and to those whom he had loved. Louis, whose whole life had been a secret, died on May 14, 1643, with a finger pressed to his closed lips. He was forty-two years old.

In eight short months the great heroes and the lesser characters in Cinq-Mars's story disappeared from the scene. But the author of the drama, who had artfully manipulated the scenes to their final conclusion, survived them all to wrest grandeur from baseness. The Spanish Queen, who had been involved in so many plots and conspiracies, who had even negotiated with the enemy in wartime, suddenly became the personification of a grand and united France. One day, as she was passing before a portrait of Richelieu, she looked up and mused, 'If that man were alive today he would be the most powerful man on earth.' Poor de Thou must have turned in his grave.

Epilogue

Cinq-Mars's conspiracy differs from the usual favourite-inspired conspiracies of the seventeenth century because he, unlike his counterparts, had no influence on the policies and the destiny of his own nation. Historians have always despised Henri d'Effiat, while poets and novelists have romanticized his memory; the historians have been too unfair and the poets too generous. He was a typical adolescent of his class who shared the aspirations of his kind to excel in battle and to conquer the beauties of his day. He was endowed with excellent good looks and with an excellent patron, who proved ironically disastrous for him. Henri was made a bait and lured into a trap which caught the King and the Cardinal and endangered the lives of millions.

Henri was Richelieu's greatest tactical error, and Louis XIII's greatest temptation to live life more fully and resign from his semi-divine duties. The King had resisted such temptations before, but he died a broken man for having almost yielded to Cinq-Mars's lure.

In order to judge Cinq-Mars we must assess whether Richelieu's policies, which Louis rigorously enforced on all, including himself, warranted the cruel sacrifices they demanded. They have been criticized and they have been highly praised; but the twentieth century has found some notable detractors, particularly outside France.[1] They have been held responsible for creating the economic and social conditions which produced the Revolution and for eliminating Germany and giving rise to Prussia in order to reduce the Austrian domination of Europe, which is supposed to have prepared the way for our twentieth-century catastrophes.

But Richelieu had no particular theories of absolute monarchy that he wished to apply. He created an absolute monarchy because he wanted to unify France and remove the constant threat of civil war, which would have brought the Bourbons to a Merovingian end. The Revolution of 1789 happened precisely when

[1] Cf. among others, Aldous Huxley's *Grey Eminence*, Chatto & Windus, London, 1941.

the monarchy proved incapable of accomplishing a royal revolution over its privileged classes—when, that is, it could not bring the Cardinal's work to its natural conclusion. The Peace of Westphalia may well have sowed the seeds of the Prussian climb to power. But Richelieu could not have been expected to make France a Habsburg satellite simply in order to prevent possible future German expansionism. In any case, such a policy would not have provided against an ultimate confrontation between the 'European bloc' and Russia or the Anglo-Saxon nations. If we consider the government of Vienna and that of Madrid still controlled by the Inquisition, we might have some idea of the disastrous effects such an arrangement would have had on Western civilization. Louis XIV and Napoleon certainly borrowed some of Richelieu's principles but they distorted them and thus smeared his reputation. No statesman can be held responsible for his successors' abuses. He was a political genius, but he was only a man and he was fallible. History, unfortunately, only elects to register the progression of evils and lesser evils, of mistakes and imperfect systems.

Every century of French history has its share of invasions and it is to the Cardinal's credit that he created a political structure which withstood invasions from 1659 to 1792. It was also during that time that France gave the world a number of brilliant men who managed to alter the complexion of the world through their respective fields of endeavour. This is enough reason to justify the Cardinal's reputation and to warrant all the sacrifices that Louis made for their sake, including the death of his dearest friend. It was these two men and their work and their deprivations which prepared the nation for its finest hour— the Sun King's golden age.

Principal Sources

Archives du Ministère des Affaires Etrangères, Paris

Archives du Vatican Nunz. Francia 91

Archives de Chantilly ms. 920

Ernest Lavisse : *Histoire de France*, Paris 1900–1911

Halphen et Sagnac : *la Prépondérance Espagnole*

Lettres, Instructions Diplomatiques et Papiers d'Etat du Cardinal de Richelieu, published by G. d'Avenel

Cardinal de Richelieu : *Mémoires* (Collection des mémoires de l'histoire de France), 1819

Cardinal de Richelieu : *Testament Politique*, Amsterdam 1688 (translated, London 1695)

Vittorio Siri : *Mémorie Recondite*, Paris 1677–79

Fontrailles : *Relation*, 1665

N. Goulas : *Mémoires*, 1879 (Société de l'histoire de France)

Montrésor : *Mémoires*, 1667

Maréchal d'Estrées : *Mémoires*, Paris 1673

Madame de Motteville : *Mémoires*, Amsterdam 1723 (translated, London 1726)

Mlle de Montpensier : *Mémoires*

Montglat : *Mémoires*

Fontenay-Mareuil : *Mémoires*, 1836

Brienne : *Mémoires*

Gaspard de Chavagnac : *Mémoires*, Besançon 1699

Henri Arnauld : *Lettres au President de Barillon*

G. Tallemant des Réaux : *Historiettes*, Paris 1834

Vincent Voiture : *Lettres*, Amsterdam 1657 (translated, Dryden and Dennis 1696)

Saint Simon : *Parallèle des Trois Premiers Rois Bourbon*

Scipion Dupleix : *Histoire de Louis le Juste*

Le P. Henri Griffet : *Histoire du Régne de Louis XIII*, Paris 1758

M. le Vassor : *Histoire du Régne de Louis XIII*, Amsterdam 1701–1711

Beauchamp : *Louis XIII d'après sa Correspondance avec Richelieu*, 1902

E. Griselle : *Louis XIII et Richelieu*, Paris 1911

F. Canu : *Louis XIII et Richelieu*, Paris 1946

Marius Topin : *Louis XIII et Richelieu*, Paris 1876

Antoine Aubery : *Histoire du Cardinal-Duc de Richelieu,* Paris 1660

Antoine Aubery : *Mémoires pour l'Histoire du Cardinal-Duc de Richelieu,* Paris 1660

P. de Vaissière : *La Conjuration de Cinq-Mars,* Paris 1928

Gabriel Hanotaux et le Duc de La Force : *Histoire du Cardinal de Richelieu,* Paris 1893–1947

F. B. H. R. Capefigue : *Le Cardinal de Richelieu* (Les Cardinaux Ministres), Paris 1865

Louis Vaunois : *Vie de Louis XIII,* Paris 1936

Auguste Bailly : *Richelieu* (*The Cardinal Dictator,* translated, H. Miles, London 1936)

Hilaire Belloc : *Richelieu,* London 1930

Saint Aulaire : *Richelieu*

Quazza Capitelli : *Marie de Gonzague et Gaston d'Orléans*

Dethan Georges : *Gaston d'Orléans, Conspirateur et Prince Charmant*

A. Delort : *Mémoires sur Montpellier,* Montpellier 1876

L. Guiraud : *Notre-Dame de Montaign à Montpellier*

Le Père Barré : *Vie d'Abraham Fabert*